LET REDPATH SWEETEN IT

LET REDPATH SWEETEN IT

RICHARD FELTOE

NATURAL HERITAGE/NATURAL HISTORY INC.

Let Redpath Sweeten It
Published by Natural Heritage/Natural History Inc.
P.O. Box 95, Postal Station O
Toronto, Ontario
M4A 2M8
Copyright © Redpath Sugars, 1993

No portion of this book, with the exception of brief extracts for the purpose of literary reviews, may be reproduced in any form without the permission of the publishers.

Editor: Wendy Thomas
Design: Derek Chung Tiam Fook
Printed and bound in Canada by Hignell Printing Limited, Winnipeg, Manitoba

Canadian Cataloguing in Publication Data
Feltoe, Richard D., 1954 -
    Let Redpath Sweeten It

Includes bibliographical references and index.
ISBN 0-920474-76-4

1. Redpath Industries – History.   2. Sugar – Manufacture and refining – Canada – History.
I. Title

HD9114.C24R44 1993   338.7'6336'0971   C93-094173-X

Contents

Acknowledgements		6
Introduction		7
Chapter 1	Beta Vulgaris	10
Chapter 2	Canadian, from the Ground up	17
Chapter 3	Growth in War and Peace	29
Chapter 4	A New Order of Business	47
Chapter 5	Sugar at War	63
Chapter 6	Is It a Brave New World or the Same Old Story?	85
Chapter 7	The British Connection	99
Chapter 8	Branching Out	119
Chapter 9	For the Times They are a-Changing	135
Chapter 10	Hard Times, and Even Harder Choices	151
Chapter 11	A New Direction	169
Chapter 12	Lawyers and Judges and Shares, Oh My!	181
Chapter 13	Winners and Losers	197
Chapter 14	Full Circle	211
Chapter 15	Something Old, Something New	225
Postscript		229
Appendix 1		230
Appendix 2		233
Selected Bibliography		235
Index		236

Acknowledgements

Following the over two years of effort required to complete the production of this volume and its predecessor, so many individuals have played parts in its development that recognition of their contributions would provide a catalogue of names beyond either the ability of my memory to accurately recount or these pages to document. Therefore to anyone who might feel slighted that their individual role was not mentioned here I apologize in advance but it was none the less valued. There were however, certain persons who must be credited for their contributions to this second volume.

As before Mr. Murray McEwen proved to be pivotal in his encouragement and support to complete this work, as were Mr. Peter Sharpe and Mr. Robert Satola (who succeeded Mr. Ed Makin as President just as this second volume was begun.)

Equally the support and teamwork provided by Barry Penhale, Wendy Thomas and Derek Chung carried me over the pitfalls of publication to enable this work to be completed.

Support must also be acknowledged from E.A. Millar, B. Easton, and M. Davidson, corporate employees who, in previous years, maintained a record of events within the corporation or who undertook to compile notes and outlines for publications by the company. Thanks to their efforts, certain features of our history which would otherwise have been forgotten were preserved for me to use as a primary source of research for this final work.

Finally, and in conclusion I hold my largest degree of expression of appreciation, credit, and debt to my wife Diane, who not only worked long and hard at my side through every stage of production of both volumes but tolerated the inevitable domestic upheaval that this work created during the past two years.

To all my heartfelt thanks

Richard Feltoe
Curator and Corporate Archivist
Redpath Sugar Museum
August 1992

Introduction

Dear Reader:

For those of you who have already read Volume 1 of this work, *Redpath, the History of a Sugar House*, you will no doubt be expecting this volume to pick-up the story where we adjourned the first part, in 1930 when the Canada Sugar Refining Co. Ltd. merged with one of its business competitors, the Dominion Sugar Co. Ltd., to create a new corporate entity. However, before we can continue to tell the story of the Canada and Dominion Sugar Co. Ltd. it is necessary to review the origins of Dominion and its use of canadian grown sugar beet as the primary source of sugar for its own range of sugar products. For this separate development had an extensive influence on the new corporation.

From that point on our book documents how the corporate entity of Canada and Dominion Sugar Co. Ltd. and its business successors Redpath Sugars and Redpath Industries Ltd., continued to develop in both wartime and peace until the present day.

Those who would compare the two volumes will note some differences in the types of information provided in them. This can be partially explained by the fact that more detailed records of the company survive from these later periods and that Dominion, Canada and Dominion, and its successors were all "businesses" whose records did not hold those personal letters found in the nineteenth century letterbooks of the Canada Sugar Refinery.

This is not to say, however, that the more formal corporate documents and reports that represented the foundation of information for this volume are without their own form of drama or even comedy, as you will discover. In comparison, it will also be found that due to the cyclical nature of governmental policies and attitudes, the problems created for the later generations of corporate executives mirror those suffered by John Redpath, George Alexander Drummond, and Huntly Redpath Drummond during their own terms of office.

As the curator of the corporate museum, I was naive enough at the beginning of this project to believe that I was fairly well versed on the history of the company. How wrong I was! And how much I have learned still astounds me. However, one fact that I recognized in my introduction to Volume I still remains the same, that "although this is the history of a company, it is also the story of the people who made this history happen."

Therefore, for all those currently working for Redpath or who have served during the times covered by this volume, this book is as much your history as it is of the

Introduction

corporation itself. I hope you enjoy some of the memories these pages are bound to evoke. Finally, to you the general reader, I hope you will find this glimpse into our history interesting and recognize that there is more to putting that simple substance onto your table than you originally thought.

Richard Feltoe
Curator and Corporate Archivist
Redpath Sugar Museum
October 1992.

UP AND DOWN THE ROWS

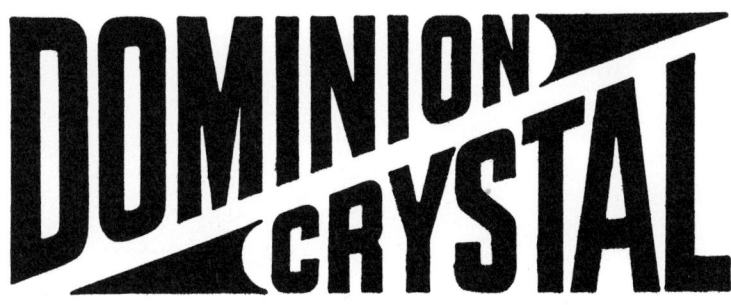

The "war" between cane and beet sugar through the eyes of a French cartoonist.

CHAPTER ONE

Beta Vulgaris

Within the mists of antiquity, the origins of nature's sweetener, sugar, lie in the realms of mythology. As a practical and commercial product, however, its history is somewhat better recorded with its extraction from sugar cane documented in India around 500 B.C. Shortly thereafter, the beet plant was also discovered to have sweetening properties and thrived in Egypt, where it was used as a vegetable and as a source of syrup for medicines. With the spread of sugar cane cultivation in the first millennium A.D., however, the beet took a back seat and was generally ignored, except as a vegetable or as a food for cattle, until 1568. At that time, tests conducted in England distinguished the white beet (now known as sugar beet) from its red cousin (beetroot), and commentaries were made on its potential as a source of sugar but without any suggestion as to how it could be extracted or concentrated.

As a result, sugar cane continued to monopolize world production of sugar throughout the seventeenth and eight-eenth centuries until the 1760s when Andreas Sigismond Marggraf (1709 - 1782) experimented with both the red and white beet and determined that the white variety produced a higher percentage of pure sugar with the residue becoming a source of alcohol. Despite these early successes, Marggraf did not advocate the manufacture of beet sugar on a commercial scale but, as a social and economic issue, he urged the extraction of syrups as a "cottage industry" to provide a sweetening agent at a lower cost than the imported colonial cane sugars.

Marggraf's efforts, although successful, were not immediately expanded upon, as the extensive financial and political power of the sugar cane suppliers was used to impede the development of this competitive method of manufacture. Therefore, it was not until Marggraf's pupil Franz Carl Achard (1753 - 1821) began to implement his own set of experiments in 1786 that the foundations of the modern sugar beet industry were laid. Working in Prussia over a period of thirteen years, Achard developed both the agricultural and industrial technology for the successful extraction of sugar from beets. Following this, he presented the first sugar loaf produced from beet sugar to King Frederick William III. The economic and political importance of this development was not lost upon the king or his ministers, and they quickly appointed a committee to supervise further trials. On April 1, 1799, Achard was commissioned to publish his findings and the first definitive work on beet sugar extraction and manufacturing was produced and distributed across Europe under the title *"Abhandlungen über die Runkelrube."* The Prussian government then compounded its support by investing substantially in the construction of a prototype beet refinery that was to be operated by Achard under government supervision.

By 1801, Achard was granted land in Silesia where a full-scale beet refinery was erected. Unfortunately, Achard's business skills did not match his scientific ones, and the facility repeatedly fell into debt throughout its operative life until 1813 when it was destroyed by French troops. It is said that despite receiving a state pension for his contribution to the development of a new industry, Achard became a disappointed and bitter man in later years.

Nevertheless, following the efforts of Achard, other individuals and business groups established beet refineries across Europe. Foremost amongst those promoting the new industry was the French Emperor Napoleon Bonaparte, who saw in the successful development of this new industry a means by which he could break the British blockade of regular sugar supplies from the West Indies.

Under this high level of sponsorship, the technologies for the extraction of beet sugar were quickly developed in France so that by March 1811 the Emperor felt confident enough to make a public pronouncement on sugar beet at the national Chamber of Commerce, which stated in part:

The Berlin and Milan decrees are the fundamental laws of my Empire as regards neutral commerce ... Commercial relations with England must cease ... I am informed from late experiments that France will be able to do without the sugars ... of the West Indies. Chemistry has made such progress in this country that it will be possible to produce as great a change in our commercial relations as that produced by the discovery of the compass. I do not say that I do not wish for maritime commerce or colonies but ... the vent of colonial commerce upon the continent being firmly shut, the English will be obliged to throw into the Thames the sugars ... for which they have exchanged the objects of their industry and which have afforded them such resources.

On the same day, he signed several decrees on the development of production for sugar beet and trade with the West Indies, that in part stated:

Plantations of beet, proper for the manufacture of sugar shall be formed in our Empire to the extent of 32,000 hectares ...The commission shall ... fix upon the most convenient place for the establishment of four experimental schools for giving instruction in the manufacture of beet sugar ... Sugar ... of the two Indies shall be prohibited and considered as merchandise of English manufacture ...

Despite these claims, the French beet industry suffered initial production problems, and it was not until January 2, 1812, that Napoleon was informed that the industrialist Benjamin Delessert had finally succeeded in making loaves of white sugar from beets on a regular basis. Without delay, Napoleon visited the plant and presented Delessert with the Legion of Honour and his workers in the factory with an additional payment equal to their regular week's wage. He then ordered the immediate construction of a series of beet plants across France. Within two years, 334 beet sugar factories were in full-time operation and produced more than 7.7 million pounds of sugar.

With the final defeat of Napoleon in the grain and

sugar beet fields outside the village of Waterloo and the opening of French ports once more to colonial cane sugars, the fledgling beet sugar industry was all but wiped out as cane sugar prices were deliberately slashed to bankrupt the beet producers. However, over the next decade the beet industry slowly recovered and regained a viable existence of its own so that by 1826, one hundred factories across France were producing 24,000 tons of sugar, all of which was either consumed in France without paying the usual import duties applied to cane sugar, or was exported, thus becoming eligible for a bonus from the French government.

Anxious not to lose the generous source of revenue provided by taxation on sugar, the French authorities quickly amended their trade laws and brought in new taxes upon the domestic product, which had the immediate impact of bankrupting almost 75% of the existing beet companies in France. In other countries too, governments began to consider whether to support beet growing by granting subsidies, or to apply new duties on beet production. The answer in each case varied according to the degree of political influence held by those commercial interests with significant investments in the cane industry. This led to a veritable European "war" of propaganda in the 1830s and 1840s between the growing beet centres of France, Germany, and Italy, and the cane-dominated sugar industry of Great Britain.

As this economic "war" was under way in Europe, the sugar beet industry of North America began in 1838 at

George Alexander Drummond

Northampton, Massachusetts, with the construction of a small factory, which worked for only a few months before going bankrupt. Similar attempts at Salt Lake City; San Francisco; Chatsworth, Illinois; Fond du Lac, Wisconsin; Alverado, California; Black Hawk, Wisconsin; Portland, Maine; and Franklin, Massachusetts likewise failed in the face of strong competition from the well-established and politically active cane sugar lobby. Therefore it was not until 1879, when E.H. Dyer organized the Standard Sugar Refining Co. in California, that an extended beet sugar presence was established in the United States. From this time on, under a substantial system of protective measures, the U.S. sugar beet industry spread across the country with centres springing up in Utah, Colorado, Montana, Wyoming, Nebraska, South Dakota, Minnesota, Iowa, Wisconsin, Illinois, Indiana, Michigan, and Ohio.

North of the border, the beet sugar industry in Canada began with attempts by George Alexander Drummond to establish a beet-processing facility at the Canada Sugar Refinery in Montreal. Quantities of beet seeds and processing machinery were purchased in 1864. However, George was unable to persuade regional farmers to cultivate this new type of crop and the idea was shelved; the machinery was mothballed and eventually sold as scrap. Some years later, in 1874, preliminary experiments were made by the Quebec Department of Agriculture resulting in the introduction of legislation by the Quebec legislative assembly for the establishment of beet sugar facilities under a government subsidy of $70,000. Taking up this offer, one group of businessmen formed La Compagnie de Sucre de Quebec in 1878. Although it was claimed that the capital of this company exceeded $500,000, there is no evidence of any factory ever being built or even of growing contracts issued to farmers. Thus it was not until 1880 with the incorporation of La Compagnie de Sucre de Betterave de Quebec in Farnham, followed by the Pioneer Sugar Co. of Coaticook, and L'Union Franco Canadienne in Berthier that the Quebec sugar beet industry became established.

Although each of these plants went into production by late 1881, they were incapable of making their operations break even, let alone make a profit, so that when the provincial government withdrew its financial support in 1883, it was quickly followed by the permanent closure of the Pioneer Sugar Co. at Coaticook and the mothballing and financial re-organization of the other two plants. By 1889 the two remaining beet companies were restructured and attempted once again to produce beet sugar, but under the combined burden of under-financing, incompetent managements, and farmers failing to supply the factories with the agreed quotas of beet, they were doomed to failure. By 1893 the Farnham plant was closed, followed three years later by the Berthier operation. Both factories were subsequently stripped of their machinery, while that of the Coaticook plant was destroyed by fire.

Co-incidentally, interest in growing sugar beet was now increasing in Ontario with the establishment of the Wiarton Beet Sugar Manufacturing Co. Ltd. Although no actual construction for a processing facility took place until some years later, it presaged the intense level of activity to come. This is not to say, however, that sugar beets were unknown in Ontario prior to 1896; in fact, small plots were grown in virtually every county settled across Ontario after 1850 with the plant being used first as a staple food for cattle and later as a crop sold to the beet sugar refineries in the northern United States.

By 1899, there was substantial pressure at provincial government levels to initiate a series of experiments to determine the viability of sugar beets as a marketable crop for a domestic industry within Ontario. Over the next twelve months teams of investigators visited factories and farms in Michigan to assess the financial infrastructure required to set up a beet industry, while in Ontario, official beet-growing experiments were begun under the supervision of Professor A.E. Shuttleworth of the Ontario Agricultural College in Guelph.

In 1901, the pace of development increased with the initial test plots around Aylmer, Welland, and Newmarket being expanded to include Alvinston, Belleville, Berlin, Lindsay, London, Mount Forrest, Peterborough, Simcoe, and Whitby, while increased volumes were being grown around Wiarton and Wallaceburg for shipment into Michigan. In all, Ontario cultivated more than 4,800 acres of beet in 1901, more than eight times that of 1900. Following the favourable reports of the Ontario Agricultural College, the Ontario provincial legislature enacted a bill

For the purpose of encouraging the growth of sugar beets and the establishment of factories within the Province of Ontario for the manufacture of refined sugar.

Beta Vulgaris

The Berlin factory of the Ontario Sugar Co. Ltd., 1902.

Under this legislation, those groups who established processing facilities within the province would benefit by receiving a bounty for each pound of sugar produced at a rate of half a cent per pound for the first two years of production and a quarter cent per pound in the third year, by which time it was assumed any such refineries would be self-supporting.

During the remainder of the year the province went "sugar beet crazy" as various municipalities sought to cash in on the provincial bounty by competing in offering lavish bonuses, tax concessions, and land grants in order to attract beet sugar plants to their towns.

First off the mark was the Dresden Sugar Co. Ltd. which was built by the American Construction and Supply Co. and had a capacity of 600 tons per day. In a similar vein, the previously established Wiarton Beet Sugar Manufacturing Co. Ltd. hired the Walburn-Swenson Co. to build a 350-ton-capacity plant. The third refinery to be completed was the Ontario Sugar Co. Ltd. of Berlin (later renamed Kitchener). Built by the Dyer Co. it had a capacity of 800 tons and while it suffered from a relativity late start in construction in 1902 it was able to process over 33,000 tons of beet in that season alone. Finally, the last contestant in the beet sugar sweepstakes of 1902, was the Wallaceburg Sugar Co. Ltd. This factory was built by Kilby Manufacturing Co. with a capacity of 600 tons per day, and was the origin of a corporate enterprise that would dominate the Ontario beet industry for the next sixty years as will be seen in this, the second part of our corporate history.

Immigrant families working the beet fields.

CHAPTER TWO

Canadian, From The Ground Up

As mentioned in the previous chapter, under the terms established by the provincial government to promote the Ontario sugar beet industry, several communities began from scratch in the development of growing and processing beets. In Wallaceburg, however, that community had a distinct advantage due to the participation of local farmers as growers of beets for the Michigan sugar plants for some years previously. Therefore, it was far more simple for these farmers to provide stocks to the Wallaceburg facility than was possible elsewhere in the province. As early as 1901, the *Wallaceburg News* was carrying editorials on the prospects of a new industry within the community. According to the various newspaper accounts, the primary financial backers for this new facility were a consortium of U.S. and Canadian financiers and industrialists who had accumulated their fortunes in the lumber trade of upstate Michigan and southwestern Ontario during the latter half of the previous century. Due to the wholesale stripping of useable timber reserves, this industry was now dying out and its backers were looking for alternative sources of income. Since many of these timber "barons" had invested heavily in the U.S. beet industry, the prospect of government-assisted development across the border acted as a natural magnet for these industrialists and their financial assets. Foremost among the group backing the Wallaceburg project was David Alexander Gordon, the descendant of United Empire Loyalists, who was born in Wallaceburg on January 18, 1858. Throughout his earlier years, D.A. Gordon had championed the economic and social development of Wallaceburg. His first business dealings were as an office boy for the *Wallaceburg Advocate* newspaper followed by a period as reporter for the *Sarnia Observer*. Due to a bout of ill health, he changed careers and entered a partnership with his uncle J. Steinhoff for the manufacture of barrel staves and cooperage stock, some of which ended up at the sugar refinery of John Redpath & Son in Montreal. From this beginning, D.A. Gordon went on to become a major local financial figure, being involved in the development of the Sydenham Glass Works, the Wallaceburg Cooperage Co., the Schultz Die Casting Co., the Sydenham

David Alexander Gordon

D. A. Gordon with his family in their Wallaceburg home.

Trading Co., the Pressure Cooker Co. of Canada, the Canadian Shipping Co., and the Gordon Manufacturing Co.

In political circles likewise, D.A. Gordon became a prominent personality, serving on the town council and acting as mayor for Wallaceburg in 1898, 1899, and 1900, before becoming the Liberal Member of Parliament for the local riding of East Kent.

With this degree of prominence, it is not surprising that with the prospective announcement of financial support from the provincial government, D.A. Gordon took the initiative and implemented plans to bring a sugar beet refinery to Wallaceburg. Following some rapid consultations and late-night council meetings, the citizens were called to a town meeting on February 20, 1901, to consider proposing a new by-law that would authorize the contribution of a bonus of $30,000 and a permanent taxation assessment of $20,000 in order to attract a beet facility to the town. This was conditional upon the facility being established within eight months, having a capacity of at least 20 tons per day, and a capital investment by the company itself of not less than $380,000. Furthermore, it was required that the proposed company agree to run for a minimum of 100 days per year for ten years and to furnish the municipality with at least 100 tons of cinders annually from its furnaces for use as road-bed material.

One week later, on February 28, 1901, a further town meeting was held for the purpose of discussing and deciding the issue. Following some lively debate, the terms were passed by an overwhelming majority of the electorate. Only one month later, D.A. Gordon submitted detailed proposals to the town for the development of a beet factory with a recommendation that construction begin immediately. He also proposed that the sum of $250,000 be raised from local investors rather than looking for funding in the money markets of Toronto or New York, in order to highlight the commitment of the region to the project.

Again, these proposals were willingly accepted and approved by the citizens of Wallaceburg at a town meeting. As a result, a citizens' committee was appointed to represent the interests of the city and liaise with the business consortium on future developments.

No time was lost in forming an official Board for the new company and on April 4, 1901, the Wallaceburg Sugar Co. Ltd. was established with a capital of $300,000.

The construction contract for the refinery was awarded to the Kilby Manufacturing Co. of Cleveland, Ohio, for just under $600,000 with a stipulation that the factory would be completed by August 1902. Following an intense period of construction, the factory was completed on time, if a little over budget, and on October 9, 1902, a celebratory banquet was held in the warehouse of the refinery. The guests included Premier G.W. Ross, Minister of Public Works J.I. Tarte, numerous members of the Chatham Board of Trade, local businessmen, and investors from across Ontario and Michigan. Deliveries of beets to the plant started later that day, with slicing commencing on November 6, 1902.

Newspaper reports on the new facility were glowing in their praise and extolled its scale of construction. The main building was 268 feet long and 65 feet wide; it stood five stories high and was constructed of stone, brick, and

Workers pose for a photograph during the drive to complete the refinery on time.

The eastern side of the completed Wallaceburg factory in 1902.

concrete. All supporting beams and pillars were of steel with scarcely any wood being used except in the window frames and doors, which vastly improved its fire resistance. Besides the main structure, a boiler house, lime kilns, and a refined sugar warehouse capable of holding 20,000 barrels completed the industrial segment of construction. However, in addition to these technical statistics, much was made by the newspapers of the fact that fifty company homes were built to house some of the corporate employees.

The first beet harvest period or "campaign" for the Wallaceburg Sugar Co. Ltd. lasted until December 30, 1902, and produced slightly under 18,000 tons of beets. This was substantially lower than had been planned or hoped for and was partially caused by inexperienced farmers planting their beet crops in low-lying areas which suffered extensive flooding during unexpectedly heavy rains in the late autumn. As a result, the books for the first year's operations recorded a loss of about $20,000 which was subsequently reduced to $2,051 following payment of the agreed bounty from the provincial government.

This was not a very auspicious start to a new industry, especially since the other three beet refinery companies fared just as badly from that season. But in his year-end report to the provincial government, Professor Robert Harcourt of the Ontario Agricultural College was able to state:

The fact that sugar beets of a high quality can be raised in Ontario is so well established that Capitalists, principally American, have already invested over two millions of dollars in extensive plants for the manufacture of sugar from beets. ... This year, for the first time sugar "made in

Ontario" from Ontario-grown beets, has been offered for home consumption.

However, in the paragraph immediately following, a word of caution was also included on a topic that was to prove to be the "Achilles' heel" of the sugar beet industry in Ontario.

The scarcity of Labour is perhaps the most serious problem in connection with the cultivation of sugar beets. ... Indeed for the last few years farmers have had difficulty in procuring the necessary help to take care of the crops. Therefore ... in order to assist their patrons with the work of cultivation the Wallaceburg Sugar Co. brought about 70 experienced labourers from Belgium. These men took contracts for blocking and thinning beets, and materially assisted the farmers ... The indians of Walpole island and of the Brant reserve also assisted with the work in different parts of the province throughout the whole season. In the neighbourhood of Berlin a portion of the thinning was done by school children after school hours and on Saturdays.

Following production, the beet sugar companies now had to obtain sales within an already established marketplace. As might be expected, the well-established sugar cane refining companies in Quebec and the Maritimes did not look favourably on new competition that would inevitably cut into their own market share. Therefore, in retaliation, a series of price cuts and competitive deals were struck by the cane refiners in 1902 - 1903 to keep customers away from the new beet sellers. However, in spite of this competition, the beet companies continued to press into the market, only to be met with a new source of opposition

A locomotive backs into the Wallaceburg factory, past the piles of beets and the factory office block.

from the wholesale importers of refined sugar, who saw the beet industry as another nail in their own business coffin. As a result, pressure was brought to bear by the leading importers upon several wholesale sugar distributors to boycott the beet sugar altogether. In response, the beet producers, led by the Wallaceburg Sugar Co. Ltd., took a dynamic step by leapfrogging the wholesale distribution system and establishing their own retail sales network. This solution eventually led to the Wallaceburg Sugar Co. Ltd. holding more than 35,000 retail accounts on its books in its peak years of sales.

During 1903, continuing strong levels of competition from both the cane refiners and refined sugar wholesalers, plus poor weather conditions, conspired to

Sugar beet cultivation near Wallaceburg.

make for another bad year for the Ontario sugar beet industry. Attempts to establish a new sugar beet plant in Peterborough failed to secure sufficient capital to allow more than a small amount of initial construction before money ran out. Somewhat more successful was the beginning of a beet industry in Western Canada where the Knight Sugar Co. was established in Raymond, Alberta, with a daily production capacity of 350 tons.

Meanwhile, for D.A. Gordon and the Board of the Wallaceburg Sugar Co. Ltd. there were financial worries based on the fact that although the actual cost of the plant had been more than $683,000, the subscribed capital amounted to only $600,000. This meant that it was under-capitalized by a substantial margin and held no working capital that could be drawn upon. To solve this problem, the Board requested each shareholder to issue promissory notes for an additional 40% of the par value of their individual stock holdings. By this method, the capital of the Wallaceburg Sugar Co. Ltd. was increased to $500,000 within one week, giving some breathing room for continued business. Following a beet campaign dominated by severe weather conditions, which prevented substantial areas of mature beets from being harvested, the records show that there was a gross financial loss incurred of $72,000 for 1903. Even the agreed provincial bounties could not neutralize this level of indebtedness and the year's net losses for the company amounted to $51,198.63.

By the spring of 1904, the initial flush of enthusiasm for developing the beet industry had begun to wane. At the provincial level, the subsidies were scheduled for termination at the end of the year (although desperate petitions by the sugar beet industry persuaded the authorities to extend them for three additional years.) Locally too, those municipalities that had originally fallen over each other to attract the beet factories now began to look for ways to recoup some of their investments and expenditures.

In Dresden, for example, the town council decided to raise the taxation assessment on the beet factory. The immediate response of its owner, Captain J.S. Davidson, was to shut the factory down, dismantle the machinery, load it onto barges, and sail it down the Sydenham River and across Lake St. Clair to Janesville, Wisconsin. At Wiarton, likewise, the initial flush of enthusiasm rapidly waned when it was revealed that due to incompetent management during the first campaign, almost half the sugar juice extracted from the beet crop had not been processed into sugar but instead had been flushed into the river. Similar problems in its second season doomed Wiarton and its assets were sold off in 1904, leaving the beet farmers with partially grown crops and no prospect of payment.

The third of the Ontario beet factories, situated at Berlin, fared only slightly better than its compatriots by breaking even in its second year of production. However, once no significant development or profit was forthcoming from this venture, it continued to founder from one financial crisis to another and was eventually merged into the Wallaceburg Sugar Co. Ltd. in 1909.

As the last of the active beet factories, the Board of the Wallaceburg Sugar Co. Ltd. took desperate measures to curb costs and look for new capital investment; it was even reported that it had been decided not to operate the factory due to the inability of the company to obtain sufficient quantities of beet. This report fortunately proved to be false and following a reasonable growing season, the 1904 campaign began on October 23 and lasted until December 21. As a result, the Wallaceburg Sugar Co. registered a self-produced profit of $68,566 which was supplemented by the government bounty to $106,439.61.

With the elimination of most of the other beet companies within Ontario, the Wallaceburg Sugar Co. Ltd. was now able to concentrate on consolidating its economic position. Contracts for acreage jumped from 4,617 acres in 1904 to 7,443 in 1905. Even so, the year-end reports still showed a loss of more than $34,000 which was only converted into a financial gain of just over $6,300 by the inclusion of the provincial bounty. Little else is recorded for this period except for a small column in the *Beet Sugar Gazette* of December 8, 1905, where it mentions that one of the centrifugal machine operators at Wallaceburg was unfortunate enough to slip and fall into the open-topped revolving basket of the centrifugal (which to the uninitiated can be likened to an oversized washing machine.) Fortunately this accident was witnessed, the machine was quickly stopped, and Andrew Thomson emerged with a broken leg, some bruises, and stark naked – all the result of the machine in question.

The following year proved to be a pivotal time in the continued survival of the company when it was recognized by the newly appointed general manager, Herman Wiese, that running a factory only two or three months of a year could not possibly yield the returns on capital required to assure the future of the company. He also recognized that the advantageous position of the refinery on the navigable Sydenham River offered an opportunity to extend this working period by importing foreign beet raw and cane raw sugar and refining them during periods not already scheduled for the processing of the local crop of beets. Taking Mr. Wiese's proposal, D.A. Gordon obtained tariff concessions from the federal government, giving the domestic Canadian beet producers the exclusive right to import, at a low preferential rate, 2 pounds of foreign raw sugar intended for refining for each pound of refined sugar manufactured domestically from sugar beet. This alteration in legislation and the subsequent re-equipping of the Wallaceburg plant with machinery to process the cane raws, secured the financial foundation of the company and eventually turned a moderately successful year into a highly profitable one, despite the termination of the Ontario government bounty. Using these advantages, the Wallaceburg Sugar Co. Ltd. went on over the next two years to quadruple its profits beyond the 1906 level, whereupon opportunity knocked once again when the financially ailing Ontario Sugar Beet Co. Ltd. was placed into receivership and its assets were ordered sold by court order.

Once again, as in 1901, D.A. Gordon was quick to recognize and take advantage of the possibilities presented by this forced sale. Within days, the corporate directorate authorized the expansion of the share capital of the company from $500,000 to $1,500,000 and changed the by-laws of the company to allow for future acquisitions in such diverse areas as land fertilizers, alcohol, beet by-products, cornstarch glucose, corn by-products, gas pipelines, natural gas wells, and railway companies. As a result, the Wallaceburg Sugar Co. Ltd. was able to successfully acquire the entire assets of the Ontario Sugar

Canadian, From The Ground Up

Head office staff, Wallaceburg, 1908.

Let Redpath Sweeten It

The head office of the Dominion Sugar Co. Ltd. at Wallaceburg, 1909.

Temporary additional office staff, working at Wallaceburg, 1912.

Dominion "Crystals" baseball team, 1911.

Inside the boiler house at the Wallaceburg factory.

Beet Co. Ltd. On June 17, 1909, the official merger took place when the corporate name was changed to the Dominion Sugar Co. Ltd.

With the combined production figures of both refineries, the newly established Dominion Sugar Co. Ltd. (hereafter also referred to as Dominion) harvested 49,250 tons of beets, which resulted in more than 12.8 million pounds of finished refined sugar. This merger also represented a major increase from 64% to 82% in the company's proportion of the overall Canadian beet industry.

From 1910 to 1914 the company continued to consolidate its advantageous position as the Canadian leader in domestic sugar production by obtaining an extension to the preferential import system secured in 1906 until 1911 (despite severe opposition by the cane sugar refiners.) Also during this period there was a steady increase in the acreage contracted and harvested, which eventually led to a scarcity of labour to work in the fields. To solve this problem, the company decided to send company officials to Belgium and Holland where they recruited experienced beet workers and then assisted the new immigrants with payment of their passage and initial settlement costs within the various communities around the refineries and beet regions. As well as field labour, an experienced factory group of workers were recruited in Italy for the specific purpose of running the new barium potash process which had been installed to increase the molasses output, thus increasing the already multicultural atmosphere of the refinery and its associated agricultural sector.

By 1913, Mr. Gordon had decided to step down as the company's President and another of the directors, H.B. Smith, became President just in time to lead the company through a period of intense disruption and change. Fortunately, through the earlier period of D.A. Gordon's presidency, the Dominion Sugar Co. Ltd. had become a solid if not vital part of the southwestern Ontario agricultural and industrial scene, a position that was to prove useful in light of things to come.

Henry B. Smith

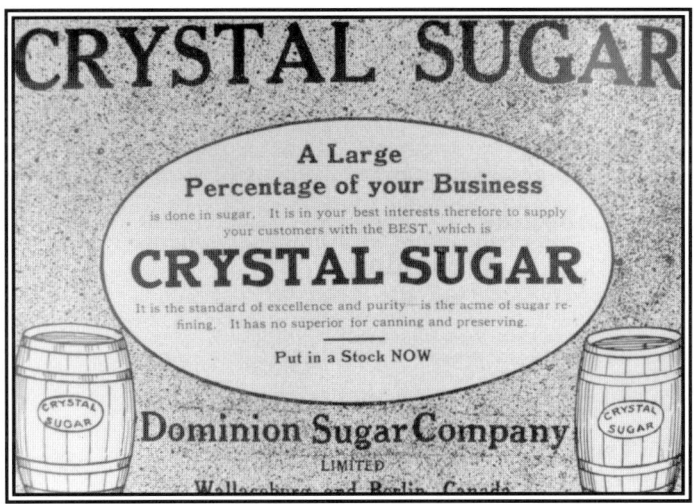

Advertisement from August 1912.

The Chatham factory during the 1930 campaign.

CHAPTER THREE

Growth in War and Peace

Nineteen fourteen proved to be an eventful period for the Dominion Sugar Co. Ltd. The year began with the announcement being made that the Knight Sugar Co. of Raymond, Alberta, had ceased operations and was in the process of dismantling its equipment for shipment to Cornish, Utah. This meant that the output of Dominion represented 100% of Canada's domestically grown sugar production, a situation that continued until a new beet factory was built in Raymond, Alberta, in 1926.

During the summer of 1914, increased rumours about the prospect of war curbed the flow of immigrants to work in the beet fields, leaving the company wondering how it was going to maintain its harvesting schedule in the autumn. With the declaration of war in August, these problems were compounded by an immediate cessation of immigration from Europe, while supplies of local labour decreased as men left the farms to join the colours or switched to more lucrative employment in war-related industries. On a slightly darker note, some farmers of Dutch or Belgian origins aggravated this labour shortage by refusing to hire any worker who had a German sounding name.

Caught somewhat unprepared by the changing circumstances, Dominion field staff looked towards the still neutral United States for additional labour. Belgian immigrants were recruited in Detroit, Illinois, and as far west as Indiana and were brought to Wallaceburg in October 1914, to harvest the beets. This solution was then repeated in 1915 and 1916 by bringing in U.S. workers on special trains in early May to thin the crop and returning them to the United States following the harvest in late autumn.

Another event for which the company was unprepared was the sudden rush by householders, retailers, and manufacturers to secure additional stockpiles of sugar, which rapidly exhausted the available reserves in the company warehouse, leaving thousands of Dominion customers clamouring for their regular and additional supplies of sugar. In response, Dominion was forced to purchase additional supplies of refined sugar in the United States and raw cane sugar from the West Indies to fill the gap until the annual beet crop was available for sale. This naturally reduced the profitability of the year, but even so, by December, the corporate profit registered over $839,000, which can be attributed mainly to the increased prices obtained for sugar.

As the war gathered momentum in Europe, the demand for sugar grew as it was increasingly used in various industries including the production of explosives, alcohol, paints, chemicals and the huge volume of preserved and tinned foods used by the military. One complication of this

The Dominion tugboat William E. Rooney.

increased demand came in the conflicting need to use more ships for transporting both sugar and other essential war materiel. Due to the ongoing shortages in shipping caused by over-demand and wartime losses, there developed an increased call for more domestic sugar production to free ships for other war work. As a result, the 1914 crop contract for 14,400 acres was expanded to 19,700 acres in 1915, and calls went out across the province for additional manpower to tend the fields. This call was met, to some degree, by the use of schoolchildren and men too young or unfit for active service. Camps were set up to house the workers near the refinery and soon these self-titled "soldiers of the soil" were found on most of the farms in the region.

Another result of this increased demand was the recognition that both of the Wallaceburg and Berlin factories were somewhat old-fashioned and needed significant modernization, nor could either of these factories cope with any substantial increase in output. Therefore it was decided that it was time to establish a new refinery in southern Ontario. To this end, Dominion approached and rapidly came to an agreement with the City of Chatham for the location of a new sugar refinery.

By this agreement, which was signed in April 1915, the company agreed to the following conditions:
- To complete the construction and installation of equipment by November 1, 1916
- To expend a minimum of $1 million in the construction and ancillary works
- To guarantee production for a minimum of ten years
- To guarantee a wages expenditure of $100,000 per annum exclusive of officers of the company and office staff.

In return, the City of Chatham agreed to:
- Provide a ground lot of sixty-four acres at a discounted price
- To assess the property for taxes at $25,000 per annum for at least ten years
- To provide water at a set price in volumes up to 50,000 gallons per day.

Construction began immediately, to the point where foundation trenches were dug and brickwork was in the course of being laid before the official paperwork giving the company title to the site or even a building permit was issued. In the meantime, in order to speed up and extend the distribution of refined sugar to the numerous stores serviced by the company, Mr. Wiese came up with a new plan by which the company purchased a series of vessels during 1915. These included two tugs, *Acadia* and *Rook*, one covered scow, six open (30 ton) scows, sixteen open (40 ton) scows, and one barge *Brothers*; all of which were soon

Growth in War and Peace

A Dominion Crystal advert from 1914.

plying the waterways of southern Ontario from Prescott to Sault Ste. Marie and moving sugar from the refineries to the company's customers.

Throughout the winter of 1915-16 and into the spring, work continued on the new Chatham factory while new equipment was installed at both Wallaceburg and Kitchener (as Berlin had been renamed due to the backlash of anti-German feeling prominent across Canada at the time) to replace worn-out machinery. Unfortunately, the primary shortage on both the industrial and agricultural sides of the industry was labour. This was particularly serious in the field labour market where the crops were threatened by severe weather conditions. Once again the call for help was answered by local groups of women and children who helped to thin much of the year's crops.

Meanwhile, to ensure adequate supplies of refined sugar, the company purchased large quantities of Caribbean and South American raw sugar for delivery to Chatham and Wallaceburg. Unfortunately, difficulties in obtaining direct shipments via the St. Lawrence River system meant that much of the sugar was transferred from ocean vessels to railcars at either New York, Halifax, or St. John, which

Installing the beet wheel, July 12, 1916.

Completing the brickwork for the beet pulp dryers.

Completing the lime kilns in June 1916.

The main framework of the Chatham refinery building.

Installing pumps July, 1916.

Hoisting the boiler tubes, August 16, 1916.

Growth in War and Peace

slowed down deliveries and increased costs substantially throughout the summer. In the autumn, the continued lack of field labour, coupled with poor weather conditions at harvest time, caused significant crop losses within the 28,200 acres contracted for in spring so that only 14,000 acres were actually harvested. This meant that a staggering 50% of the crop failed to be available for processing as opposed to a normal average loss of between 8 to 10%.

The steamer D. A. Gordon of the Canadian Shipping Co. This vessel transported numerous cargoes of raw and refined sugar for the Dominion Sugar Co. before being sunk while on war service off the coast of Spain in 1917.

An unusual picture, showing Dominion brand sugar products derived from cane instead of beet.

This led to the embarrassing position of the country's only beet company having a year-end output of sugar that was more than 80% derived from sugar cane sources instead of the intended beet.

On the positive side, however, the new Chatham refinery was completed on time and immediately went into production, running from December 13 to December 24, while Wallaceburg ran from October 12 to December 9 and Kitchener from October 12 to November 13. On December 20, 1916, the official head office of the company was relocated to Chatham, reflecting the increased importance of this new factory within the corporate structure.

Additionally, plans were laid to purchase numerous plots of land around the region for development as weigh stations.

Despite the harvesting setbacks of 1916, the Dominion Sugar Co. Ltd. pressed ahead in the early months of 1917 with plans for the coming year. These took the form of cutting back on what were recognized as unrealistic levels of contracts in light of the shortage of labour, coupled with a substantial rise in the prices to be paid per ton of beet in order to persuade farmers to offer more money to their labourers.

Other developments occurring at this time included the purchase of properties across the region for use as storage and weigh stations and three canal boats named *Mesler and Pease*, *Libbie and Sadie*, and *Mamie Petrie* to expand the small fleet of boats already in use to distribute the refined sugar around Ontario. Within the refineries, too, measures were taken to improve production efficiency by installing new processing machinery at Wallaceburg and Kitchener to match that already in place at Chatham.

But as in the often-quoted saying "the best laid plans ..." all these investments and operational plans were swept aside in June 1917 when the federal government took total control of all aspects of acquisition, distribution, and pricing of foodstuffs, fuel, etc., under the administration of W.J. Hanna, the new Food Controller.

As mentioned in the previous volume of our corporate history, *Redpath, the History of a Sugar House*, Mr. Hanna was totally unfamiliar with the complexities of the sugar situation and his biased judgements did much to injure the Canadian sugar industry as he sought to impose his own view of food control at every level of consumption. No example of this disastrous lack of comprehension is clearer

The first delivery of beets at Chatham, October, 1916.

than when the Food Controller ordered that all refiners who distributed through the wholesale trade cease shipping to retailers as well. To the government, this measure made sense as it reduced the channels through which sugar was distributed, thus making control easier. To the cane refiners across the country, this measure was a major inconvenience and meant loss of revenue, but it was one they could learn to live with. For Dominion, however, it was nothing short of disaster, as it would wipe out overnight almost 92% of the company's sales.

Immediate telephone calls and telegrams to the government outlining the magnitude of the catastrophe this regulation would cause were met with bureaucratic prevarication and departmental "passing of the buck." Therefore it was not until Dominion was able to enlist the aid of the other sugar companies for a joint petition to the government, calling for the exemption of Dominion from this prohibitive order, that matters returned to some degree of normality for the beet sector of the Canadian sugar industry.

By early 1918, the chronic labour shortage within the beet industry had reached its peak. Local labour was virtually unavailable due to the attractive wages being offered by competing war production plants in Toronto, Hamilton, Windsor, and Detroit, while farm workers from the United States were equally unavailable once that country finally entered the war in 1917. Extreme measures now had to be employed to secure workers for the 1918 beet crop. Following considerable negotiations and "red tape," a co-operative scheme between the Dominion Sugar Co. Ltd. and the federal government was developed to use imported Mexican labourers, who were subsequently brought from Mexico by train across the United States under a bond agreement paid by the company.

The first batches of these workers arrived in Chatham from El Paso, Texas, where armed U.S. marshals had previously "escorted" them in a forced march from the Mexican border to the train, to avoid any of the migrants absconding. Having experienced the nature of American hospitality, and after three days in a sealed train, when the Mexicans arrived in Canada to be met by a committee of company officials and wives bearing baskets of fruits and baked goods, it is little wonder that the over 200 men, women, and children felt somewhat bemused and were uncertain of what to expect next.

To house these new field workers, a site alongside the refinery had previously been set aside and a large, specially built dormitory-type building was erected. This large structure was subsequently nicknamed the "Titanic" by local residents, although the reason is not known. Within the "Titanic," each family, irrespective of its overall size, was allocated a single room to live in. Subsequently, most of the migrants were relocated to various field districts around the region, and accommodation was arranged through the combined efforts of the company field agents and individual farmers.

As a result of the work done by the local and imported field labour force, the 1918 crops were harvested and produced a record 21,000 acres, the highest level ever recorded since production began in 1901. The three refineries worked a record number of days (92½ in Wallaceburg, 74½ in Chatham, 74½ in Kitchener) and produced a satisfactory 39.5 million pounds of sugar, more than double that of 1917.

At the end of the campaign most of the Mexican workers returned home, but a few hardy or perhaps foolhardy families elected to stay on through until the next year. Unfortunately, they were far from prepared for the severity of a Canadian winter and initially suffered great hardships through lack of proper clothing, food, and heating in the drafty "Titanic." One local area historian recalled that in her youth she participated with her mother and neighbours in preparing baskets of food and clothing for distribution to the desperate Mexican families.

Following the signing of the Armistice in November 1918 and the ending of the Great War, much was expected of the future, but for the beet industry the problems of lack of labour still exerted a strong influence on plans laid by the company for 1919. Repeating the successful 1918 example of importing Mexican labour, over 300 men, women, and children made the journey from El Paso to Chatham in 1919 to supplement the new increasing supply of labour available as war industries cut back on production and laid workers off. Additionally there was, once again, a ready supply of willing workers wishing to emigrate from war-ravaged Europe and the slow start to this flow in 1919 gave little indication to the large numbers that were to arrive later.

Regrettably, the weather in 1919 did not co-operate with this new opportunity to harvest the beet crop, and nearly 43% of the originally contracted beet crop failed. On another level, problems continued for Dominion as governmental regulations and restrictions implemented for "the duration" were maintained long after the end of the war. Normal sales patterns and pricing were totally disrupted by bureaucratic decrees. In addition, due to a projected world shortage of sugar, the Canadian government now implemented a policy under which the refiners were forced, against their better judgement, to purchase huge volumes of raw cane sugar at inflationary prices. In return, the government made vague promises of assistance should prices fall and overt threats of retribution if they failed to obey these government demands.

While these measures had most impact on the cane refining companies across Canada, the Dominion Sugar Co. Ltd. was also bound under this arrangement, although to a significantly lower level as its beet production insulated it from acquiring too much cane-type sugar during this period of rapidly rising prices. In fact, due to the world price of sugar reaching new high levels, the company was able to offer its farmers a substantially higher price for their beets, so that for the proposed 1920 crop a rate of $12.84 per ton was announced compared to the $6.32 paid in 1916 and $5.85 in 1914.

Ralph Gilchrist

This prompted farmers into contracting over 34,000 acres and produced more than 32,000 acres leaving only 5.7% unfulfilled.

The spiral of increasing world sugar prices could not continue indefinitely, however, and in September of 1920 the "bubble" burst. Raw sugar prices then collapsed, leaving the cane refiners with huge stockpiles of raw sugar bought under governmental directive. When the refiners appealed to the government for the assistance previously promised while prices were rising, the government reneged on its written commitments, abandoning the refiners and leaving them scrambling to unload the unwanted sugar as quickly as possible to avoid bankruptcy (for details see Chapter 26, "Dance of the Millions" in *Redpath The History of a Sugar House.*)

At Dominion, this price collapse represented a disturbing but not disastrous turn of events. Cushioned by the nature of its business in beet, it was generally felt that the losses incurred in the company's small holdings of cane sugar could be worked off in a reasonably short period of time compared to the years required for the cane refiners. This is not to say that it did not have its own impact in the longer term, as the general fall in Canadian prices reflected back on the beet industry through the lower level of payments offered in contracts to farmers for the 1921 crop.

The S.S. Maplebranch unloading sacks of raw sugar at the Wallaceburg refinery wharf.

The S.S. Ralph Gilchrist taking on boxes of refined sugar at the Wallaceburg refinery.

In a more contradictory manner, while it might be thought that lower prices would now stimulate general purchasing, the opposite reaction occurred, whereby retailers held off buying sugar in hopes of getting better prices later. This led Dominion to initiate a novel incentive to improve sales by delivering sugar to its retailers on consignment. The retailers were instructed to maintain each week a record of their stocks, from which the company billed them according to the going rate for sugar at that time.

With the effective collapse of the eastern Canadian sugar industry in 1920-21, the members of the Board for the Dominion Sugar Co. Ltd. saw a significant opportunity to extend their share within the Canadian market. Led by their new President, R. Gilchrist, they used their financial reserves to embark on a major programme of upgrading and expanding the Wallaceburg and Chatham refineries while closing down the Kitchener plant, thus concentrating their operational capacity in a single geographical area. To balance this production concentration, however, they also purchased a significant number of plots of land adjacent to various railway sidings across the region which were developed into transfer and weigh stations. This now allowed more distant farmers to benefit from lower costs and faster delivery of beets to the factory, which in turn reflected back in a higher price for the beets as there was less time for sugar content to deteriorate prior to testing. The company also embarked on an active programme of recruitment for field workers from Europe by sending representatives to Holland, Belgium, France, Germany, and Italy. These representatives were selected specifically to match the cultural, religious and language backgrounds of the different regions chosen for visitation and they were also authorized by the company to advance transportation fares, negotiate with government agencies for legal documentation, and arrange for credit at stores in Chatham and Wallaceburg to aid in the easy assimilation of the new families into life in Canada.

Fortunately, the company also received substantial co-operation from the federal government, who saw in this programme a means of expanding Canada's population with productive citizens.

Once the new immigrants arrived in Canada, they were either housed in the refurbished "Titanic" or a new series of prefabricated barracks until separate accommodation could be supplied in the various field districts. Many farmers (some of whom were from earlier batches of beet immigrants) also established small houses to accommodate their new workers, which encouraged the new families to remain within the area and work on additional crops as well as the sugar beets.

Similar activities occurred in 1922 and into 1923 to such an extent that the area around the refinery where the new immigrants were housed became nicknamed "Little Holland" despite the fact that the Dutch were only one of many nationalities drawn into the area.

Meanwhile, world sugar prices in the early 1920s fluctuated wildly as a result of extensive commodity speculation in various stock markets in Europe and especially the United States. This led to a period in which the beet industry was forced to reflect these swings in the prevailing prices for beet offered to the farmers. Naturally the farmers began to raise an outcry, calling for more stable pricing. Unfortunately this demand occurred at the same time as one of the price fluctuations reached its peak; thus the calls of the farmers were augmented by everyone from the housewife to the commercial food processor, who accused the sugar refiners of profiteering at the expense of the public. This resulted in the establishment of a special committee of the House of Commons, which summoned the head officials of the individual sugar companies to Ottawa to account for the wild changes in sugar prices over the previous few months.

Charles Henry Houson

In a series of meetings, all the corporate leaders of the major sugar companies testified as to the uncontrollable nature of the prices being demanded for raw sugar around the world and each called for the need to stabilize the Canadian market. The Dominion Sugar Co. Ltd., although among the smaller companies involved in this matter, added its voice to those of the other refiners calling for a stabilization of prices in order to allow it to set and maintain its own beet prices. Eventually, the special committee reported that, in its viewpoint, the sugar refiners were not responsible for the rises in sugar prices and cleared them of all blame. Co-incidentally, shortly thereafter the world price of sugar fell and appeared to maintain a steady level for some time. This then encouraged certain members of Parliament on the special committee to claim to the press

The S.S. Jack arrives with a cargo of 1,260 tons of raw sugar on May 14, 1925.

The S.S. Edmonton manoeuvres alongside the Wallaceburg refinery dock on June 4, 1927.

that they had "put the fear of God into the sugar barons," ensuring themselves of a claim to be used in their next re-election campaign.

In 1924 Dominion once again found itself with a new President as Charles Henry Houson took over from Mr. Gilchrist. Mr. Houson had originally joined the Wallaceburg Sugar Co. Ltd. at its inception in 1901 as a general accountant and had worked his way through the corporate hierarchy. One of Mr. Houson's first actions was to react to the announcement that two new sugar beet production facilities were to be opened. The first was scheduled for development in Manitoba, followed by a second in Raymond, Alberta. This would cause Dominion to lose its exclusive position as Canada's only domestic sugar grower and forced it to look more closely at its own economic position in a market very much more crowded with sellers than before. During the next three years, a great deal was done to improve the efficiency of transporting and

processing the beets with the introduction of more transfer weigh stations, mechanical unloading systems at the refinery, and improved types of machinery within the plant. By these methods, the 1924 contracted harvest of more than 31,000 acres only lost 1.5% on its original level. In a like manner, the harvests of 1925 to 1927 kept losses well below the 10% rate, thus helping to maintain the company's position in the face of increased competition.

By 1928 matters had settled into a routine as the Canadian sugar market adjusted to the additions of the new facilities out west. But shortly afterwards, the Canadian government implemented a trade agreement with Cuba, the wording of which contained several loopholes that allowed the Cubans to export large quantities of refined sugar to Canada, where it was then sold at prices far below those of the Canadian sugar companies. Since most of this influx appeared in and around the Ontario market, Dominion was particularly threatened with a severe cut in its sales. Claims

Preparing the fields for seeding on the farm of James Anderson, Lot 3, Concession 16, Chatham Township.

Thinning the seedlings on the farm of John Deweyn, Lot 17, Concession 5, Sombra Township.

Working the rows of beets on the farm of W.T. Fox, Lot 3, Concession 3, Chatham Gore Township.

Cultivating and hoeing on the farm of Isaac Skinner, Lot 9, Concession 3, Chatham Gore Township

were rapidly made by Dominion and the other Canadian refiners against the Cubans for dumping sugar at an unnaturally low rate into Canada. Unfortunately, when the government looked into the matter and proposed implementing a dumping duty to protect the Canadian industry, the Cuban sugar industry countered by sending envoys to claim their rates were not dumping prices but were merely equal to those in Cuba (neglecting to mention that these domestic Cuban prices were deliberately set far below normal market levels to ensure that the exports could be justified in exactly the manner being used in this case.) As a result of these statements, the Canadian government then withdrew its threat, and Cuban sugar began to flood into the Canadian market, putting even more pressure on the already hard-pressed sugar companies. These imports continued until later in the year when the Cuban government took control of its own sugar industry and cut back production drastically in order to force-up prices. In reaction to this cut-back, the world sugar market immediately went on a buying spree. This forced-up prices as the Cuban's wished, but it also had the effect of draining away sugar supplies from the Canadian market. Initially this was welcomed by the Canadian refiners, but when it continued and began to threaten their future supplies of raw material, opinions changed, and the major cane refiners went on a panic scramble in order to secure their raw sugar requirements. At Dominion, however, this cut-back was nothing but good news, and the company was able to offer its farmers an additional bonus for the planting of extra acres beyond their previously signed contracts. Additionally, Mr. Houson had been pressing the government throughout the summer for legal and financial measures to actively protect and support the development of a domestic beet growing industry. The government's response was to implement a new tariff schedule, substantially increasing the duty on raw cane sugar while leaving beet unchanged. This left the cane refiners crying "foul" as it would virtually eliminate 80% of their output and make production totally uneconomic. Following consultations, the tariffs were amended, but the cane refiners were now in no doubt that those in power in Ottawa were intent upon expanding the beet sector at the cost of cane production. As a result, rumours began to circulate about secret negotiations between some of the cane refiners that could lead to consolidations and mergers; but when questioned on the matter, all the companies reputedly involved denied the prospect.

It is likely that things would have continued in this vein without any substantial change except that in October 1929 the growth in the world economy reversed itself, leaving many investors totally without capital to cover their debts. This sudden collapse, followed by a protracted period of downward spiralling of prices, values, and employment, led to the so-called Great Depression and threw everyone's plans for the future out the window.

One immediate consequence of the economic downturn was the recognition by all the sugar companies that their sales figures were bound to suffer as both domestic and industrial consumers cut back on their purchases. Anxious to maintain their individual trading levels the refiners now began a "war" of price cuts and extended credits which did nothing to actually promote sales and only succeeded in cutting profit levels for the companies involved. Another source of concern for the Canadian refiners at this time was the growth in sales for a new type of

A Dominion Sugar Co. Ltd. railcar tanker for molasses and sugar syrups.

sugar product called liquid sugar. Produced primarily in the United States, liquid sugar held significant technical advantages over crystalline sugar in such manufacturing processes as jam, candy, chocolate, soft drinks and canned fruits, and vegetables. Unable to immediately match the established liquid sugar production of the United States refiners, the Canadian sugar industry acted with a show of rare unanimity by pressing the Canadian government to temporarily assess liquid sugar imports on the same basis as granular sugar instead of the then existing rate as a blend or dilute syrup. In return, the industry committed itself to develop a liquid sugar production capacity and sell the product at a price below that of the imports and at a higher quality.

Naturally, the commercial food manufacturers (who were taking advantage of the lower priced import) objected strenuously to any change in the tariffs. However, when the sugar refiners submitted technical reports that showed the similarity of liquid and granular sugar, the government sided with the refiners and raised the applicable duties. In response, most of the food manufacturers dropped their use of liquid sugar in favour of the older, but cheaper, method of remelting granular sugar and here the matter rested until more than twenty years later, when the technology of liquid sugar came once more to the forefront of the industry's attention.

As the world economy continued to deteriorate in 1930, one noticeable consequence for Dominion was the suspension of recruitment of new immigrant workers from Europe, for with unemployment within Canada rapidly increasing, there was no justification for seeking labour abroad. Furthermore, there was an increased reluctance on the part of many Europeans to pull up their roots and start again halfway around the world during such a period of uncertainty. On the other hand, many Ontario farmers saw in sugar beets a means by which they could ensure their continued existence in the face of falling prices for other crops. Therefore those farmers who had previously grown moderate-sized beet crops began to clamour for larger contracts; while farmers who had been sporadic or had even rejected invitations to become beet growers flocked to the company offices to attempt to secure contracts to ensure an income for themselves. This forced the company to implement a system of rationing and to refuse contracts to new growers because the combined output of the Chatham and Wallaceburg refineries could not cope with more than the production from 38,000 acres.

Despite these obvious difficulties, the Dominion Sugar Co. Ltd. was generally in a better financial position than the cane sugar companies, who were still suffering the lingering effects of the financial woes inflicted upon them in 1920. Additionally, the beet industry was aided by the expressed policy of the government to support and, if possible, increase the proportion of beet sugar sold within the Canadian sugar market. As a result, rumours began to circulate once again about certain refiners holding talks on mergers or shutting down production entirely.

Within this atmosphere, C.H. Houson took what might be considered a highly speculative step by actively investigating the acquisition of one of the cane sugar refiners. Initial approaches to the St. Lawrence Sugar Co. Ltd. in Montreal were not successful, so his sights were switched to the country's oldest sugar company, the Canada Sugar Refining Co. Ltd.

Following a series of negotiations with the Canada Sugar Refining Co. Ltd. President, Huntly Redpath Drummond, an agreement was reached whereby the Dominion Sugar Co. Ltd. would effectively take over the Canada Sugar Refining Co. Ltd. and the two would form a new enterprise under the title Canada and Dominion Sugar Co. Ltd. (hereafter also referred to as Canada and Dominion or C and D) as of December 30, 1930.

Under the new business structure, the corporate head office would be located in Chatham, and of the ten directors on the Board, seven were previously executives of Dominion. This arrangement indicated clearly which side of the business was to dictate the terms for future decision making.

Huntly Redpath Drummond

NOTHING EQUALS SUGAR

The Montreal refinery in 1939.

CHAPTER FOUR

A New Order of Business

With the merger of the Dominion Sugar Co. Ltd. and the Canada Sugar Refining Co. Ltd. into the Canada and Dominion Sugar Co. Ltd., the new corporation became the largest sugar company in Canada. It was also something of a business anomaly as it now held substantial interests in both the beet and cane industries. This could and did lead to eventual conflicts of interest when attempting to sway government policies on sugar, since any significant preference for one type of sugar would inevitably have detrimental effects on the other.

It seems evident from those documents that have survived that C.H. Houson and his other business associates recognized that the Canada Sugar Refining Co. Ltd. was a major player in the Canadian industry and that they were getting something of a deal through this acquisition. What they did not anticipate, was the substantial amount of additional investment required to modernize the Montreal refinery and the phenomenal dominance of the *Redpath** brand within the Canadian market. Sales figures, for example, revealed to the new owners that in comparison to the *Dominion Crystal** brand, *Redpath* outsold *Dominion* virtually throughout eastern Canada. For the Maritimes and Quebec, this was only to be expected, but even in Ontario some of the margins were surprising. For example, in the Kingston – Ottawa region, *Redpath* sold 10,000 pounds of sugar for each pound of *Dominion*. Elsewhere, margins were not quite so dramatic, but still significant, as can been seen by the fact that in Toronto, Hamilton, Kitchener, North Bay, and Winnipeg, *Redpath* was outselling *Dominion* by a margin of 2 to 1; while even around London, Chatham, and Windsor, *Redpath* held an edge of 3 to 2. In fact, it was only in the market of Fort William that the records showed *Dominion* outselling *Redpath*. This must have come as something of a shock to the directors from the Dominion side of the business, that even in their own backyard they were being consistently outsold by *Redpath*, a circumstance that obviously could not continue without severe embarrassment to the "beet" men so dominant on the Board of Directors.

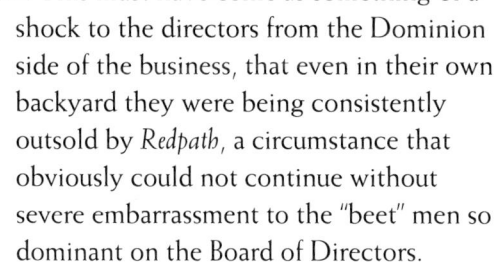

Therefore, it is not surprising that at the first Board meeting of the new corporation, held in the Mount Royal

---

* To differentiate the product brand names from the Corporate name, the products will hereafter be delineated by italics.

Hotel in Montreal, one of the first priorities on the agenda was to re-apportion the individual sales areas in order to give *Dominion* a much greater segment of the Ontario sales market. From this meeting the new joint sales department of the company was subsequently instructed to place *Redpath* into those territories requiring the lowest freight rate in Quebec, the Maritimes, and eastern Ontario while leaving the western Ontario market exclusively for *Dominion*, regardless of freight rates.

Another matter discussed was whether *Redpath* should now be sold direct to retailers in the style of *Dominion*. This proposal was strongly opposed by Huntly Redpath Drummond as he felt that it would alienate many of the wholesalers that were the cornerstone of the *Redpath* business. Following some intense discussions, Huntly Redpath Drummond was overruled on the grounds that the change would reduce the credit risk of the refiners since several wholesale distributors in Ontario and Quebec were known to be in financial difficulties.

The final matter on the agenda for this initial meeting was the urgent requirement for the upgrading and modernizing of refining equipment at Montreal and, to a lesser extent, at Chatham and Wallaceburg. It was decided to invest over $200,000 into new machinery, divided as follows: Montreal $116,000, Chatham $104,000, and Wallaceburg $8,500. A courageous decision in light of the state of the economy at that time.

Another repercussion of the Depression developed the following month when the Michigan Sugar Beet Co. announced that it would no longer seek to contract for beet acreage from its traditional suppliers in southwestern Ontario. This left those Ontario farmers who had previously supplied the Michigan Sugar Beet Co. desperate to find a new market for their crop, and they naturally turned to C and D to bail them out. Regrettably, the company was already under considerable pressure from its regular farmers to expand their acreage. Therefore it was forced to turn down any new contracts while rationing its own suppliers to an upper limit of 30,000 acres.

By April 1931, the redefined sales area for the company meant that *Redpath* was sold only as far as Hamilton with opportunities further west only if *Dominion* was unable to supply its customers. The decision to go direct to the retail trade in Ontario seemed to be working well, but as Huntly Redpath Drummond had previously warned, the Quebec wholesalers reacted negatively to this intrusion into their business by withdrawing substantial future orders from Redpath and giving them to St. Lawrence and Atlantic Sugars. In another aspect of the business, it was found that many of the smaller cartage companies, traditionally used by both the cane and beet refineries to distribute their finished sugar, were no longer in business due to the Depression. To alleviate this problem, the Board began negotiations with the Canada Steamship Lines to undertake shipments by lakers from the refineries to various distribution terminals around the Great Lakes corridor, including those at Three Rivers, Quebec City, Cornwall, Kingston, Sarnia, Owen Sound, Collingwood, Gore Bay, Blind River, Port Stanley, Windsor, Toronto, and Hamilton.

Over the summer, while the new equipment was installed at the Montreal and Chatham refineries, measures were undertaken to increase sales through an extensive advertising campaign. Unfortunately, the financial climate was not supportive of this attempt and little change resulted

A New Order of Business

Immigrant labourers working on the Wilfred Craven farm, Lot 8, Concession 15, Chatham Gore Township.

An unusual perspective in a beet field belonging to W. H. Rabideau, Lot 4, Concession 18, Dover Township.

Beet harvesting on the farm of W. H. Racher, Lot 7, Concession 4, Camden Township.

A couple pose beside one of the huts provided by the company on some of the regions farms.

in the already dull levels of sales recorded earlier in the year.

Towards the end of the year, when the beet harvest was tallied, it was found that a number of the farmers had exceeded their acreage quotas to ensure a full contract return. Left with the choice of refusing the crops from these extra acres and creating a source of bad feelings or buying these extra crops, the company chose the latter option. This was then accompanied by a warning that the continued severe competition from imported refined Cuban sugar would make the likelihood of repeating this additional purchase virtually impossible next year.

As indicated by its warning to its farmers, the impact of the imported Cuban sugar was indeed severe, especially in the Toronto and south central Ontario market, and greatly affected the *Dominion* sales. To counter this, the company organized a joint programme with the farmers' advocacy groups and the municipal governments from those counties where large crops of beets were grown, to petition the provincial and federal governments to act to curtail this flood of foreign sugar and protect employment in Ontario. This led the Minister of National Revenue, the Hon. E.B. Rychman, to announce a new ruling on the duties applicable to imported refined sugar as of mid-February 1932. This new measure effectively eliminated the advantages held by the Cuban and to a lesser extent the U.S. refineries, thus returning some degree of protection to the Canadian industry.

The S.S. Canadian, berthed at the Wallaceburg refinery.

Furthermore, there was talk of increased support for the beet sugar industry through new legislation being considered by a parliamentary committee on agriculture, which would specifically allocate a set percentage of Canadian production to beet facilities.

In March, the new proposed contract for beets was issued by the company. Due to the prevailing weakness in the economy and the continued drop in sugar prices worldwide, the 1932 contract was set at $4.98 per ton. This shocked many farmers who were hoping for the $5.63 per ton provided in the 1931 contract and it was feared that the response would be correspondingly low. However, due to those same pressing economic conditions, farmers recognized that even a low price was better than no price and the entire quota of acres was quickly signed up.

In June 1932 the financially troubled Atlantic Sugar Refineries Ltd. attempted to reorganize itself with only a mixed degree of success, and throughout the summer there were rumours of plans for a merger between Canada and Dominion and Atlantic, although in the end nothing positive actually occurred. Elsewhere in Canada, the agricultural sector of Manitoba was crying out for assistance in the face of increased bankruptcies by farmers.

The Chatham factory beet yard during the 1931 campaign.

This led the Manitoba provincial government to respond with a guarantee of $600,000 to assist in the establishment of a sugar beet industry in Manitoba. This was, of course, bad news for Canada and Dominion, who saw in this the elimination of yet another of their sales markets.

Problems continued during the latter part of the summer, when heavy rains alternated with periods of extreme heat creating poor growing conditions for the beet crop. Even so, when the full harvest estimates were tallied, enough acreage remained to exceed the original established quota. Once again, in a gesture of support for its suppliers, the company agreed to purchase the excess crop, even though it did not have a sales market in which it could economically dispose of the product. Meanwhile, on the cane side, sales were so slow that all purchases of raw sugar were suspended for the duration of the shipping season as earlier shipments had accumulated to the point where there was enough raw sugar available to last through until the spring of 1933. By the end of the year, although the sales record showed some growth in Montreal, the Province of Quebec sales region, and around Ottawa, it was overshadowed by the plummeting sales figures for the Toronto, Hamilton, Kitchener, Windsor, Chatham, and western sales regions. Nor did things improve during January and February 1933, leading the sales department to increase its discounts in an attempt to boost sales in the face of a declining market.

Matters worsened in March 1933, as the government sought to extract money from additional sources by implementing a new excise tax of 2 cents per pound on sales of granulated sugar. In the domestic sales market, this was a severe blow, but to the commercial sales sector it proved disastrous, as this tax added as much as 45% to the cost of sugar for food manufacturers. The results were obvious and immediate as sugar consumption plummeted and refined stocks remained unsold. In desperation, the refiners sent numerous telegrams, both individually and as a representative body, to press for a special exemption for the domestic beet industry, but without success.

Similar protests and petitions by the food manufacturers were also ignored, causing a significant increase in the smuggling of sugar across the border from the United States by several major food producers, who could obtain their sugar supplies in the United States at almost half the Canadian price.

Seeing its financial difficulties mounting, the company gave serious consideration to implementing lay-offs and even the shutting down of the Montreal refinery for an extended period (despite the better level of sales emanating from that plant as compared to Chatham and Wallaceburg) as the "beet" dominated Board of Directors

The head office of Canada and Dominion at Chatham.

sought to protect their preferred production of beet at the expense of the cane facility. However, vigorous opposition from Huntly Redpath Drummond at a succession of Board meetings prevented these measures being adopted, and instead, production continued at Montreal while the planned beet crop for 1933 was restricted to 1932 acreage. Additionally, the Wallaceburg refinery was selected for a major overhaul to bring it up to the production efficiencies being enjoyed by Montreal and Chatham.

By the end of the year, a successful beet harvest (that did not exceed the contracted acreage) allowed Wallaceburg to run for 60½ days producing 37.4 million pounds of sugar, Chatham ran for 64 days resulting in 47.6 million pounds, while Montreal's output exceeded 224.1 million pounds. One additional point that came to the notice of the directors at this time was that there was still a significant preference by both retail and wholesale customers for the *Redpath* brand over the *Dominion* product, despite the deliberate attempts of the company to encourage the switching of allegiance by its customers to the beet line. In response, such was the determination by the "beet men" to promote this sector of the company's business that all advertisements inserted in the *Canadian Grocer* magazine throughout 1933 and 1934 were exclusively for *Dominion Crystal* with no mention or advertising for the *Redpath* brand being included.

Early in 1934, due to the extra revenue earned in 1933, the federal government extended its taxation on sugar by applying it to all products containing sugar instead of simply on the sugar itself. The result of this measure was a major explosion of indignation and protest from across the nation by every food manufacturer. This led Finance Minister E.N. Rhodes to reconsider his position and propose that the excise tax be cut to 1 cent per pound as of July 1, 1934. Still not satisfied, the food manufacturers continued their campaign of pressure so that on May 20, 1934, Prime Minister R.B. Bennett intervened on the issue by initiating the cut as of that day instead of the announced July 1, which gave the sugar industry some hope for a rebound from the tumbling sales figures being reported by their sales and marketing departments.

Meanwhile, at the offices of C and D, three other matters were being discussed that were affecting prospects for the future. First, was the announcement that the Quebec provincial government was considering re-establishing a beet-processing industry in their province. Second, in the United Kingdom, the British government policy of giving substantially preferential rates for British West Indies raw sugar resulted in an almost total withdrawal of normal supplies destined for Canada as the Caribbean companies sought better markets in the United Kingdom. Third, was the development in Toronto of a new refining operation by Crosse and Blackwell in their food-processing factory at the foot of Bathurst Street. This facility was rapidly capturing a sizable part of the city's market as it offered discounts far above those justifiable in the existing economic circumstances and well beyond those that could be offered by C and D for either of its brands.

In response to these circumstances, the company executives decided to protect the beet division by cutting back output at Montreal to the point of establishing a process for making sugar syrups at Wallaceburg (a product previously exclusive to the Montreal refinery) and also making semi-refined sugar for the manufacturing trade that was sold in used raw sugar bags.

Unfortunately, Mother Nature did not co-operate with these protective company measures as the driest summer in many years withered the beet crop, forcing many farmers to attempt re-planting very late in the season. This, in turn, exhausted the reserve stocks of beet seed held by the company without the possibility of obtaining any more except at a premium price. By the end of the year, the company's financial outlook was decidedly gloomy because the already mentioned poor crop results were compounded by several additional factors including supplies of contaminated replacement beet seed stock; major repairs and re-equipment needs at all three refineries; the sinking of the M.V. *Clan Mackay* with 8,500 tons of Australian sugar bound for Montreal; and the loss of export sales to the United States due to undercutting of prices by Cuba for the U.S. market.

The only two relatively good pieces of news were that first the Crosse and Blackwell sugar plant was in financial difficulties, which had brought about a meeting of its creditors, and secondly the general sales reports showed a slight recovery from the previous year's low point.

Moving into 1935, recognition was given to the contribution of Huntly Redpath Drummond in the corporation, when he was elevated from his position of Director in Canada and Dominion to Vice-President. This move possibly indicated a reconciliation of the cane and beet factions within the Board, whose earlier differences had undoubtedly been a cause for unhappiness since the merger in 1930. Shortly afterwards, the Annual General Meeting of C and D took place and its minutes contain some interesting points that highlight the state of the company in the midst of the Depression.

On the positive side, a proposed increase on the excise tax for sugar did not occur, which prompted a rapid growth of sugar sales in the latter part of the first quarter of the year. Additionally, the company was able to purchase land adjacent to the Chatham plant at a good price for an expansion of the storage and ancillary capacities of the refinery. Technical improvements within the two beet plants allowed an increase in the daily processing capacity from 2,500 tons to 5,000 tons. Finally, new lower rates for rail transport made shipment of refined sugar by rail more economic and allowed deliveries to be made in a shorter time than by using the earlier ship-borne method.

On the negative side, however, the former Crosse and Blackwell Sugar Refinery in Toronto had been re-formed as the Beamish Sugar Company thus threatening an even bigger drop in Toronto sales than had previously been occurring.

The Canada and Dominion "float" in the 1935 Silver Jubilee parade for King George V.

Similarly in the west, the Canadian Sugar Factories Ltd. of Raymond, Alberta, was producing plans to build a factory at Lethbridge, while a U.S. consortium was developing a proposal for the establishment of a beet plant in the Red River Valley area of Manitoba.

C and D initially planned to match this latter proposal by establishing a beet plant of its own, but following discussions between C.H. Houson and the Hon. J.S. McDiarmid, the Manitoba Minister of Mines and Natural Resources, it was decided to drop the C and D proposal and concentrate on development within Ontario instead. To this end, the company initiated funding for research at the Ontario Agricultural College in Guelph in co-operation with the University of Toronto and the Ontario government to develop new and improved strains of beets that could be grown to produce seeds instead of relying upon supplies that originated predominantly in Germany.

Once again, however, circumstances combined to cause problems for the company, when in May 1935, labour activists attempted to expand unionized worker influence within a substantially non-unionized industry by recruiting beet workers. Posters were put up across the beet districts claiming that the sugar beet growers were miserably underpaid for their efforts and that the "sugar barons" were making huge personal profits off the backs of the exploited workforce. A mass meeting was called for May 30, 1935, at Tecumseh Park in Chatham where union activists pressed for people to join the union with promises that the sum of $19 per acre would be demanded and achieved (instead of the current $14 per acre) by unionization.

When this call was largely ignored by the beet workers, the union resorted to a series of smaller local meetings, coupled with "flying squads" of union militants who toured the beet fields to persuade workers of the advantages of following the union. When this did not work, certain extremist elements took matters into their own hands by advocating and occasionally using intimidation tactics, followed by a call for a strike of all beet workers until their "grievance" was settled. Again these tactics failed, and the small number of workers who did stop work abandoned their strike on June 10. Some farmers did, in fact, pay between $16 and $18 to their field labour but most stuck to their original scale in the face of the economic conditions of the industry at that time.

In reviewing the singular failure of this attempt to unionize beet workers, it can be seen that the union did not recognize two major factors. First, the continuance of the Depression made even the relatively low pay for beet work better than no job or money at all, but more important was the fact that most of the field labourers and farmers were originally immigrants recruited by C and D. These people maintained a strong loyalty to the company that had paid their passage to Canada and provided them with assistance during their initial period of adjustment. In response, they now repaid this generosity by ignoring the call to strike.

By year's end, the corporate reviews could be said to be mixed. The sugar beet crop was only moderate in quality, having suffered from leaf blight in August; however, the availability of labour was plentiful, which allowed the crop to be harvested in record time. Additionally, discussions with farmers on the introduction of mechanical seeders, thinners, and harvesters progressed to the extent that certain farmers agreed to experiment with machinery on parts of their acreage during part of the season the following year. Within the refineries, increased efficiencies produced by updated equipment reduced costs of production, while between workers and management, negotiations were begun for the introduction of a pension fund. Significantly, this fund was originally proposed and pressed by Huntly Redpath Drummond, who felt that the contributions made by long-term employees required recognition in a tangible form.

At the next Board meeting, held in Toronto on January 23, 1936, the prospects for the upcoming year were discussed. They indicated that sales in the Toronto area were substantially down (71 million pounds for 1931 to 52 million pounds in 1935) as a result of the price undercutting done by the Beamish Sugar Company. In retaliation this forced C and D to cut its own Toronto prices to the point where it was losing money just to retain its share of the market. On the other hand, in Montreal, exactly the opposite was occurring, with sales climbing higher than ever (44 million pounds in 1931 to 67 million in 1935.) Elsewhere, the trend seemed to be slightly upwards but without significant hopes for a rapid growth within the next year.

Next on the Board's agenda came a report from the cane section of the company wherein it was recorded that it was having difficulties obtaining regular and reliable supplies of raw sugar at favourable prices, despite the fact that there was a current world surplus of raw sugar of more than 9 million tons. This was then followed by observations from the beet section that the world surplus had caused an extended drop in the price of sugar, which in turn reduced the prices that could be offered by the company to farmers for their beet crops and still remain competitive in the Canadian market. Unfortunately, this did not help the farmers, as their costs of labour, machinery, and fertilizers were all escalating, forcing some farmers to reconsider their commitment to growing sugar beet in favour of less labour-intensive crops.

Finally it was revealed that the federal government was considering cancelling its 1932 duty on refined sugar imports. If implemented, this measure would once again allow significant volumes of Cuban and U.S. sugar to be imported, flooding the Canadian market, to the detriment of both the beet and cane refiners in Canada.

By the middle of the year, the earnings of the company were down considerably, which would usually indicate cutbacks in expenditures, but due to the extremely low world price for raw sugar, the company decided to invest in purchases of raws with the intention of stockpiling up to 20,000 tons through the next winter in expectation of higher prices in 1937. For the beet division, the company co-ordinated with the Sugar Beet Growers Association to first pressure the government to exempt beet sugar from the excise duty as a means of encouraging employment. Secondly, it was the joint opinion of the company and its growers that a new round of recruitment for field labour from Europe was required as settled immigrants and Canadians seemed increasingly reluctant to do the manual labour required for the proper cultivation of beets.

A third issue on which the company and the Growers Association co-operated was in their response to the government announcement of a possible re-establishment of preferential tariff concessions by Canada with the British West Indies, as had occurred in 1927. Fearing another influx of imported products undercutting their own, the combined forces elicited the additional support of the other sugar companies and various beet-growing municipalities, to persuade the government to drop the idea for the time being. At a more local level, however, this co-operation was perhaps best seen in the funding and support given by the company to the establishment of beet "clubs" for boys, who were given lectures and taught how to cultivate beets in small plots by company employees. These boys were supplied with beet seed by the company and at harvest time they were paid for their crops in proportion to the regular farmers and awarded prizes for particularly high yields.

In August, news was released that the Beamish Sugar Co. in Toronto had grossly overextended itself financially due to its deliberate cut-pricing policy and was being pressed for re-payment by its creditors. This forced Beamish to put its prices up to a more realistic market level, causing many customers to return to the *Redpath* and *Dominion* brands. At the end of the year, the reports that have survived give very little indication of the status of the Montreal refinery as almost all documentation emphasizes the continued preference of the executives for the beet division.

One other point worth noting to conclude 1936 was the introduction of the pension plan championed by Huntly Redpath Drummond which applied to both current and previously retired employees and gave the previously retired workers a grant of $35 per month for life.

With the arrival of 1937, the season's round of negotiations for beet prices came up once again. The company proposed to contract for 40,000 acres at the same price given in 1936 due to the low price for world sugar. However, since competing crops such as corn, grains, and tobacco were currently enjoying a rise in value, many farmers refused to grow beets, resulting in only 18,000 acres being eventually signed up. This forced the company to increase its offer (despite the financial losses involved) by a dollar per ton, which drew in additional contracts to an eventual level of 30,000 acres. Unfortunately, heavy spring rains and extensive flooding prevented many farmers from planting at the right time, and only 26,000 acres were actually started.

For the cane division, 1937 was also a period of unsettled business due to increased competition as each Canadian sugar company attempted to maintain or even increase market share by offering discounts. This was compounded by the International Sugar Conference held in London, England, which resulted in an agreement to curb overproduction by ensuring exporters a guaranteed market with selected importing countries for a specified quantity of sugar. On the face of things, this might have appeared to be a beneficial opportunity for C and D, but due to the wording of the terms of the agreement, Canada now became obliged to bring in substantially more refined sugar imports than in the past, so that by September 1937 they had reached a volume more than double that imported for the entire year in 1936.

Certain of their impending extinction if things remained unchanged, the Beet Growers Association pleaded with the government to remit the excise tax on beet production, but once again their calls fell upon deaf ears. This caused some farmers to abandon their already planted beets in favour of other crops and as a result only 24,000 acres were eventually harvested. Faced with the choice of shutting down one plant entirely or splitting the harvest between the two refineries, the company chose the latter

Planting beets and the floods that followed in April 1937.

option. This meant the two refineries each had to cut back their "runs" so that at Chatham, instead of the 68½ days of production experienced in 1936, only 37½ days were actually worked, while Wallaceburg's production was similarly sliced from 65 days to 34½, a figure not experienced since 1907 and one that did not portend well for the long-term future of the Ontario sugar beet industry.

As a result of this reduced production period, the *Dominion* sugar supply was unable to meet the increasing demand being enjoyed by the sales department during the first quarter of 1938. This led to the necessary expedient of transferring *Redpath* sugar into the markets of Chatham, Wallaceburg, and Windsor, much to the chagrin of those corporate executives who had been deliberately fostering the beet product as the primary corporate line. In the company's western market area too, problems were developing as the Alberta Sugar Beet Co. offered its product in the Winnipeg market at a price 10 cents per pound below that of *Dominion*. This forced the company to slice its own prices to match, thus eliminating any profit for sales in that area.

Problems mounted for the beet sector of the company in February 1938 when it was reported that many farmers were reluctant to sign beet contracts. Upon investigation it was found that most of the farmers had concerns about shortages of labour coupled with the overall trend of downward prices for raw cane sugar, which would inevitably reduce their returns for the year if they grew beets.

In response, the company accelerated its attempts to recruit skilled labour in Europe, and teams were sent to Belgium, Holland, and Czechoslovakia; while at home, the company raised its price for beets by one dollar per ton to $6.25. This persuaded some additional farmers to sign up, but even so, only 27,000 acres were contracted in 1938, a far cry from the 30,000 acres easily obtained in 1935.

Obviously, matters in the beet industry were not as they should be, and the company made a great effort to look for long-term solutions to the continued difficulties of the industry. Experiments were made with mechanical seed planters, beet blockers, mechanized harvesters, and lifters with various degrees of success, while co-operative plans were implemented with the Ontario Agricultural College to develop improved varieties of seed and crop-disease controls.

As the summer progressed, the continued drop in world raw sugar prices led to some discussion at Board level about dropping the additional one dollar per ton previously offered to the farmers. The proposal was not implemented, however, as it was felt that the negative reaction from farmers and the likelihood of triggering a wholesale boycott of sugar beet in 1939, outweighed the short-term financial loss that would be suffered due to the additional payment.

As the harvest time approached, estimates showed that only 25,000 acres would be available, leaving the company with the difficult choice, once again, of where to process the crop. After much discussion, it was decided that both plants would again be run on a reduced schedule, following which a decision would be made on whether to mothball one refinery for a season or two.

One interesting fact that appeared in the annual sugar beet crop report for this year that is worthy of mention was the significant increase of direct deliveries to the plant by farmers. This was due mainly to the increased use of motorized tractors instead of horse-drawn wagons, and it had the added effect of reducing the need for the numerous weigh stations situated across the growing districts; the change allowed the company to reduce its costs by closing down several stations in 1938.

Plans for 1939 were now drawn up, and prospects looked somewhat uncertain as rumours of war continued to circulate despite the Munich Treaty. Additionally, world raw sugar prices continued to fall and so the 1939 contract was initially offered at $5.75, fifty cents less than the 1938 crop. In past years, this cut would normally have raised a storm of protest from the farmers, but due to the uncertainties of the world political and economic climate, most farmers put off signing and took a wait-and-see attitude.

Meanwhile in Montreal, the company's cane refinery was experiencing its own difficulties. These centred on the fact that while most new cargo ships were substantially larger than their earlier counterparts, the Lachine Canal had not been widened or deepened to accommodate these newer vessels. As a result, only small cargo ships and towed barges could now unload directly at the refinery, while larger ocean-going vessels were forced to dock over a mile away at Windmill Point on the St. Lawrence River. From there, the bags of sugar were transferred manually onto trucks and driven to the refinery, adding significantly to the initial costs of production. Feeling that this lack of access reduced the value of the Montreal property, the company applied for a reduction in the taxes applied by the City of Montreal. Naturally, the city refused this application and called for the full tax assessment to be paid by claiming that it was not its fault that ship sizes had increased or that the federal government had neglected to expand the canal system. In reply the company took the matter to court, where it succeeded in obtaining a small reduction in its tax levels. Ironically, at the same time, the federal government department that supervised the lands along the bank of the Lachine Canal, and from whom the company had leased a

Let Redpath Sweeten It

Supporters and members of the Montreal refinery baseball team in 1937.

strip to construct special ramps for loading refined sugar directly onto lakers, decided to impose a special surcharge on all cargoes of refined sugar moved across the government's strip of land. In response, the company launched another court appeal while making plans to use Windmill Point for output loading as well as input unloading.

Throughout March and April 1939, the federal government was investigating its current trade agreement with the British West Indies, and much pressure was being put on the government to terminate the deal. Such a termination was greatly desired by the beet sector of the industry as it opened up an opportunity to press for a larger sector of the Canadian sugar market and greater protection from low-priced cane sugar. On the other hand for the cane refiners, any abrogation of the treaty could lead to a greater instability in the supplies of raw sugar, a situation not at all desirable. In the end, as might be expected, the executives of the company sided with the beet lobby and co-operated with the Ontario Sugar Beet Growers Association to send a deputation to Ottawa to call for the ending of the trade agreement and the removal of the federal excise tax on beet sugar.

As the political situation in Europe deteriorated in the early summer of 1939, the volume of sugar sales began to rise as nervous individuals decided to stock up "just in case." This led to a general rise in the price of refined sugar, which caused many farmers to finally decide to take up the preferred contracts for beets in 1939, and more than 37,500 acres were signed up in short order. One worrying point, however, was the dominant percentage of beet seed that was supplied by German growers. In case of war, these supplies would inevitably be immediately cut off, so the company went on an extended purchasing spree, acquiring additional seed supplies from Holland, Belgium, Italy, Hungary, Poland, and Denmark as well as from Germany; in addition, contracts were signed with North American agricultural groups to expand beet seed crops for 1940.

In July, the *Redpath* line introduced its newest innovations for the sale of sugar. These included a new 5 pound and 10 pound paper bag for white sugar and a cellophane 2 pound package for Golden Yellow. Both these lines were aimed at the convenience domestic market and under normal circumstances could have been expected to do well; unfortunately, circumstances beyond anyone's control were shortly to intervene and severely curb their availability to the public.

The Chatham Daily News

CHATHAM, ONTARIO, WEDNESDAY, MAY 28, 1941.

Let Us All Help To Arm the Wall!

Day by day the hearthstones of Canada are protected by a wall of Britain's guns, ships and planes in the hands of men whose high morale and unflinching courage commands the admiration of the civilized world.

Day by day this wall must be bolstered — rebuilt. More ships— more guns — more planes — more food—must go to Britain in ever-increasng measure. A surplus must be built up to insure a British offensive—a victory—and finally—PEACE!

War weapons must be bought with money — YOUR money. Thanks to the workings of democracy you HAVE money. You have but to put that money to work!

Let Canada use some of your savings for a while. Invest NOW in priceless security for your home —your family — all that you hold dear!

Help To Arm the Wall!

BUY VICTORY BONDS

TO THE LIMIT OF YOUR RESOURCES

Canada and Dominion Sugar Co. Limited

CHAPTER FIVE

Sugar At War

With the invasion of Poland by the armies of the Third Reich, the prospect of war became inevitable. This led to a frenzy of sugar buying across Canada which far outstripped the levels of the similar occurrence of 1914. Despite having stockpiled additional supplies for the previous two months, all the refineries were soon emptied of refined sugar. Much of this can be blamed on the retailers who, in some instances, saw the opportunity to sell other goods by linking sales of sugar to equal value purchases of other products or by selling sugar by the hundredweight to individual customers who had previously thought twice about buying more than 10 pounds at a time. At the industrial level, too, demands for sugar supplies rose with the outbreak of war. This was because sugar was now needed both for its easily recognizable traditional uses in prepared foods, medicines, and drinks and also for its inclusion in such diverse war products as varnishes, dyes, alcohol, synthetic rubber, plastics, and even explosives. Fortunately, Canada had a total of six cane and five beet refineries from which to draw its supplies, but even so, estimates of the required wartime needs for sugar indicated that every plant would have to work at full capacity to supply the domestic, industrial, and military demands that were likely to arise.

On September 3, the Wartime Prices and Trade Board (W.P.T.B.) was established and called a conference of all the national refiners to seek a solution to the immediate shortage of sugar. From this meeting, a consensus was reached that each refinery would attempt to increase current output by 25% and maintain the established prices without change. To Huntly Redpath Drummond, this must have brought back strong memories of 1914; once again, Huntly was involved in the group of industrialists who helped establish the system of centralized sugar purchasing and distribution that was to be used throughout the war and beyond.

Meanwhile, the level of panic buying continued unabated, providing plentiful material for newspaper reports on suspected black market rings, hoarders, fifth-column threats to production facilities, and threats of government takeovers of the entire industry. Within a week, the Canadian sugar industry was working flat out to increase sugar supplies. C and D initially shipped large amounts to Manitoba, followed by several train loads to the Niagara region where a bumper crop of fruit was in danger of rotting due to a lack of sugar for canning and preserving.

To supplement these increases, the W.P.T.B. took the initiative a step further and persuaded several large manufacturers to sell back part of their refined sugar in their possession to the government. By this means, 1 million pounds of sugar was obtained from the Coca-Cola Company while the Pepsi-Cola Company contributed 800,000 pounds. Spurred by this success, the W.T.P.B. issued telegrams to the twelve biggest industrial users of sugar stating:

> *The Wartime Prices and Trade Board would appreciate expression of your willingness to release your refined sugar supply in excess of two months requirements for general distribution.*

As a result, an additional 25.4 million pounds of sugar was secured for re-use within forty-eight hours.

Despite these efforts by the government and the full co-operation of the sugar industry and its customers, numerous complaints came in to the W.P.T.B. through various M.P.s, Chambers of Commerce, and Boards of Trade, claiming that their own communities were not receiving their normal proportion of sugar supplies. In every case, subsequent investigation showed that deliveries by the refiners to those locations were *at least* 25% higher than the average for 1938. A more legitimate petition was, however, submitted by the apiarists of the country, who petitioned the government to grant them special buying privileges for sugar, especially during the forthcoming winter when their bees would be fed on a solution of white sugar and water. The government acceded to the request and subsequently divided the country into sectors under which Canada and Dominion supplied the beekeepers in Manitoba and Ontario, while the St. Lawrence Sugar Co. got Quebec.

By the beginning of October 1939, the initial chaos caused by the advent of war had subsided, but in this new wartime environment, the government was determined to completely control all matters related to sugar. In support of this determination, S.R. Noble, the assistant general manager of the Royal Bank of Canada, was appointed Canada's Sugar Administrator. His mandate and authority stemmed directly from the government with the power to undertake all future negotiations with the U.K. Sugar Controller for arranging supplies of sugar to be imported into Canada, as well as having total supervision of the purchasing, shipment, and delivery of sugar to and from the refiners of Canada.

At the recommendation of the refiners, one of Mr. Noble's first acts was to purchase all current supplies held by refiners and then immediately re-sell it to the refiners at a higher price. The official reason for this action was that it was a means by which to accumulate a fund to safeguard the refiners in the event of a post-war slump in prices and avoid a repetition of the events of 1920. His next act, however, was not quite so popular with the refiners as he eliminated "temporarily" the dumping duty applied against Cuban and U.S. sugars in order to accelerate the recovery of sugar stocks by encouraging more imports. For the refiners, this was not welcome news as it was felt it would set a precedent for similar action in the future, but in view of the extreme shortage they felt there was little that they could do and so they did not object to the ruling.

Shortly afterwards, Mr. Noble extended his attempts to acquire a fund for future use by implementing an additional excise tax on sugar sales. Despite some misgivings, the cane refiners generally acquiesced to this new tax. For the beet refiners, however, the tax was an unacceptable additional burden that had to be fought. As a result, they argued for the exemption of beet sugar from the tax as a means of encouraging farmers to increase their crops of beet and as a way to reduce the reliance upon imported sugar supplies that could be threatened by enemy surface and submarine activity. Unfortunately these arguments were dismissed out of hand by Mr. Noble and the tax was applied across the board.

Mr. Noble's failure to act to ensure the maximum production of beet through financial incentives and positive legislation may at first seem odd; however documents held by the Public Archives in Ottawa include numerous private memoranda between Mr. Noble and the W.P.T.B. that reveal a deliberate bias on the part of Mr. Noble and the government against the beet industry. Part of this bias was based on the pre-war undertaking made by the Canadian government at the International Sugar Conference in 1937, that it would not expand the beet sugar industry by subsidies but would instead maintain its purchases of raw cane sugar from fellow Commonwealth sources. But most telling is the revealed fact that the government did not want to set a precedent of subsidizing or encouraging an industry that was known to have an active political profile and that could cause problems in a post-war environment if subsidies and protective measures were subsequently dropped. Therefore, in private, it effectively meant that it was preferable for the Canadian public to suffer shortages of sugar and possible future rationing rather than do everything possible to maximize production of beet sugar.

In public, the government put on an entirely different face by instituting a Tariff Board inquiry on the domestic production of sugar and how it could be developed. Teams of specially selected "investigators" visited both the Chatham and Wallaceburg refineries and met deputations from the Ontario Sugar Beet Growers Association, who called for subsidies on beet in a manner already well established for other crops being grown. They even heard a proposal from Mr. Houson that C and D was prepared to establish a new beet facility in Manitoba at no cost to the public purse. But to these and other supportive proposals made by the producers of beet, the government investigators made only passing and dismissive mention in their eventual report to the government and even referred to the beet industry as "localized" with little capacity or ability to grow. This now allowed the federal government to continue in its pre-set policies and leave the Ontario beet industry to attempt to supply eastern Canada's increasing sugar needs without proper backing. In comparison to this negative central government attitude, the provincial government of Saskatchewan announced financial support for experiments in beet growing in the Qu'Appelle River Valley, and the Manitoba government began the construction of a refinery for beets at Winnipeg.

Despite these apparent problems, the beet sector of the company pressed ahead, and through some additional support at harvest time from local teams of high school students, a crop of almost 36,000 acres was collected. In the cane sector, production continued unabated as supplies of sugar increased to the point where the Sugar Administrator was able to officially declare the shortage crisis ended, and then re-establish the old dumping duties as in pre-war days.

Early in 1940, rumours began to appear in various trade journals and newspapers of a forthcoming increase in

Promoting the war effort at Wallaceburg.

the federal excise tax on sugar. This precipitated another round of increased sales as people stocked up on sugar, which in turn depleted the raw cane supplies held by the company at Montreal. Anxious to maintain their production, the company contacted the Sugar Administrator to warn him that while their reserves should last until the opening of navigation, any delay in the arrival of vessels would inevitably lead to a shut-down of the refinery. Mr. Noble immediately replied that to avoid this possibility a quantity of 6,500 tons of raw sugar would be trans-shipped from the Maritime ports with the additional costs being absorbed by the Sugar Control Board.

Meanwhile, in Ontario the negotiations on the new season's contract between the company and its beet farmers were not going well, with the growers complaining loudly that since the new contract was basically the same as that proposed in 1939, they would refuse beets in favour of corn, soya beans, and vegetable products. Although the company could not offer a higher beet price for the 1940 season (due to restrictions imposed by the Sugar Administrator,) the timely payment of a bonus for the bumper 1939 crop persuaded many farmers to sign up and 40,000 acres was under contract by mid-March.

In May the Sugar Administrator took new action to extend his control over sugar and raise money for the government by using an Order-in-Council which invested authority in the W.P.T.B. to require all sugar refiners to sell their entire raw and refined stocks to the government, who then immediately increased the price and re-sold the sugar to the sugar companies for a profit of 30 cents per ton on raw alone. For the refined side, he increased the list price from $4.80 to $5.15 per 100 pounds and levied an additional assessment of 33¼ cents per 100 pounds on all refined stocks currently held or held in the future by the Canadian refiners. He also ruled that a similar levy would be imposed on all refined beet sugars. This effectively stopped the beet refiners from offering additional money to the beet growers for their new crops, which obviously caused resentment by the farmers, who erroneously concluded that the sugar company was siphoning off the extra money for their own benefit while cutting the farmers out.

As the summer progressed, the drain of manpower to military service and war industries left the beet refineries short of labour. This shortage also worried many farmers, and their response was to besiege the company offices, threatening to tear up "your" beets if the company did not supply them with the required workers. Similarly in Montreal, labour shortages within the cane refinery raised the question of shortening the working week. In all three cases, additional efforts by company officials resulted in labour being found to allow normal operations to continue.

The Canada and Dominion choral group.

By October 1940, the new Winnipeg beet plant came into operation, which helped Canadian sugar supplies but decreased the sales market for the company. Fortunately the huge demand for sugar in Great Britain allowed the company to obtain export permits with the added bonus of being able to use newly approved measures that allowed companies to purchase raw sugar, import, refine, and re-export it under bond and reclaim 99% of the original tariffs.

When the season's beet crop came in, the company records show that despite the continuing difficulty of lack of labour and an extended period of poor weather prior to the harvest (which turned many of the fields into quagmires of mud), some 38,000 acres were actually harvested. Both Wallaceburg and Chatham ran for 72 days, and refined sugar production amounted to over 98 million pounds.

As the war intensified in Europe, the demand for servicemen, backed by additional military production, drained Canadian manpower into either the armed services or the mushrooming industrial centres of Detroit, Windsor, London, Hamilton, and Toronto, leaving some farmers almost without workers in 1941. Unfortunately, the counter-remedy of offering more money was not a viable option for the farmers of Ontario as they were already suffering from increased costs of fertilizers, machinery, gasoline, and in some cases the loss of useable acreage as military bases were established on prime agricultural land for pilot training centres under the Commonwealth Air Training Scheme. Neither could the company supply additional money in 1941 as it too was suffering a lack of spare parts, machinery, gasoline, and other essentials of production, while its prices were deliberately being held at current levels under the control imposed by the Sugar Administrator. As might be

A field worker hut.

expected the farmers looked for alternative ways of alleviating their problems, and with the support of their municipal governments and local members of Parliament, they petitioned the federal government to either drop its $1.35 per 100 pounds tax on sugar when applied to beet supplies or advance a subsidy of one dollar per ton for growing beets. Some militant farmers even went so far as to advocate a total strike on producing beet until either the government or the company guaranteed more money. Eventually, following much internal wrangling, a deputation of farmers went to Ottawa but, as expected, received very little support for their ideas. The farmers were now left in the position of either accepting the current contracts or finding alterative crops. As a result, although the acreage contracted for in 1941 fell to just over 32,000 acres, it still represented a moderately good return for the company in the light of circumstances prevailing.

At the end of March 1941, the Sugar Administrator was once again instructed by the Minister of Finance to raise government revenues. In response, Mr. Noble repeated his purchase and re-sale system for all sugar supplies raising the prices from 4.89½ cents to 5.89¼ cents per ton. Additionally, in view of the speculation of an increase in sugar duties in the forthcoming budget, a pre-budget levy of 1 cent per pound was imposed overnight to prevent hoarding. Then in a move that can only be described as crafty, the Sugar Administrator instructed the sugar companies to collect the new tax and forward all monies to Ottawa, thus forcing the company to absorb the administrative costs and to bear the inevitable brunt of criticism from the customers paying the tax.

Throughout the summer, the shortage of experienced labour continued to be a problem, and it was only by resorting once again to college and high school volunteers that the required blocking of the crops was achieved for the required acres.

Even so, the inevitable toll on productivity occurred so that although almost 30,000 acres was eventually harvested, the sugar content was lower than normal, which resulted in lower payments back to the farmers in accordance with the terms of the standard contracts. This was the last straw to many farmers and led many of them to state categorically that without substantially higher payments of one kind or another, they would switch to other crops that were already partially or fully subsidized by existing government measures. In fact, they noted that not only was sugar beet the only major crop being grown in Ontario that was not currently supported by governmental

One view of wartime sugar rationing.

funding, but it was the only crop penalized by an imposed excise tax that acted as a specific disincentive to any prospective grower or producer.

To the company, this complaint was not only expected and understood, but it was also heartily supported by complaints of its own about the way the beet sugar industry in particular was being suppressed by government policies in a time when every pound of sugar was needed. However, the government authorities and the Sugar Administrator reacted with what can only be described as mild shock and surprise that they could be criticized for anything they might have done, or more appropriately, not done.

Following discussions held between the company, the Beet Growers Association, and Mr. Noble, the government acceded to the growers' demands and agreed to advance a small additional payment for the 1941 crop based upon volumes still unsold by January 1, 1942, and a remission of part of the stabilization fund tax, which was considered something of a victory by all those involved in calls of support for Canada's domestic sugar production. Unfortunately this small victory did not last long as the benefits won were counteracted almost immediately afterwards by the introduction of sugar rationing on January 25, 1942. The initial quota was set at 12 ounces of refined sugar per person per week and it was unlawful to maintain more than a two-week supply of sugar at any one time. No coupons were required and exceptions from the holding clause were made for those who lived in remote areas so they could purchase up to six months' supply at a time. Nevertheless a buying panic set in once again, depleting the accumulated refined stocks of the refiners. The Sugar Administrator now issued new edicts to the refiners to accumulate additional raw sugar inventories with assurances that since world prices for raw sugar were rising, any additional costs involved would be secured and protected by the maintenance of current control policies if hostilities ceased and there was a sudden drop in prices. Recognizing that this was an exact duplication of the promises given by the authorities in 1917 and 1918, and with the bitter memories of what had happened in 1920, the Canadian cane refiners, led by Huntly Redpath Drummond (who was running the company while Mr. Houson was ill) took a determined stance opposing these demands.

At the same time, the company's beet sector had its own problems when dissatisfied farmers rejected the new beet contract as being insufficient to yield profits back to the farmers once the increased costs of production had been deducted. In return, the company stated that they had no real control over the stated price as pricing authority was now in the hands of the Sugar Administrator. Unwilling to accept this claim, many farmers held off from signing contracts when their representatives, the Ontario Beet Growers Association, publicly advocated that farmers not sign sugar beet contracts with Canada and Dominion as a pressure tactic to gain concessions. To complicate matters one local M.P., C. Desmond, addressed several hundred beet growers at a meeting in London and charged that the Sugar Administrator was "a cane man" and was not in sympathy with the needs of the beet growers.

With these kinds of accusations flying around, many farmers decided to switch to alternative crops. When this information was relayed to the authorities by the company, the Minister of Finance announced a belated attempt to remedy matters on February 17 by cutting the excise tax once again and advancing the list price of sugar. But it was already too late to stop the swing away from beets by the farming community of southern Ontario.

Tragically, at this crucial time in the company's history, its President, C.H. Houson, died as a result of his earlier illness. Huntly Redpath Drummond declined to take on the presidency due to his advancing years and his commitments to the Bank of Montreal, of which he was currently President. As a result the mantle of responsibility fell to the Secretary Treasurer, William J. McGregor.

To properly characterize W.J. McGregor would be impossible in the limited space available here but one of his employees, M.William Davidson, recorded the following in a biography of Mr. McGregor:

William J. McGregor

> W.J., as he was known by his associates was over six feet tall, muscular, had the short thick neck of a wrestler, and was as bald as an eagle ... W.J. was a round-the clock President ... with no family, no relatives and no sort of consuming hobbies ... he was brought up by a widow mother in the town of Wallaceburg where ... he joined the company as an assistant in the laboratory in 1905 ... Over a period of forty years he worked his way up through the positions of general sales manager and Secretary - Treasurer, (and) had made himself so indispensable to the Company that when Mr. Houson died in 1942 ... there was only one possible candidate to succeed.

As stated, his entire devotion seems to have centred on the company, especially the beet sector, and when Mr. McGregor saw or imagined anything that smacked of a threat to "his" beets, he applied with vigour the old adage "The best form of defence is attack." Unfortunately this attitude had its drawbacks as it would place him very much at odds with various government officials and lead to some extremely bitter confrontations over the next few years.

Immediately upon being appointed President, "W.J." went all out in his efforts to change the state of the Canadian sugar industry. He cabled Mr. Noble and subsequently held several meetings with the Sugar Administrator to argue the case for guaranteed additional support for beet production; however, Mr. Noble would not agree to more than a verbal assurance of future backing for sugar in general. Without a written guarantee, W.J. then refused to offer more money to the beet growers over the 1942 crop price as it could leave the company liable to provide the funds if prices fell by harvest time and the government failed to fulfil its obligations. Here things ended while matters were taken to the Ontario Beet Growers Association to elicit their reactions and proposals.

During the first two weeks of March, a number of stormy meetings between Mr. McGregor, Mr. Noble, and the Growers Association took place, but they failed to come to an agreement. This led Mr. McGregor to write to Mr. Noble on March 12, 1942:

It is imperative in my judgement to operate our beet sugar plants at Wallaceburg and Chatham to their maximum capacity this season, as a safeguard to National security. The Canadian public would consider it a matter of serious defection on the part of the Government and its sugar control policy if either of these plants should stand idle for even part of the operating season ... At this moment our contracting has reached an absolute impasse notwithstanding that we have offered the farmers the most favourable contract in the Dominion ... The governing factor which is retarding the contracting is price alone ... The Federal Government has guaranteed bonuses for 1942 over 1941 prices ... on tomatoes ... shelled peas ... green and waxed beans; all these without any corresponding revenue by way of excise taxes. On the other hand the Government collects an excise tax on sugar of $1.50 per hundred pounds ... The farmers are anxious that the beet sugar industry be not abandoned, but they are obviously unwilling to grow sugar beets to support the industry under what they consider a substantial sacrifice in their farm returns.

To this impassioned argument, Mr. Noble was brief if not terse:

It would be better if the farmers understood immediately that they can expect no further relief from Ottawa ... You can take it as definite that nothing further can be expected from the Sugar Administration.

Determined to end this situation, Mr. Noble obtained an Order-in-Council on March 12 which established the Ontario Sugar Beet Marketing Scheme, under which certain conditions and restrictions were imposed upon both the company and the farmers. In compliance with this new scheme, a series of telephone calls took place between Mr. McGregor and Mr. Noble which lasted until April 4, 1942, when a tentative solution was found whereby the company would offer a higher price for better quality beets but in return, no guaranteed minimum payment would be offered on tonnages.

The very next day, Mr. McGregor was shocked to read in the newspapers that Mr. Noble had announced publicly that he had approved the new beet contract of increased values for higher quality beet and a guaranteed minimum sale of payment. In a private memorandum between Mr. Noble and the Wartime Prices and Trade Board on April 6, 1942, Mr. Noble revealed his attitude over this issue.

There has been continuous wrangling for weeks past between the beet growers and the company in regard to next years prices of beets ... The meeting broke down without an agreement largely because the farmers would not accept at face value and apparently could not be made to understand the offer which the company made ... I talked to Mr. Perkin [the growers' representative] who wanted a fixed minimum price ... It had previously been understood in our discussions with Mr. McGregor in Toronto that no minimum guarantee was involved ... Not withstanding the fact that Mr. McGregor had previously understood there would be no minimum I said I would make such a recommendation ... Mr. McGregor strenuously objects that this is setting a precedent for the future, and there is no doubt something in what he says ... As administrator I have full power to fix prices and while it is regrettable that I took this decision without full discussion ... I was convinced further discussion would inevitably delay a final agreement ... while my action will probably be resented by the Board of the Company, it is my feeling that I have saved them from themselves.

To say that Mr. McGregor and the Board of the company resented this blatant betrayal of an agreement is to put it mildly and Mr. McGregor sent a telegram to Mr. Noble stating:

I can only recommend to my directors that we confine our sugar beet operations this year to acreages already committed ... We have gone the limit in our offer and must advise you that my directors unanimously reject minimum guarantee and definitely state this is our limit and we cannot go beyond.

In response Mr. Noble wrote:

I agree that you should not have had first knowledge of this from press but also knew that further discussion with you would not lead to agreement ... I have full authority to fix prices and am now exercising this authority ... and I want to know at latest this week ... whether we can expect your full co-operation. If you and your directors cannot give this assurance ... The Company will not be permitted to follow any such course as you state.

In support of this position Mr. Noble subsequently travelled to address the next meeting of the Board of Directors. Here he stated his opinion that C and D would not be taking any chances under the imposed scheme as his treaty with the British authorities would maintain controls in the event of peace until all sugars currently contracted for were sold off. When, in return, the company asked for written confirmation of this guarantee, Mr. Noble still refused to give one. This led to an explosive exchange between Mr. McGregor and Mr. Noble until Huntly Redpath Drummond intervened saying:

As the government has the power to fix prices we had better accept the situation, bearing in mind our patriotic duty to safeguard the National Security and do our utmost to secure a maximum acreage.

In support of the company, however, Huntly also expressed his view that the Sugar Administrator and the government must regard their actions as placing themselves

Chatham office staff "pitching in" during the 1942 campaign.

under a moral obligation not to reduce the returns on refined beet sugar until the year's crop was disposed of. When Mr. Noble agreed to these implied conditions, W.J. McGregor reluctantly ceased his argument and the company accepted the imposed contract, although it must be admitted that it left a very sour taste in the mouth of the company and W.J. McGregor in particular.

Having gained everything they had demanded, the Beet Growers Association now supported the contract for 1942. But the damage had already been done and only 23,000 acres were actually contracted for. Furthermore, due to heavy rains throughout the spring and early summer, not all of this acreage actually got planted or properly tended when the workers failed to arrive, as they were unwilling to work in fields that resembled vast mud puddles. To alleviate this shortage, the company called upon the government to direct workers from the compulsive selective service scheme or Italian prisoners of war for work in the fields. But the government chose not to take these proposals forward. Instead, they decided to use recently interned Japanese Canadians from the west coast. Some 500 single male volunteers were anticipated and camps were established at Essex, Valetta, Chatham, Dover Centre, Wallaceburg, Dresden, Petrolia, Glencoe, and Centralia under the supervision of the R.C.M.P. Payment for work was set at a rate equal to locally recruited labour plus a 75 cents daily allowance for food and board.

Being desperate, the company went along with this proposal and made arrangements to receive the first batch of workers in late May. However, in accepting this solution the company failed to anticipate the overtly hostile and racist reaction that came from certain elements of the communities destined to receive these Japanese Canadians. Despite the already multicultural base of the beet industry, racism reared its ugly head as mass meetings, petitions, newspaper editorials, and even formal resolutions made by the councils of Chatham and Essex criticized and condemned the bringing in of these Japanese Canadian workers.

This prompted an immediate counter-

A sugar cargo damaged in rail transit from a port on the Gulf of Mexico.

programme by the company of articles and open letters explaining the value of the policy; these were backed by letters of support from the Sugar Administrator and the Minister of Agriculture, P.M. Dewan. Fortunately, when the first group of 345 men arrived at Chatham, only a few isolated incidents of open racism were reported, although the general atmosphere was distinctly unfriendly for these young men. As a result, there was little encouragement for these individuals to pitch in, and the actual amount of work that eventually emerged hardly justified the expenses or trouble the company expended in trying to get them onto the farms. Finding itself still well short of its required labour force, the company put out yet another appeal for general help which was fortunately answered by volunteers from schools, service clubs, and even employees and staff from the company. Even so, not enough beets were projected as being available to harvest to justify the running of two beet plants. Eventually, the difficult decision was made to run only the Chatham plant, due to its larger daily slicing capacity, while Wallaceburg would remain closed and be used only as a receiving centre, a situation that had not occurred since its opening in 1902.

If these domestic events were not enough for the company to contend with, the cane refining sector of the company was also undergoing severe difficulties caused by the failure of the U.S. Navy to protect shipping travelling up the eastern seaboard. This allowed the Nazi submarines to freely roam the main shipping lanes, often within sight of the U.S. coast, and sink vessels almost at will. Over 11.25% of Canada's annual imports were now being lost to enemy action, which in the case of sugar amounted to 200,000 tons of vitally needed product.

To the Canadian authorities, the simple solution was for the U.S. Navy to improve its patrols and create a safe travel zone for Allied vessels. However, instead of admitting its failure and working to improve its tactics, the U.S. Navy, backed by its government, pressured the Canadian authorities to divert all sugar ships coming from the Caribbean and central America, away from their regular port destinations in Canada to sites on the Gulf of Mexico. Here the sugar was now unloaded for rail shipment across the United States to the Canadian refineries. Naturally, this now added to the problem of delays in maintaining a steady supply of raw sugar, not to mention an increase in damaged shipments and the costs of production for the sugar industry, and the cane refiners let their opinions be known to the government in no uncertain terms. Another effect of the submarine menace on Canadians was felt that summer, when communities on Prince Edward Island and Newfoundland, as well as isolated sectors of Nova Scotia, Labrador, and Quebec were overlooked by the Canadian Shipping Board when it was allocating vessels for food deliveries. As a result, some Canadians were left without sugar and other staple needs for weeks at a time until the administrative error was corrected.

By late July the sugar shortage had still not improved and the government decided to apply new measures to obtain more sugar supplies for Canada. However, instead of encouraging expansion of its under-utilized beet industry, the government chose to implement changes that would benefit only cane sugar production. To add insult to injury, current attempts by the company to make up for the perpetual lack of labour by purchasing a number of mechanical beet unloaders from the United States were being repeatedly blocked by bureaucratic red tape. As these new machines could drastically cut the consumption by farmers of other vital war material including gasoline and rubber tires, the company argued that no efforts should be spared to clear the equipment for immediate delivery. Eventually, after much effort and the personal intervention of the Agriculture Minister, P.M. Dewan, these beet unloaders were obtained and immediately pressed into service as the beet campaign was about to begin. Unfortunately, regardless of this mechanical help, a mixture of heavy rains, freezing temperatures, and early snows throughout the campaign hindered the workers so that 10% of the already realized crop acreage remained unharvested. Just over 20,000 acres of crop was left, which produced 55 million pounds of sugar compared to the 85 million pounds in 1941, a far from satisfactory situation in light of the national shortage of sugar and a strong indication of the obvious failure of government policies regarding beets.

To round out the already busy year, the Munitions and Supply Department determined that the priority of needs for alcohol to manufacture synthetic rubber, explosives, and ethyl gasoline outweighed the requirements for consumable alcohol, and so the production of liquor was banned. This led to the decision by C and D to convert its Montreal Products Distillery, located within the old Montreal refinery, from using molasses to grain and to increase its output for wartime uses for the duration of the conflict. At the same time, the Sugar Administrator decided that current sugar production used too much manpower, fuel oil, and electricity and ordered that certain refineries must cease production in order to allow others to maximise their output. As a result, some very rapid negotiations took place

"Doing it differently this year". Rationing sugar in 1943.

between the various sugar companies that resulted in an agreement being made between C and D and the St. Lawrence Sugar Refining Co. Ltd. Under the terms of this arrangement, the St. Lawrence Co. refinery would be shut down for the rest of the war and the Canada and Dominion Montreal plant would increase its output and manufacture sugar under both brand names. Profits and costs would be split 60% - 40% in favour of C and D. Any additional plant machinery or personnel required by C and D would be transferred from the St. Lawrence factory with an understanding that they would be returned at the expiry of the agreement.

With the advent of 1943, company representatives were thrown once again into the annual round of negotiations for beet contracts and prices. As in previous years, the farmers' groups urged both the company and the government to increase payments substantially, arguing that they were having to absorb the higher costs of fertilizer, while paying out higher rates for labour, mechanization, and transportation, all of which reduced their returns on growing beets. In equal measure, the company stressed its position that it had already exceeded, by a wide margin, the price that would result in a fair return for the company and that it could not offer more in 1943.

Hopeful of getting additional money from the company through governmental directives, the beet growers pressed the Sugar Administrator to side with them, but this year he decided that prices should remain as in 1942. As a result, most of the previous year's farmers refused outright to sign beet contracts for 1943, and despite extensive personal appeals by company field agents, only 16,500 acres were contracted by mid-March. In April even this small amount of acreage was reduced when virtually continual rains prevented many farmers seeding in time or getting their fields properly thinned. This led to serious discussions at boardroom level as to whether the entire season should be abandoned and the beet plants stay closed. In the end, however, it was decided to open only Wallaceburg for the season and supplement any shortage of beets with output from cane sugar, which the Sugar Administrator agreed to provide. At the same time, the federal government attempted to promote additional acreage by reducing the excise tax applicable to beet sugar by 50 cents per cwt, and specifically stipulated that the full benefit of this reduction be passed onto the growers, while the provincial government provided for a bonus of 55 cents per ton on all sugar beets produced in 1943 to be paid directly to the grower.

Despite these assurances, many farmers still refused to sign up for beets preferring to grow other crops instead. For those who did join the rolls, their efforts to grow a decent crop were thwarted by a combination of heavy rains throughout April, May, and July, separated by a month of extreme heat in June. By August, the field reports projected that the year's crop would amount to just over 9,200 acres, which represented a loss of 40% on the original contract acreage and the smallest potential campaign in 30 years.

As if these facts were not bad enough, there was the continued need to acquire labour to work in the fields. Due to the hostile response given to the single Japanese Canadian men by the local citizens of Chatham and elsewhere, most of these individuals were unwilling to return to the area in 1943. Anxious to obtain its workers, the company now worked in co-operation with the Beet Growers Association, local agricultural representatives, the Ontario government, and the B.C. Security Commission to recruit Japanese Canadian family groups for work in the same manner as had been successfully achieved in Alberta. Following a survey of beet growers who were willing to accommodate these prospective workers, a company employee, Bev Easton accompanied by Robert McPherson from the federal government, went to British Columbia and attempted to persuade families to come to Ontario. Regrettably, the result was that only a half-dozen families ended up arriving to help in the Ontario beet season of 1943. This left the industry substantially short of workers so conscientious objectors were called up by selective service and placed in camps for sugar beet work.

Having temporarily dealt with the labour problem, the company now introduced two programmes which it hoped would provide long-term benefits to the company. The first was the modernization and mechanization of the beet processing and unloading facilities at Wallaceburg, with plans for a similar programme at Chatham in 1944. The second programme was the wide introduction of a new strain of "segmented" beet seed, which had been specifically bred to complement the development of mechanical seeders and beet blocking equipment. Unfortunately, this was not the best of times to attempt new or innovative measures in the beet industry as many farmers were suffering a severe cash-flow problem and could not afford the new types of machinery or even the gasoline required to run them. As a result, the segmented seed did not come into general use until some years later.

Meanwhile in Quebec, the Redpath refinery had to contend with a new competitor as the provincial legislature funded the National Sugar Co. Ltd (hereafter also referred to as the Quebec Sugar Refinery or Q.S.R.) at St. Hilaire under the specific assurance that:

it is not the intention of the government to keep control of the new establishment indefinitely, but to give it back to a farmers co-operative society as soon as the expenses incurred have been recovered and the enterprise placed on a safe basis.

Regrettably this was to become a promise this and successive provincial governments were to find impossible to keep.

In September, the previously announced federal reduction in excise duty on sugar was implemented and the provincial subsidy took effect, which was good news for the industry. But this was immediately followed by declarations by the Sugar Administrator that effective immediately, molasses, corn syrup, cane syrups, maple sugar, maple syrup, and honey were all to be rationed to domestic users, while industrial users required special exemption permits from the W.P.T.B., otherwise they were banned from using the designated sweeteners.

When the time came for the 1943 beet crop to be harvested, the weather was unusually cold, which raised the potential of sugar losses through the beets freezing if they were left unprocessed for an extended time. Therefore, in an effort to maximise the potential crop, the weigh scales were opened for business earlier than normal. At the same time, the Wallaceburg plant, which had been processing raw cane sugar since August, was switched over to receive the beets. Despite these additional measures, however, the losses on the year's contracted acreage reached the second highest in the industry's history at 44%, amounting to only 9,287 acres successfully harvested. This pathetic crop was processed in a mere 35 days and yielded 18.6 million pounds of refined sugar, only 14% of Canada's total beet production for the year.

In the annual beet crop report made up for 1943, the catalogue of the year's problems fill thirty-six pages of a thirty-eight-page report, while the final two pages outline projections for 1944. These prospects are worth reproducing at this point for comparison with the realities of that year that will be outlined below.

> *The outlook for sugar beets in 1944 undoubtedly is better than for 1943.*
> *First: The laws of chance make it extremely unlikely that we will have in 1944 what the Beet Growers report said of 1943, namely ... the least favourable [weather] experienced in this area for a great many years.*
> *Secondly: The closing of the Chatham plant has had a profound effect upon the local farm organizations, businessmen and politicians. Every effort will be made by these to secure sufficient acreage to operate the Chatham plant in 1944.*
> *Third: The labour situation is easing off ... Indications are for more labour to be available [from wartime industries] in 1944 and there are indications of this labour being keener for employment.*
> *Fourth: There is hope for a substantial price increase which the newly constituted Agricultural committees of the Provincial Government are recommending to the Government of Ontario.*

At the outset of 1944, discussions took place between the company and the Ontario Minister of Agriculture, Colonel Kennedy, based on the aforementioned proposals of the Agricultural Committees. As a result, the province proposed a direct payment of a subsidy to Ontario farmers for beet crops at the rate of $1.55 per ton up to a maximum tonnage of 145,161 tons, which equalled $225,000. For its part, the company supplemented this figure by guaranteeing to pay an additional $1.55 per ton for any amount in excess of the provincial upper limit as its contribution to the war effort for 1944, conditional only upon the maintenance of current federal policies and the essential point of a minimum of 16,500 acres being contracted for.

Armed with these new arrangements, the company went into its new season of contracts confident that farmers would return willingly to sugar beet production. Within a couple of weeks, this optimism had died as only 13,500 acres were contracted by the end of March. This left the company with little alternative but to take some drastic action, and so they published an open letter in the company newsletter *Up and Down the Rows* which stated:

COMPANY FACES TASK OF MOVING BEET FACTORIES

> *The financial statement of this Company will shortly appear and will show that, on its overall operations, the company made a substantial net profit in 1943. Many people will conclude from this that the Company made money on its 1943 beet sugar operations.* THIS IS NOT THE CASE. *The company lost heavily on its beet sugar operations in 1943 and the profits shown on the financial statement all came from other departments of the business.*

In other words, THE COMPANY WOULD HAVE MADE MORE MONEY IN 1943 IF NO SUGAR BEETS HAD BEEN GROWN AND PROCESSED.

This is not the first year that the company has operated its beet sugar factories at a loss. It happened several times during the years 1930 to 1939. The cause of losses during those years was the extreme low price of sugar. The prices paid for beets were low, too, but even so, the beet prices paid by the Company were higher than were justified by the depressed level of sugar prices. The company was operating its beet sugar factories on a very slender margin and it took only a slight turn of conditions to wipe out that margin entirely and show a loss on operations during those years.

The Company is again operating on a narrow margin but the cause of the loss in 1943 was the failure of a sufficient supply of raw material – sugar beets. Industrial concerns often carry on through periods of low prices even if they do lose money, in order to hold the business together for better days. But if its supply of raw material dries up, no industry can keep on operating. This fact is perfectly obvious to everyone.

The Company is now faced with this condition. In 1942 only one of the Company's two beet sugar plants was operated, though it was at full capacity. In 1943 only one plant was operated and that at only one-third of capacity. So far this season, we have but 15,000 acres of beets under contract. If this is all planted and if there is only average spring shrinkage of acreage and if the yield per acre turns out to be normal – a lot of IFS – we should have enough beets to operate one plant to HALF CAPACITY. *To put it another way, from two-thirds to three-quarters of the Company's beet sugar plant will stand idle in 1944 for lack of raw material.*

This, of course, cannot go on. The Company is now face to face with the grim prospect of relocating its beet sugar plants at places where its raw material – sugar beets – can be obtained.

Fortunately this document had the desired result as more farmers added beets to their crops, resulting in 17,334 acres being eventually contracted – still far short of the amount required to run both refineries, but sufficient to allow the management to decide to run the Wallaceburg plant for 1944, supplemented by an additional period for cane operations. So much for prediction number two!

For its labour in 1944, when local newspaper appeals failed to attract sufficient workers, the company was forced to resort to the use of conscientious objectors, a small number of Japanese Canadians, and more than 350 German naval prisoners of war from a camp near Chatham, although the beet reports state:

> *The prisoners were not very speedy in the execution of their tasks. However ... they rescued 566 acres of sugar beets which would have been lost. Those growers who accepted the Prisoners of War labour hesitated so long about placing their order that the beets and weeds had reached the height where it would almost have been impossible for the most experienced beet workers to do a good job.*

Bang went prediction number three!

Once the harvest campaign began in October, although a period of exceptionally good dry weather helped in the speedy collection of the 14,500 acres that represented the year's crop, it also had a negative effect by producing so much congestion at several of the regional rail depots and weigh stations that the railway company could not cope with the influx and declared a temporary suspension on additional beets being loaded onto railway cars or full cars entering the rail system. This delay caused some beets to rot before they were processed and further reduced the already diminished volume of beets available to the company for the year. This on balance gave no luck on prediction number one, and left only prediction number four as having any prospect of coming true, and one out of four is not exactly a good rate in anyone's book.

At this time, the minutes of the Board reveal that thought was being given to the prospects for the company in a post-war world. Much was made in Board discussions of the fact that the past year's continual use of the Montreal refinery for the production of both its own brand and the St. Lawrence product had increased the rate of wear on all production equipment, while spare parts were becoming less and less available. Furthermore if the worn-out equipment at Montreal was to be replaced with the new technologies that were available for the making of both granular and liquid sugar, a huge amount of capital would have to be committed by the company over a period of at least two years. In like manner, both the Chatham and Wallaceburg plants were in need of extensive work to bring them up to par.

Off the official record, discussions took place on another and somewhat serious matter. This concerned the fact that stock counts had revealed that considerable volumes of sugar were vanishing from the inventories of the Montreal refinery. Initial enquiries by company officials and even an outside detective agency hired by the Board had failed to uncover the reason for the losses, so it was agreed that a detective would be placed undercover inside the refinery. Within a few weeks, the man had discovered an organized black market operation, which subsequently led to the arrest and conviction of two truckers, three checkers, and a foreman from the plant for the theft of 80,000 pounds of sugar. The sugar had been sold to at least seven local merchants and candy manufacturers, who were also charged and convicted under the applicable war measures. Roughly speaking, the scheme was that the foreman would turn a blind eye while the checkers, who were in charge of a number of labourers, would order fifty sacks of sugar for an order requiring only forty. The accomplices driving the trucks were then informed of this "extra" in their loads, which they delivered to special clients in the black market. The resulting money was later divided among all concerned.

At the national level, both Canada and the United Kingdom were now entering a period where their supplies of sugar were stretched to the limit, and matters were not helped by the cynical U.S. attitude of paying lip service to rationing while in reality increasing its domestic consumption at every opportunity, to the detriment of its allies. Matters came to a head over this issue in November 1944 when the combined Sugar Committees of Canada, the United States and Great Britain determined that the projected deficit in sugar supplies would equal 12 million tons. Both Britain and Canada argued for an equal distribution of this shortfall between the three countries to which the United States reluctantly agreed. However within days, the United States announced its own domestic allocations of sugar for the first quarter of 1945. These allocations completely ignored the current shortfall and used the dominant position of the United States as the major supplier of transport for sugar cargoes to claim almost 75% of the available sugar exclusively for U.S. consumption. Despite immediate condemnation by its allies, the U.S. authorities refused to re-consider their stated demands to allow the shortfall to be distributed equally. This led to a showdown on November 28, 1944, between the Minister of Supply and Food for Great Britain, the Minister of Agriculture, Munitions and Supply for the Canadian government, and the Secretary of Agriculture and War Food Administration in the U.S. government. At this meeting, following some strong demands from the Canadian and British representatives, the Americans reluctantly agreed to moderate their position, although both Canada and Great Britain recognized that at the end of the war, the United States would almost certainly rapidly abandon its position, de-ration sugar as soon as possible, and then go on a buying spree to acquire as much sugar as possible before either the British or Canadians could react. As a result, it did not take long for the two countries to come to an agreement to extend their joint rationing and purchasing controls over sugar beyond the end of the war to ensure equity of distribution for what sugar might remain available once the United States had taken its excess share from the market.

As a final point for 1944, in December the Quebec Sugar Refinery at St. Hilaire actually went into production but instead of the much publicized output of 20 million pounds, just over 3 million was actually produced, leaving little hope that the Quebec government would obtain a quick return on its investment.

As the nation entered into 1945, having suffered six years of war, rationing, and personal losses, many people looked forward to peace, the return of their loved ones, and some of the luxuries of life. For the beet industry of southern Ontario, three consecutive years of inadequate supplies of sugar and labour shortages had to be reversed if it was to have any kind of a future. Fortunately, the industry now had the strong backing of the Ontario provincial government, who had agreed to continue their subsidy for the beet growers on the same basis as in 1944. This caused the company to also repeat its offer to pay the equivalent of the Ontario subsidy for excess tonnages over the provincial limit. In a series of newspaper, magazine, and radio releases during January, February, and March, the joint forces of the C and D agricultural department and the provincial agricultural ministry "blitzed" the farming community of southern Ontario, while personal visits by company field representatives eventually persuaded enough farmers to contract almost 21,000 acres for 1945.

Regrettably, Mother Nature was once again to thwart much of this effort, as one of the severest winters in many years gave way to one of the wettest springs in recorded memory. This led to most of the beet crop being planted very late in the effective growing season and discouraged many workers from signing up in time to thin the crops so that eventually 900 prisoners of war from four separate camps were used to supplement locally hired labour. The weather also affected the introduction of additional mechanized crop machinery, which became repeatedly bogged down in the heavy mud that constituted the soils of southern Ontario during that spring.

By May 1945 the state of the beet industry in Ontario was definitely in the balance as poor weather continued to hamper proper tending of the crops and the effective growing acreage fell rapidly. Nor could the company counterbalance the projected shortfall of beets by increasing its cane output as the quantity of raw sugar being brought into Canada dropped when increased volumes of sugar were diverted to the newly liberated territories of Europe to alleviate their desperate need for sweeteners.

Appeals to the Sugar Administrator were met with responses indicating that the entire Canadian sugar industry was in a similar plight and that Mr. Noble had a new solution to the problem. When it came, however, it was not a welcome solution as he chose to remedy the situation by cutting the national ration scale for the second time that year to a new all-time low, with warnings of the prospect of further cuts in the next quarter if matters did not improve. When by June things had not improved to his satisfaction, Mr. Noble sliced the ration once again to 1 pound per person per month — only 50% of the 1941 level for general users — while industrial users suffered in equal proportion. Additionally, new orders were issued by the Sugar Administrator requiring statistics from each refinery on their production rates and energy consumption levels in order to determine which refineries could be shut down to conserve supplies.

Determined to protect his own company's interests in the light of this implied threat, W.J. McGregor initiated a new publication, *Sugar Facts*. This paper was composed of articles and facts related to the sugar industry and was circulated to all Canadian daily newspapers and radio stations. Its objectives were simple, to protect the company, especially its beet division, and to influence the Sugar Administrator; as such, it certainly could not be called an objective publication, although it did bring out many interesting facts on the state of the industry at that time. Understandably, Mr. Noble was not enthusiastic about this new publication as it frequently highlighted inconsistencies, failures, and embarrassing contradictions in the governmental policies emanating from his administration. Not surprisingly the degree of tension and lack of co-operation between the Sugar Administrator and the company increased dramatically in the coming years. This was particularly unfortunate as the ending of hostilities should have ushered in a new period of hope and optimism. Instead most reports indicated a substantial period of continued governmental control of the sugar industry and its pricing, and the weather forecasts for the beet growing areas continued to report one rainy period after another. It was definitely not a good way to usher in the post-war era.

NO 1 - GENERAL VIEW - SEPT. 1/49

A view across the Montreal refinery yard to the old (arched) raw sugar shed and the refinery coal yard.

CHAPTER SIX

Is It a Brave New World or the Same Old Story?

As the echoes of the celebrations ending the war died away, discussions of prospects for the future now came to the fore. The way matters stood, the current low levels of rationing were certain to remain in effect for the foreseeable future since the devastated factories in Europe and the Soviet Union would take years to become re-established as fully effective sugar suppliers. In the meantime, much of the world's sugar would have to be re-directed to these regions to prevent starvation, leaving Canadians suffering the inconveniences of rationing. Nor was there much hope of increasing domestic beet production, while government policies that acted as disincentives to grow sugar beets continued to be implemented. Even the much subsidized St. Hilaire sugar beet factory in Quebec was considered by the new National Union government of Premier Duplessis to be a total economic failure. Despite this admission, however, the Unionists deemed it prudent to continue to pour more money into the project in hopes of getting something back. In Montreal, the company was informed that the co-production agreement between Canada and Dominion and St. Lawrence was extended by governmental decree until at least April 1946. This was not welcomed by the Board as it wanted to re-equip the refinery and install new innovative technology to produce liquid sugar, a plan that could not be implemented until at least the following year.

By October 1945, the extensive modernization of the Chatham plant, which entailed a complete new boiler house, plus alterations to the beet receiving yards and beet flumes, had made the refinery almost ready for the year's crops. Unfortunately, for yet another year the weather experienced in southern Ontario proved to be wet in the extreme, eight inches of rain falling in September alone. The crop reports later recorded:

> The early part of October was also very wet and those growers who harvested their beets during that period did so in a sea of mud. Many growers lifted their beets, rolled them with the land roller, lifted them the second time and then harrowed them to remove the soil ... The entire crop of approximately 164,000 tons [17,705 acres] was processed at the Chatham factory ... The Ontario government subsidy was the same as that which was granted in 1944 ... The Canada and Dominion Sugar Company ... therefore ... paid a subsidy on 19,005 tons at a cost of $29,457.75.

In the company publications *Up and Down The Rows* and

Sugar Facts, these points were reiterated with the additional point that much of this year's labour had come from prisoners of war, a source of labour that would obviously not be available in the future. Therefore, the farmers were urged to implement the widespread introduction of mechanized beet machinery onto their farms. In the meantime, however, the company took concrete action to widen its base of labour for the new year by working in co-operation with farmers' groups to assist refugees and displaced persons from Europe to come to Canada to begin a new life by initially helping in the sugar beet fields.

At the end of January 1946, the Ontario Minister of Agriculture, Col. T.L. Kennedy, announced that for the fourth year in succession, the provincial authorities would provide a subsidy to beet growers, although this year the level would be cut from a maximum of $225,000 to $112,500. Fortunately, some small additional aid was now forthcoming from the federal authorities in the form of a payment of 60¾ cents per 100 pounds of production for all of the 1946 crop. On top of this, the company also agreed to maintain its additional payments, giving Ontario's beet farmers the highest potential level of payments available in many years.

Despite these relative gains, many farmers were worried about the lack of immediately available labour and were unwilling to expend the funds to modernize or mechanize their production of beets, so they held back from signing contracts. This led to extensive behind-the-scenes negotiations, and unofficial assurances were made by government authorities that the prisoners of war used in 1945 to harvest the crops would also be available in the spring season of 1946. This was in spite of the return of thousands of ex-servicemen who, according to one report, were unemployed but still reluctant to take positions as "hired men."

In March, the national sugar ration was raised for industrial users but general household rations were

Loading a railcar tanker with molasses.

continued as before, leading to a further period of loss of revenue under the current scheme of distribution. The following month at the Annual General Meeting for C and D, W.J. McGregor overcame his extreme reluctance to speak in public by addressing the assembled shareholders. In his speech, Mr. McGregor stated that there had been a decline in the net operating profit for the company of some 35% due mainly to the substantial financial losses incurred by the sugar beet sector of the company in each of the last three years. Furthermore, although the costs of labour, fuel supplies, and packaging materials had risen by some 112%, the selling of refined sugar and molasses had remained fixed at government ceiling prices that were so low that even allowing for the extremely small crops actually harvested the losses were severe. Ironically, during the same period, the company collected and paid over to the government over $1 million in excise tax on its production. Furthermore, during the war as a whole, government aid had amounted to some $2.4 million while the taxes collected had exceeded $6.1 million and clearly indicated the reality of the government's so-called support for its domestic industry.

In concluding his presentation, Mr. McGregor commented on the fact that there were prospects of a third western beet refinery being built near Lethbridge, Alberta, while in Quebec, the provincial government had announced a guaranteed high price and machinery bonus plan for the Quebec sugar beet growers. In comparison, the Ontario farmers were being abandoned by their own government at both the provincial and federal levels, leaving the company having to consider whether to close both its beet refineries in the near future if matters did not improve.

Difficulties for the beet sector of the company continued as the month of June brought with it yet another period of extensive rains, which caused widespread flooding across most of Kent County and lasted for several weeks, severely damaging the beet crops. This was then followed by a long dry spell and high temperatures, which baked the ground into a brick-like consistency that proved impossible to cultivate. To attempt to regain some of the lost acreage, the company offered free beet seed to any farmer willing to re-plant his land, which resulted in just over 350 acres of the 1,600 originally lost being reclaimed.

Fortunately, the latter part of the season proved to be more propitious and October turned out to be a favourable month for harvesting. The labour situation, too, was substantially better than in previous years, as the programme of obtaining displaced persons from Europe supplied much-needed workers to augment the joint teams of prisoners of war and locally hired labour. Eventually, some 23,000 acres were harvested producing over 232,000 tons of beet, which were then processed in the Chatham plant between October 8, 1946, and January 9, 1947. As the acreage harvested exceeded the provincial subsidy limits, it meant that the company paid out $22,350 in additional subsidies, a cost that was beginning to drain the already strained financial reserves of the company and one from which the company began to look for ways to extricate itself in 1947.

On the other side of the corporate coin, operations continued at C and D's Montreal refinery in 1946, under the joint production programme with St. Lawrence Sugar as the Sugar Administrator extended the system yet again from April to December 1946. Rationing was eased somewhat during the summer but rumours began to circulate that controls on pricing and production might be extended as far as 1950. This speculation prompted some very pessimistic reports and articles in national newspapers criticizing the government for its mishandling of Canadian needs and buckling under to U.S. intimidation when that country decided to increase its domestic consumption at the expense of its neighbour. One particularly outspoken critic of the government was John G. Diefenbaker, who stated in early December:

> *At the moment there is a strong agitation in the United States to cut other countries off from supplies of sugar controlled by the country [the United States]. At the same time the government of that country is making valiant efforts ... to encourage a greater production of beets. [while] ... Here in Canada, we tolerate, or at least the government tolerates a production of beet sugar considerably less than it should be.*

In a final note on 1946, two other incidents are worth reporting. First was the exposure of another black market sugar operation that was centred in the Montreal docks. There, a group of dockers and truckers unloading raw sugar from a West Indies ship hijacked a truck load of 10,000 pounds enroute to the Montreal refinery. Fortunately, smaller losses that had occurred in the previous months had been noted, and R.C.M.P. surveillance officers were in place when the actual hijack occurred. The vehicle was tailed and the individuals involved arrested, although it took four months for 9,650 pounds of the stolen sugar to be returned. Where the other 350 pounds disappeared to, no one could positively state. The second event concerned the veteran Board member, sugar maker, and businessman, Huntly Redpath Drummond as he concluded his active career with the Bank of Montreal. Since his first days as a Director in 1912, Huntly had served in numerous posts with the Bank of Montreal, concluding with a term as Chairman of the Board, a position he had held since 1942. He now retired from the bank's Board by accepting the position of Honorary President, a position granted only once before, to Sir Donald A. Smith, Baron Strathcona and Mount Royal.

Once more the calendar brought round the annual contract negotiations for the new beet crop, which this year were highlighted by proposals by the Beet Growers Association to the Sugar Administrator for a massive expansion of the domestic beet industry coupled with a price increase to encourage farmers to participate. Although the Sugar Administrator admitted that increased volumes of sugar were required, he refused to pay for home production despite the fact that the costs involved would be lower than those being currently expended for bringing in foreign sugar.

The eventual contract included the Ontario government subsidy but this year the company felt it could not add to this amount. Fortunately, due to the recent steep increases in world prices for raw sugar, a change in federal government policies led to the list prices of sugar being raised by a dollar per 100 pounds for the first increase applied to sales since March 1941. Since this would in turn reflect back on increased revenues for farmers, the acreage contracted for 1947 did increase over that of 1946, but once again nature had its part to play in eliminating most of the gains of the year.

The wet weather officially began on March 24 and continued until June 15, a full eighty-four days during which rain fell on no fewer than forty-three days. Drainage systems and rivers overflowed their banks and extensive flooding took place around Wallaceburg, Dresden, and Chatham, preventing any sugar beets being planted in April.

During this period, other events were happening that also affected corporate decisions for the future. Prominent among them was the increased level of criticism and condemnation of governmental policy over sugar by various opposition M.P.s led by John Diefenbaker. Mr. Diefenbaker's views led him to exchange heated words with various government ministers in the House of Commons over the relative merits of domestic sugar production. This was then followed by calls to cut through the "red tape" that was preventing hundreds of willing and experienced beet workers from coming to Canada under the emigration schemes developed principally by Canada and Dominion in co-operation with farmers' organizations. As a result of these parliamentary exchanges, some of the impediments delaying the new immigrants were subsequently overcome and eventually 283 new workers arrived during the next few months. The majority of these came from Holland and Belgium but there were also recruits from Switzerland, Palestine, Poland, Germany, England, and France. About sixty additional workers whose papers were cleared from Czechoslovakia did not arrive, however, due to their own government denying them exit visas at the last moment.

In June 1947, the United States introduced its long-expected legislation and de-rationed sugar. This led to many questions being asked in the Commons as to what prospects for a similar release could be expected for Canadians. The government's answer was "None," at least for the foreseeable future. Once this attitude became known by Canadians, it fostered an interesting phenomenon in near-border cities as cross-border shopping in sugar increased to the extent that Customs officials were compelled to apply for additional assistance at various crossing points to deal with the increased flow of traffic.

As the pressures to de-ration sugar in Canada continued to mount, increased uncertainty across the sugar industry led to fears being voiced of another 1920 "Dance of the Millions" unless long-promised pricing supports were maintained until current stocks were disposed of. On top of this, the long-needed overhauls on equipment at the company's refineries could now no longer be deferred or attacked piecemeal. Therefore, despite this period of uncertainty, massive amounts of work were authorized for all plants, with a special concentration on Chatham to allow it to be ready for the harvest period.

When the time came, the abundance of the new immigrant labour and additional mechanical loaders, aided by good weather conditions, made it possible for the region's farmers to deliver half the total crop in only eleven days of work. At its peak, vehicles were being unloaded at the previously unheard of rate of one vehicle per minute, which led to optimistic reports being made on the economic viability of the industry for the future.

In the midst of this harvest, the government finally announced that sugar was to be de-rationed in Canada. Under normal circumstances, this would have been a cause for celebration within the sugar industry. However, the stream of additional governmental directives that accompanied the announcement of de-rationing left the industry uncertain of its prospects for the future.

For example, while the officially authorized price for

An Athey Mobiloader, used to transfer beets from storage piles to the factory process area.

sugar was increased by one dollar per 100 pounds, the sugar companies saw none of the extra funds, as the government used the money to implement an equal value drop in the excise taxes. Second, while the government claimed it had guaranteed the availability of supplies of sugar for the next twelve months, these supplies were almost totally from cane sugar sources, leaving the beet sector with the bad news that the government had terminated its subsidization of the beet crop for 1948.

Finally, while the official rationing of sugar would cease for consumers, the sole authority for the purchase and distribution of supplies of both raw and refined sugar were retained by the government with no indication of when these controls would be lifted.

Over the next few months, repeated appeals by beet lobbies failed to budge the government from its announced position, which discouraged the farming community from signing its 1948 contracts with the company and eventually led to a total of only 27,607 acres being signed up. With this level of response, the inevitable conclusion for the company was that only one of the now extensively (not to mention expensively) overhauled plants would be required for beet operations. As a result, Chatham was chosen for the year's beet run while Wallaceburg was operated for a time using imported cane in a manner akin to earlier years but without the benefit of the main beet production.

Throughout the summer, repeated contradictory statements emanated from Ottawa about the potential de-controlling of sugar, tariff levels, and industry protection on current stocks. This left the company and W.J. McGregor, in particular, worried about a proper transition back to a free-market system.

Eventually, following a season of mixed weather, the Ontario beet crop was again harvested. The now successful programme of bringing in European workers, plus the continued increase in use of mechanized equipment, yielded exceptionally good results with record volumes being successfully delivered and unloaded at the Chatham plant in an amazingly short period of time.

Meanwhile, on the cane side, the partial modernization of the production facilities in the Montreal plant allowed the company to introduce four newly designed package lines for fine granulated, tea cubes, special icing, and golden yellow sugars. For its industrial market, the first shipments of liquid sugar began to emerge, resulting in some very positive comments by customers who saw in

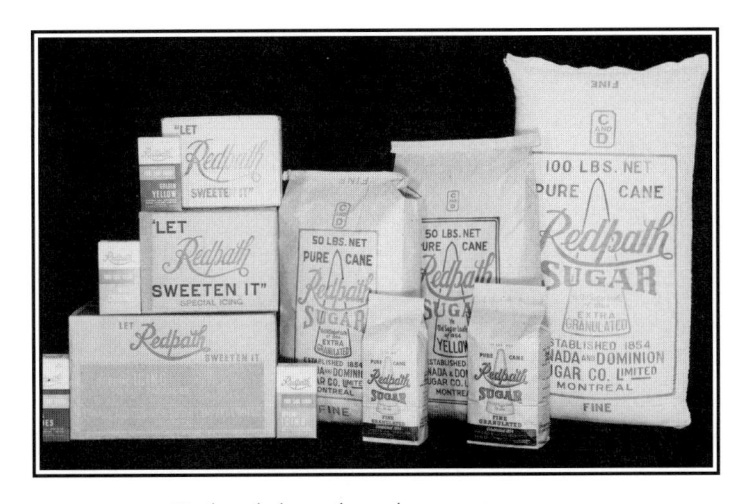

Redpath brand packaging in 1948.

Dominion packaging in 1948.

this new line a significant advance in sugar usage and reduced costs of production for their own lines. Following these developments, a new and dramatic alteration was now proposed to replace the main raw sugar shed with an entirely new structure of a radical design. Instead of the traditional arched roof design of earlier years, a new prismoidal structure was proposed, measuring 500 feet by 120 feet to hold 40,000 tons of raw sugar. Furthermore, storage within the shed would not be in the old style of hogshead barrels or 250 pound jute bags, but in open bulk form, and represented a complete break with the methods used for 1,000 years in the transportation of the raw sugar.

In the new year, the company was pleased to note an overall improvement in field labour supplies coupled with the prospects for freer market conditions. This finally encouraged Ontario farmers to return to beet growing, and

the acreage eventually signed up totalled more than 34,000, which led to the welcome decision that both refineries would be run for the first time in seven years. On top of this, the Wallaceburg plant began to refine raw sugar at an all-time early date in order to make 60 million pounds of refined sugar, guaranteeing 350 men employment well into the spring.

To ensure that enough labour would be available, the company worked in co-operation with the Federal Department of Labour to bring in 100 displaced persons representing a cultural mix of Poles, Italians, Danes, Ukrainians, Yugoslavs, and Germans, supplementing the already substantial number of Dutch and Belgian workers from earlier years. Upon arrival at Chatham, in June 1949, these new immigrants were housed in three new camps established at Chatham, Wallaceburg, and Glencoe. The

Displaced persons from Europe arrive at Chatham.

Daily life in the camps provided by the company for field labour.

Is It a Brave New World or the Same Old Story?

Heading out to the beet fields.

Food supplies in the camp kitchen.

Night school.

Time to relax.

Let Redpath Sweeten It

A liquid sugar tanker in 1949.

Inside the refined sugar warehouse at Chatham in 1949.

The new agricultural office building at Chatham.

camps deserve some description as they represented a substantial improvement over the old "Titanic" used in World War I. The Chatham camp was a labour hostel that was used as a dining and recreational area, while nearby tourist cabins were used for sleeping. Wallaceburg's camp consisted of two company-owned houses and the Glencoe camp was a building at the local fairgrounds where modern facilities were installed. At all three camps each man was issued with two blankets, mattress cover, pillow, and a towel. Each camp had a manager and food was supplied by local caterers. For recreation, movies and English classes were provided free of charge by the company.

This programme of having a guaranteed pool of labour encouraged many farmers for the year and more than 1,000 acres of beet were blocked by this group of workers alone. On July 23, the three camps were closed for the year, and workers were transferred to individual farms to continue the season's work. As a result of excellent weather during the latter part of the season, harvesting took place under much better conditions than those of 1948. This allowed additional mechanical harvesters to be used successfully for the first time since their introduction in

1945. In all, in excess of 30,000 acres were harvested, resulting in 335,000 tons of beets and 93 million pounds of sugar. Chatham ran for seventy days while Wallaceburg ran for fifty-nine. The "good old days" seemed to have returned, and by the end of the year, the company magazines were expounding on the good prospects for the future of the industry. Even at Board level, the tone of the minutes was decidedly more optimistic and major investments were approved for 1950. At Chatham these were to include the construction of four huge sugar silos designed to hold 30 million pounds of refined sugar; the modernization of the packaging lines; the re-equipping of the centrifugal systems; the construction of a new centralized agricultural department for the proper storage of seed, fertilizer, and implements; and finally the installation of a new hydro power station in which, through a co-operative agreement with Ontario Hydro, the company could provide steam for the Hydro facility during non-processing periods. At Wallaceburg, investments included an entirely new power house building and turbine generator powered by fuel oil instead of the old coal-fired system, plus a new river water pumping system.

Finally for 1949, in the minutes of the meeting of December 20, 1949, two other references that were to have profound and lasting effects on the future of the company appear. First was the report of discussions being initiated with the Toronto Harbour Commission for the prospective purchase or long-term leasing of an area of 7.2 acres of new landfill on the Toronto harbour waterfront. This land was initially scheduled for use as a distribution centre and possibly a new refinery sometime in the future to coincide with the development of the proposed St. Lawrence Seaway.

This now led to the second point, which in the long term was even more influential in the corporate future, since it was recognized that to develop a brand new refinery, technical expertise beyond that currently available to the Canada and Dominion Sugar Co. Ltd. needed to be obtained. The choice was therefore made to approach the British sugar firm of Tate & Lyle for a co-operative technological agreement, subject to the proviso that Tate & Lyle continued to exist in 1950, as it was deeply involved in a bitter dispute with the British Labour government over that government's plans to nationalize the British sugar industry.

Is It a Brave New World or the Same Old Story?

Aerial view of the future site of the Toronto refinery (waterfront centre.)

A line-up of vessels unloading raw sugar at Windmill Point, Montreal.

CHAPTER SEVEN

The British Connection

Following the ending of government price controls and having regained some direction of their own industry, Canadian sugar companies were quick to re-equip and modernize their separate factories to take advantage of the developments in technology that had occurred during the war years. Unfortunately, ongoing arrangements between the British and Canadian governments required the Canadian refiners to continue purchasing most of their sugar from parts of the British Empire through the sole agency of the British Ministry of Food. As the Canadian government had now discontinued the post of Sugar Administrator, there was no longer any official representative authorized to speak on behalf of the refiners. Led by W.J. McGregor, the eastern Canadian refiners wrote to the Chairman of the Wartime Prices and Trade Board, K.W. Taylor, requesting official permission to establish an industry-run central purchasing agency to liaise with the British Ministry of Food. After consultation with his colleagues, Mr. Taylor approved this arrangement on February 9, 1950. Also at this time, the new beet contract was issued by the Chatham head office and netted 40,000 acres, the highest level ever recorded in the history of the industry. At the Montreal refinery, a five-year technical agreement was concluded between the Canada and Dominion Sugar Co. Ltd. and Tate & Lyle Technical Services to study the current operations of the Montreal refinery and propose improvements in its capacity and efficiency. The man placed in charge of these studies (later a Director of C and D) was Geoffrey Fairrie, the Managing Director of Tate & Lyle. This was an ironic twist of fate as Mr. Fairrie came from a long-time Scottish sugar refining family with whom John Redpath had held extensive communications on technological developments while planning his original Montreal refinery in the 1850s.

Construction and renovations at each of the company's three plants continued in the following months, creating a new profile on the skyline at Chatham as the silos neared completion; at Wallaceburg, the newly reconstructed ship wharf received the first of several water-borne cargoes of raw sugar to be delivered that year on board the lake vessel *Easton*. Meanwhile, the year's beet crop was not faring well due to a combination of heavy rains in May followed by an extended dry period that

Geoffrey Fairrie

Construction of the new Montreal refinery raw sugar shed on the site of the old coal yard.

Construction of the raw sugar conveyors for the new raw sugar shed.

Inside the framework of the new raw sugar shed, February, 1950.

The completed raw sugar shed, June 1950

killed off so many beets that the company issued free beet seed to encourage re-planting. On the labour front, the company programme of assisting its farmers to sponsor relatives for emigration to Canada had almost reached its limit and so the previous year's successful system of using displaced persons was introduced once again with some 124 men from Germany arriving at Chatham on June 1. The three labour camps were used under the same arrangements as 1949 and were closed in late July when the blocking and thinning of the crop had been successfully completed. One tragic note from this general period of good news occurred at Chatham during the early stages of construction of the huge silos. On June 19, an elevator tower suffered a structural failure while a load of concrete was being hoisted, killing two of the construction workers. All work was immediately suspended while an inquest was held, which recorded that the deaths were accidental and not attributable to negligence by any of the parties concerned. Following the inquest, the construction commenced once again to ensure its completion by harvest time.

During the same period, the world political situation had deteriorated with the development of the conflict in Korea, which raised fears of another international war. This led to a rapid increase in the purchasing of sugar by consumers in duplication of the "runs" of 1914 and 1939 to such an extent that by the end of July, the shortages of

M. V. Easton.

Construction of the Chatham refined sugar silo, May, 1950.

Before and after the collapse of the tower at the Chatham factory, June, 1950.

Completing the silos at Chatham, August, 1950.

production could be countered only by raising prices. For the larger industrial customers, this shortage was further complicated by a railway strike that held up large shipments of refined sugar until additional trucks were rented to deliver the orders.

By September 1950, the new bulk raw sugar shed at Montreal and the refined sugar silos at Chatham were completed and put into immediate use; at Wallaceburg, the new powerhouse was almost complete and was certain to be ready for the following month, when its coolant water intake was blocked by a collapse of the river bank. The immediate reconstruction both to repair the river bank and free the coolant intake cost over $18,000. Subsequent investigation determined that the erosion of the river bank had been caused by the propeller wash of the additional vessels used through the summer to deliver raw cane sugar and led to added work orders being issued for further strengthening of the river bank to prevent its re-occurrence the following season.

At the next meeting of the Board of C and D, Mr. Fairrie presented his preliminary results of the required alterations within the Montreal refinery. These included:
– the construction of an entirely new refining building with a daily capacity of at least 2.5 million pounds,
– the construction of a new charhouse or the complete upgrading of the current system of affination machines,
– structural alterations to the main refined sugar warehouse to raise its efficiency to modern standards,
– the total re-equipment and streamlining of the packaging processes used by the company.

The estimated cost would exceed $6.5 million, an amount that shocked many of the Canadian directors. As if to add insult to injury, Mr. Fairrie also intimated that the company needed to re-evaluate the efficiencies and quality of its refinery and support staff. As might be expected, while the Board was expecting an expensive list of alterations, they were not prepared for such a sweeping catalogue of apparent failure by what was considered to be an outsider. As a result, although some strong words passed between the Board members, they all agreed that the refinery did need modernization. Therefore, following some further discussion, it was agreed that as much work as possible would be done using the existing building structures rather than erecting entirely new ones, and so the modernization programme for Montreal was approved. Similarly, at this meeting approvals were made for Chatham with the additions of a new vacuum pan, three centrifugal machines, and the building of a concrete "runway" on the beet piling ground at a cost of $100,000, while Wallaceburg was to receive a new packaging line costing $75,000.

In October, the

Weighing in the first load of beets for the 1950 campaign.

The tug Atomic doing duty as an icebreaker.

year's harvest began and yielded 104 million pounds of refined sugar from the more than 33,000 acres harvested, an all-time record. On the negative side, however, the Chatham plant seemed to suffer a spate of bad fortune; first, part of the soil embankment surrounding the sediment settling basin adjacent to the factory collapsed, releasing a huge volume of high-lime-content water across nearly 100 acres of cropland. This was followed in November by the application for a court injuction on behalf of a number of residents living near the factory to prevent the factory processing beets because of an alleged smoke nuisance emanating from the factory. Finally, as if to fulfil the saying that bad luck comes in threes, on December 6, 1950, John Wood, a switchman on the rail yard at Chatham, fell from an overhead crane and was dragged along the track for several yards by moving beet wagons before breaking free at the cost of some severe cuts and bruises. With the new year of 1951, although it was hoped that the bad-luck cycle had been ended, it seemed instead to renew its force as massive ice jams on the Thames River caused the flooding of some 10,000 acres of nearby land. Since much of this land was scheduled for beet crops, the company felt it had a strong interest in eliminating this current problem and ensuring that it did not re-occur in the spring. Therefore C and D became one of the first companies to contribute money and support to the local Kent County Council's Ice Jam Relief Fund, which led to the hiring of the ice breaker tug *Atomic* from Amherstburg to break up the backlog of ice and release the pent-up water.

The elements continued to cause problems for the company when shortly afterwards a large fire broke out in one of the Wallaceburg storage sheds destroying some supplies and the building itself. Less visible but nonetheless severe damage was caused on January 30, 1951, when the Minister of Agriculture, the Hon. James G. Gardiner, made a speech to the Kent County Federation of Agriculture. In this speech he let it be known that the unofficial position of the government regarding sugar beets was that farmers should abandon beet growing in favour of soya beans and allow the nation's supplies of sugar to be derived from cane sources. Naturally, this infuriated both the beet farmers and their growers' association, not to mention W.J. McGregor, who responded by sending searing telegrams to all levels of government. Within days, the agriculture minister was backtracking on his statement, claiming that he had been misquoted and misinterpreted by the press. His protests did not carry much weight as a disclaimer since most of the complaints had originated with beet farmers who were in the audience that night.

When the eventual total of acres contracted for the year was announced and it was seen to be down 30% on the

Let Redpath Sweeten It

Construction of the refined sugar silos at the Montreal refinery.

The Montreal refinery in December, 1951.

year before, W.J. McGregor was reported to have loudly condemned the statements of Mr. Gardiner as one major reason for the lower numbers. He also blamed the situation upon other government officials attending the international conference on tariffs in Torquay, England. There the Canadians were being criticized by other Commonwealth countries for negotiating a huge trade deal with Cuba to reduce the Canadian tariff on Cuban sugar in return for reciprocal reductions by Cuba on Canadian products. Despite these criticisms, Canada disregarded the complaints and signed a three-year deal to purchase a minimum of 75,000 tons of Cuban raw sugar each year, but without stipulating a specific price. This loophole allowed the Cubans to inflate their prices at will, secure in the knowledge that the Canadian government would use its influence to force the refiners to absorb this excessive amount of sugar without regard to previous contracts or long-term commitments with other countries at lower set prices.

At the Montreal refinery, the approved modernization was begun, but it quickly became clear that far more work was required than earlier thought. At a result, the technical service agreement between Canada and Dominion and Tate & Lyle was re-negotiated for the installation of two quadruple effect evaporators, eight white centrifugal machines, two refined sugar silos, and the introduction of a new system of filtration called carbonatation. This latter carbonatation process was not familiar to the current Montreal refinery staff and it was agreed that experienced Tate & Lyle personnel would be made available to ensure the correct installation and subsequent running of the system.

Also agreed upon at this time was the future development of the proposed Toronto waterfront site. As it

Cutting-in at the raw sugar shed.

was felt that 7.2 acres might not provide sufficient space for future development, the purchase was increased to 10.5 acres. The first structure scheduled to be constructed on this site was a refined sugar warehouse and distribution centre. This would then be supplied from the refineries of Montreal, Chatham, and Wallaceburg, until the future refinery project was decided upon.

By October the new carbonatation system was installed at Montreal. Initial production tests revealed that it would produce a significant improvement in the quality of the refined liquor. However, some problems were experienced at another point in the production cycle called the "mud" presses. These could not keep up with the new improved syrup volumes, so the management had to consider installing additional presses to re-establish the balance. Another problem at this time came in the training of the Montreal refinery employees by the Tate & Lyle staff. Initially, there was some resistance by the local labour, especially when some of the new English engineers were appointed to positions of authority over Canadians who had worked for many years in the Montreal plant; when J.H. Magee, the process manager of Tate & Lyle's Liverpool refinery, was appointed as refinery manager for Montreal, some tempers began to flare. Fortunately, Mr. Magee's skills as a professional sugar maker and his aptitude as a personnel manager soothed the ruffled feathers, and he was able to lay the foundation for welding together the separate elements of the refining staff into a highly efficient workforce.

One of Mr. Magee's first submissions to the Board for its approval was the restructuring of the old and now obsolete refined sugar warehouse to facilitate the loading movement of the newer and larger delivery vehicles. Even the new raw sugar shed did not escape his notice as he proposed the expansion of the bag receiving system to allow a speedier "cutting-in" and dumping to take place.

Back on the beet side of the company, the year's harvest was taken from just over 31,000 acres without any significant interruptions by poor weather and yielded 341,000 tons of beets. Following processing, a total of 93 million pounds of refined sugar was stored, although some 6,000 pounds were later destroyed when a spontaneous combustion fire erupted in the Wallaceburg warehouse on October 26. Fortunately, the fire was discovered before it became too large and was quickly extinguished by refinery personnel, otherwise an estimated 40% of the total year's supply of sugar could literally have gone up in smoke overnight.

Early in 1952, two major developments occurred in the Canadian sugar industry. First was the announcement by the British Ministry of Food that it was curtailing its activities as the sole agent through which Commonwealth sugar could be traded at the end of 1952, thus ending twelve years of controls, during which it had effectively directed Canadian sugar policies. This was, of course, good news for the Canadian refiners, who now felt they could develop a free market once more. Unfortunately, this was not to be the case, as the second development occurred with the announcement by the Canadian government that although it was their policy not to interfere with the refiners and their business methods, the fact remained that as well as the contract for 75,000 tons of raw sugar previously signed with the Cubans, the government had now added similar contracts with the Dominican Republic and Haiti and it "expected" the sugar industry to "adjust" its purchasing plans in order to absorb these volumes without delay. Shocked by this new "expectation," the industry attempted to explain to the government the impossibility of this request due to the long-term pre-planning of raw sugar contracts generally done by the industry. In reply, the government merely repeated its declaration of "expectations" with the added clause that due to the "failure" of the sugar industry to take up the full 1951 quota of Cuban sugar, the outstanding volume from 1951 would be added to the 75,000 tons for 1952 making a new required quota of 121,264 tons from Cuba. When this was added to the original quotas from the Dominican Republic and Haiti it amounted to a grand total of 172,960 tons of which C and D was "required" to take 59,000 tons. Despite repeated calls by all the sugar refiners to revise this new volume requirement, the government stood firm on its position and claimed that in the long run the refiners would thank them for making such a good deal with the Cubans. These thanks were not likely to occur, as soon afterwards large quantities of Cuban refined sugar began to appear across Quebec and Ontario, at prices well below that of Canadian-made sugar. When enquiries were made by the Canadian refiners as to the means by which this refined sugar could be brought in, they discovered to their horror that the government's so-called "good deal" had a huge loophole that allowed unlimited volumes of Cuban refined sugar to be sent to Canada as well as the 75,000 tons of raw. Recognizing the severe threat this new flood represented to the Canadian sugar industry and his beloved beet sector, W.J. McGregor began what was to become a running battle with government bureaucrats in an attempt to close the loophole.

In January 1952, the full-scale production use of the affination and carbonatation systems, began at the Montreal refinery, while the new vacuum pans, centrifugals, and packaging equipment were either in the process of being installed or were scheduled for delivery. At Chatham the old steam cranes were converted to diesel fuel, new baling machines for the packages of sugar arrived, and an innovative method of preserving harvested beets by using forced-air ventilation was introduced in the main yard. Wallaceburg was included in the improvement programme through the installation of new pulp driers and the development of a concrete "runway" for that site's beet yard.

At the agricultural level, the 1952 beet contract was issued at the same rates as the previous two years and netted 34,000 acres. For the season's influx of workers from Europe, the camps at Chatham, Wallaceburg, Dover Centre, and Petrolia were refurbished to accommodate the 140 Italian and 70 French single men who eventually arrived. In addition, twenty-three family groups were placed in renovated company-owned houses.

Harvesting beets during an early snow fall, October, 1952.

By mid-summer, while the beet crop was developing nicely and was projected to be a bumper crop, the continued increase in the volume of Cuban refined sugar being pushed onto the Ontario market at cut-rate prices caused the company to consider closing down at Wallaceburg permanently. Alarmed by the prospect of seeing their year's efforts ruined by these foreign supplies, farmers' groups turned to the company for assistance and guidance. As a result, a combined barrage of telegrams, letters, petitions, and resolutions were sent to the attention of Mr. Howe and his ministry officials. The gist of these messages was to first of all complain that in the initial negotiations the government had failed in its duty to Canada's farming community, and secondly to call for immediate remedial action to stop the dumping of Cuban refined sugar onto the Canadian market.

In reply, Mr. Howe notified the farmers' groups that technically no "illegal" dumping was occurring, as the prices for refined sugar in Cuba were lower than the sums charged for the product coming to Canada. What he failed to mention, however, was the fact that the Cuban sugar industry had deliberately slashed its normal domestic price of refined sugar to almost give-away levels in order to specifically circumvent the dumping regulations of Canada.

Naturally, neither the farmers' lobby nor W.J. McGregor were fooled by this bit of double-talk and efforts were redoubled by all concerned to change the government's mind. As the weeks passed, the momentum of the campaign increased as local boards of trade, women's organizations, private citizens, and local newspapers joined their voices to those of the farmers and W.J. McGregor in drafting letters. In the House of Commons, opposition members representing beet-growing areas were more than willing to join in and attack the government in general and C.D. Howe in particular.

Finally, stung by this campaign into giving a response, Mr. Howe announced that he had scheduled a tour of South and Central America and would extend this to Cuba to see what could be done to resolve the issue. In the interim, the sugar industry and the various lobby groups should simply trust in the government to do what was best.

Not content to let matters rest or "simply" trust in the government to sort matters out, W.J. McGregor continued to co-ordinate the stream of media releases, telegrams, and articles in the corporate newsletter, *Sugar Facts*. These hinted that if no remedy was forthcoming soon, both C and D beet plants could be closed in 1953.

The following February, C.D. Howe departed on his announced tour hoping to escape from his critics. Unfortunately for him this was not to be, as a company official, M.W. Davidson, later wrote:

He was already grumbling about the campaign ... before he left, but an incident in Bolivia, while inspecting the depths of a tin mine, was the last straw ... The Ministers party could hear the echo of running footsteps getting closer and closer ... until a runner from the Canadian embassy came into view. He delivered to the Minister a decoded message from the farmers of Thedford, Ontario, urging him to get on with stopping the flow of Cuban refined sugar ... and when C.D. Howe disembarked from his D.C.3 in Ottawa he could hardly wait to reach the House of Commons to deal with the perpetrators of the resolutions on Cuban refined. He had decided that Canada and Dominion Sugar was the architect and that he would abuse his parliamentary immunity to focus his attack on the President, W.J. McGregor.

According to an article printed in the Ottawa Sentinel, this attack was delivered because:

Mr. W.J. McGregor ... had cost him [C.D. Howe] his sleep ... by urging policies with which Mr. Howe did not agree. So Mr. Howe entered the House of Commons on February 11 determined, in his own words "to do a real job" on Mr. McGregor. First he accused Mr. McGregor of conducting the most aggressive pressure campaign of Mr. Howe's experience. Then he contrasted Mr. McGregor with other men in the sugar refinery business who, said Mr. Howe were "men of integrity." Then ... he left the clear insinuation that Mr. McGregor's policies were motivated by ... greed ... Veteran Parliamentary observers agreed that it was an unprecedented verbal thrashing by a Minister of the Crown to a private citizen.

For several days following this tirade, the national papers were full of editorials on the issue. Opposition papers were openly critical and condemned Mr. Howe's statements, while papers that supported the government tried to justify the case on the grounds that there had indeed been a strong campaign centred on the opinions of W.J. McGregor against Mr. Howe and the government. However, even they could not avoid the fact that the authority of the national government had been used to defame a citizen of the country without that individual having an equal opportunity to defend himself. In fact, no response came from either Mr. McGregor or the company for several days while various legal options were considered. When eventually a prepared statement by Mr. McGregor was released, it contained no excuse or apology "for any effort of mine in promoting the well-being of the sugar beet industry" but did itemize the factual errors inherent in the minister's statements about corporate profits and various business dealings in the sugar industry.

Matters continued to develop when on February 13, 1953, Mr. Howe summoned a delegation of the refiners to his office. Under normal circumstances, Mr. McGregor would have automatically been part of this group, but in light of the current atmosphere, two other representatives from the company were sent instead. At the appointed hour, the delegation was ushered into Mr. Howe's office but were not welcomed or invited to be seated. Instead they were left standing while Mr. Howe pronounced that in his judgement the Cuban authorities had assured him of their willingness to hold back from exporting refined sugar directly to beet-growing areas of Canada until an official negotiated settlement was concluded. He then instructed the refiners to send a delegation directly to Cuba, there to negotiate with the Cubans under the supervision of the Canadian Embassy. At the end of Mr. Howe's statement, the visitors were summarily dismissed and escorted from the office. When the sugar industry subsequently made up its list of representatives, Mr. McGregor was included on behalf of C and D. Upon seeing this, Mr. Howe was reported to have "exploded" and declared Mr. McGregor as

An aerial view of the Montreal refinery in 1953.

"banned," leaving the industry with no alternative but to send another individual in Mr. McGregor's place.

One major fall-out of these events was the rise in uncertainty amongst the Ontario beet growing community and it led to difficult negotiations between the company and its farmers. This difference eventually had to be arbitrated by the Chatham Board of Trade before a settlement was reached that gave the farmers a higher return on their beets. Even so the scepticism of the farmers kept contracts down and eventually only 25,570 acres were signed up.

To everyone's surprise, a new announcement now emerged from the office of C.D. Howe, indicating that an embargo was to be placed on all direct shipments of refined sugar from Cuba. However, over the next few weeks, the sugar continued to pour into Ontario prompting one beet farmer, Wilfred Brockman, to question Mr. Howe at a banquet of the Perth County Federation of Agriculture. According to the subsequent reports in various newspapers, Mr. Brockman asked Mr. Howe if he was aware that, despite his claim of an embargo being in place, at least twenty-five railcar loads of Cuban refined sugar had been delivered to Perth County since the minister's statement. Mr. Howe replied that he had said there would be no "direct" shipments, and since these carloads had not come "directly" they did not count. "Then the statement you made in the House was of no value," said Mr. Brockman. "It was only a shield?" Mr. Howe had to admit, "That's right."

This admission now led to yet another round of newspaper editorials on the value of a government minister's word, while an opposition Member of Parliament, J.W. Murphy, quoted from the conversation in the House and pressed Mr. Howe for direct action to uphold the spirit of

Packaging 5 pound bags of sugar.

the statements he had made. Angered by the continuous attention this issue was receiving, Mr. Howe attempted to shift the blame away from himself and called Mr. Murphy a "stooge" for Mr. McGregor. When called upon by the Speaker to retract his "unparliamentary statement," Mr. Howe altered his accusation to describe Mr. Murphy as an "emissary." This still infuriated both the opposition benches and Mr. Murphy in particular, who stated he wanted it clearly understood that he was "no emissary for Mr. McGregor or for anybody else in the processing industry" but rather that he was simply a beet farmer who wanted justice for his industry.

Although these incidents were distinctly unpleasant for the image of the sugar beet industry, and the company in particular, they did seem to have the required effect as the volume of refined Cuban sugar diminished rapidly. How much this was due to the actions of Mr. McGregor and his campaign, and how much to the simultaneous circumstance of events that took place at the International Sugar Conference in Geneva (where Canada was singled out for criticism by her Commonwealth partners over its deal with the Cubans) no one can tell.

In April, Mr. Fairrie found it necessary to resign from the Canada and Dominion Sugar Co. Ltd. Board due to his commitments in the United Kingdom with Tate & Lyle. This led to the President of Tate & Lyle, Lord Lyle of Westbourne, being appointed in his place. In June, an agreement was made by the company for Tate & Lyle to negotiate raw sugar contracts on behalf of C and D and to develop these shipments as true bulk loads of raw sugar (i.e., loose in the holds of the ships) instead of the current inconvenient method of delivery in sacks, which then had to be "cut in" at the raw sugar shed before the sugar could be piled in bulk.

By the end of the year, although the beet campaign was reasonably successfully carried out, the fact that only 22,000 acres were available did not make for a successful campaign in the eyes of Mr. McGregor. Furthermore despite the fact that announcements were made that the Canada-Cuba trade agreement would not be renewed, rumours began to circulate that in retaliation, the Cubans would again start shipping refined sugar into Canada. To circumvent this possibility, W.J. McGregor took matters into his own hands and visited Cuba with J.R. Crawford, the Vice-President of St. Lawrence Sugar. In a series of meetings, they successfully negotiated an agreement whereby the Canadian refiners would buy specific quantities of Cuban raw sugar; in return, the Cubans would refrain from shipping refined sugar into the Canadian market. Obviously this rapid success by his severest critic caused C.D. Howe considerable embarrassment, especially when he had earlier publicly declared the refiners' trip a waste of time and he was reported to have made some unprintable comments about Mr. McGregor when he heard of the deal.

With the securing of a firm agreement between the Canadian refiners and the Cuban sugar producers, a feeling of optimism returned once more to the beet industry, although it took some time for its effects to show as contracting for the 1954 beet crop progressed slowly to an eventual level of 28,844 acres. Unfortunately, weather conditions conspired to disrupt plans once again, as high levels of rain during the seeding period followed by a full five months of drought significantly reduced the actual amount of beets planted and harvested.

Nor was the rest of the company free from ill luck, for in March, Lord Lyle died in England. This created a gap in the Canada and Dominion Board and temporarily stalled the plans for the development of the Toronto site. So it was not until August, when Ian D. Lyle, the Chairman of Tate & Lyle, was appointed as a Director, that discussions resumed on the construction of the Toronto refined sugar warehouse and prospective refinery complex.

On a more pleasant note, August also represented the one hundredth anniversary of the original opening of John Redpath's Canada Sugar Refinery. To celebrate this milestone, a special publication was commissioned documenting the story of the Montreal site; as in past anniversaries, the employees of the company and members of the Redpath and Drummond families joined together for a celebratory function that culminated in a commemorative photograph. Of interest is the singular absence of W.J. McGregor, who was reportedly on vacation in Europe. The chairmanship of this celebration was therefore taken by one of the other directors, the Honourable George B. Foster, Q.C., who led

Special packaging for the 100th Anniversary.

An early version of a bulk granular truck.

the descendants of the founding families on a tour of the refinery before the senior surviving family member, Huntly Redpath Drummond, made special presentations to long-service employees and gave a short retrospective talk on the state of the sugar industry.

September 1954 saw the introduction of a new system of sugar deliveries to industrial customers in the form of large "bulk" containers fixed on railcars or trucks. This represented a quantum leap in large sugar shipments as it eliminated all packaging, which in turn allowed greater discounts to be made in prices compared to an equivalent volume of bagged sugar. At the other end of the scale of sugar products, the tea cube system was approved for a major upgrading to eliminate the time-consuming manual methods currently being used, and experiments were begun on the use of a new type of packaging machine to produce small envelopes filled with loose granular sugar. These Individual Serving Envelopes, or I.S.E.s, it was claimed, would revolutionize the small-volume sugar market as the bulk deliveries would the large.

Bad luck returned for the company in the final quarter of the year, beginning with torrential rains that accompanied the passage of Hurricane Hazel across the province of Ontario. More rain fell in seventy-two hours at Chatham than had occurred during the previous five months. As a result, the fields became unworkable and some 758 acres of beets had to be abandoned due to the heavy mud conditions. So poor was the rate of harvesting that, for the first time in the industry's history, the Chatham plant shut down in mid-campaign due to a lack of beets; it then re-opened for a second, short run about a week later once the final crops had been harvested.

The British Connection

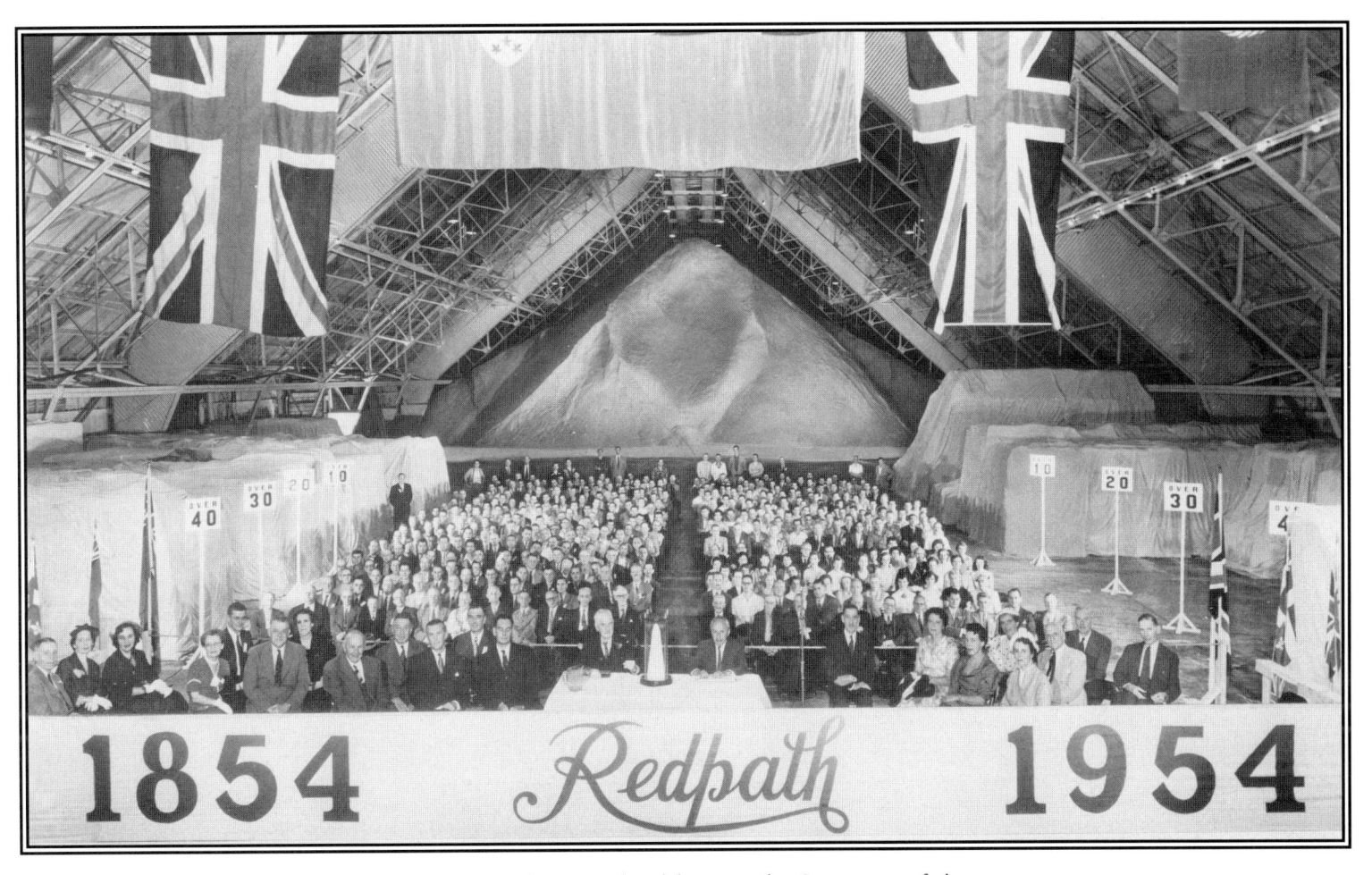

The commemorative photograph celebrating the Centenary of the company.

The molasses spill at the Chatham refinery.

To add to these difficulties, on the last day of operations at the Chatham plant, one of the main molasses tanks ruptured and poured most of its contents out into the factory yard. Many workers who had already completed their last shift for the season and had left to go home had to be recalled to the site to aid in clearing up the sticky mess.

Seeking to break this cycle of bad luck, an increased effort was subsequently put into developing a new beet contract that would substantially increase the acreage contracted for 1955. But despite the inclusion of several new clauses, including a guaranteed minimum price, many farmers were reluctant to sign up, citing fears that their expenditures on fertilizer, seed, and labour would be lost if the disastrous weather conditions of 1954 were repeated. This now led to intense discussions between the company and the Ontario Sugar Beet Growers Marketing Board, who proposed that the Ontario government be approached for a subsidy to the industry. Unable to wait for a possible subsidy, the company representatives eventually succeeded in signing just over 20,000 acres, which prompted W.J. McGregor to make one of his few public appearances to address a meeting of beet farmers wherein he warned:

> *Our shareholders received no dividends from beet sugar operations for the last decade. The company was obliged instead to siphon off earnings from our other operations for improvements at Chatham and Wallaceburg beet plants and mechanization at receiving stations ... No industry can survive without satisfied shareholders who cannot be criticized if they expect some reasonable return on their investment.*

Money was now becoming increasingly tight for the company as a whole, and the situation was not helped when a major fire broke out in the warehouse of the Workman Bay Co. Ltd. immediately adjacent to the raw sugar shed at Montreal. The fire not only gutted the Workman warehouse but destroyed 86,000 bags of C and D raw sugar stored inside, for an estimated loss of $250,000.

Discussions now began to take place within the Board on what cost-cutting measures could be introduced; it was agreed that the construction of the new Montreal central office block that had been started at the end of 1954 should be completed as planned, but the proposed development of a new Toronto refinery facility was definitely in jeopardy. This led Ian Lyle to submit a major proposal at the next Board meeting on April 29, whereby Tate & Lyle would not only participate in the technical end of designing the proposed refinery but would aid in the financing as well up to a maximum of 25% of the costs in return for a proportion of Canada and Dominion shares.

Unwilling to make a snap decision on such a vital question, the Canadian members of the Board deferred their discussion of the question of financing until the year's beet crop was harvested and the state of the company could be assessed, although the public announcement of the plans for the refinery at Toronto were released the next day.

During that summer, each of the company facilities received much needed investments of capital and equipment to maintain their efficiency in a competitive market. In June, the Montreal plant received the first of its new bulk raw sugar deliveries aboard the M.V. *Canadian Highlander*. The vessel was unloaded at Windmill Point by cranes normally used to empty coal barges into trucks which then delivered the loose sugar directly into the raw sugar shed.

Another first for the company came in the use of a new mobile irrigation system at the Wallaceburg experimental farm. This system proved so successful that it was subsequently loaned out to other farmers to use on their fields during what proved to be another dry summer in southern Ontario. On the labour front, when the expected influx of immigrants failed to materialize, many farmers blamed the company, although the real reason was that higher levels of unemployment across Canada had dissuaded many new immigrants from leaving their home countries where conditions were beginning to improve. As a result, no labour camps were established for the year; instead, teams were sent to Toronto, Hamilton, Welland, Niagara Falls, and St. Catharines to recruit workers. Unfortunately, the attractive wages being offered by the major construction projects of the St. Lawrence Seaway and the Windsor-Toronto section of Highway 401 had already drawn most labourers away. This led Mr. McGregor to pen several memorandums to government employment agencies to see if additional manpower could be obtained. Fortunately, volunteers from the local communities and teams of children tided the

The new office block for the Montreal refinery.

Loading trucks with raw sugar in bulk at Windmill Point.

Delivery of the bulk raw sugar at the Montreal refinery.

industry over until harvest time, when the increased number of mechanical harvesters that had recently been introduced came into their own. A total of 18,914 acres were then harvested, with record yields being recorded per acre, but the low total acreage curbed the campaigns of the plants so that Chatham ran for fifty-nine days while Wallaceburg was closed after only thirty-five days. When the accounts were drawn up, they revealed, as feared, that for yet another year the beet sector had run at a loss. At the next Board meeting, the proposal made by Tate & Lyle for joint funding and a minority share holding were accepted, with Tate & Lyle acquiring 50,000 shares of Canada and Dominion as of October 31, 1955. A new player had just been added to the game.

The new warehouse at Toronto.

CHAPTER EIGHT

Branching Out

Immediately following the addition of Tate & Lyle as a minority shareholder, there were distinct signs of changes in the direction taken by the Canada and Dominion Sugar Co. Ltd. Primary amongst these was the decision that the Montreal Products alcohol plant was no longer a viable proposition. This was in part due to the growth in production of industrial grade alcohols from wood pulp and petroleum byproducts, which had all but eliminated the sales of the molasses-based product made by Montreal Products. As a result, it was decided to close down the distillery, dismantle its equipment, and convert the current alcohol storage building into a refined sugar warehouse. On the beet side, consideration was begun on the viability of maintaining a two-plant operation when regional farmers had only agreed to contract just over 21,000 acres, an amount that could easily be processed by a single refinery. Meanwhile, outside the company, other events were occurring that affected the future of the company. These included, first, the fact that the west coast refiner, B.C. Sugar Co. Ltd., had gained a significant proportion of the outstanding shares of the Manitoba Sugar Co. Ltd., effectively giving B.C. Sugar the control of the Canadian market from the Ontario – Manitoba border to the Pacific and making a certainty of a regional price war for sales in Manitoba.

Second, a change in the regulations on sugar duties created a loophole that allowed U.S.made refined liquid sugar to be brought into Canada under a lower duty schedule that had previously only included low-grade molasses. This represented a major threat to the growing trade in liquid sugar being enjoyed by C and D and was perceived as the thin edge of a very large wedge that could cause trouble in the future if it was not curbed immediately.

Finally, at the international level, the Canadian government signed a new concession on its duties under the General Agreement on Tariffs and Trade (G.A.T.T.) which would allow Canadian wineries to directly import foreign-made refined sugar for use in the manufacturing of wine products for domestic consumption at only 1% of the rate normally applied to regular shipments of refined sugar. This now placed the Canadian refiners at an impossible disadvantage in comparison to the U.S. and Mexican producers, who saw the opportunity to eliminate the Canadian competition by offering expanded discounts to the wineries in return for long-term contracts.

Over the next two months, the Board kept a wary eye on the international developments while awaiting government responses to their complaints on the liquid sugar and winery sugar situations. In the meantime, a more immediate and visible problem had developed in the beet sector, where weeks of continual rain had washed out much of the germinating beet plants to the point where it was seriously suggested that the year's crop be abandoned. However, some rapid and extra hard work by field representatives resulted in some acreage being reseeded while awaiting the arrival of the year's labour force from Europe. This new volume of workers was the result of an extensive recruiting drive undertaken in England, France, Belgium, the Netherlands, and Germany by a team of company representatives and led by B.E. Easton, the Agricultural Supervisor. Initial reports indicated that more than fifty families were tentatively "recruited" but due to various reasons, only seventeen eventually made the journey. At the same time, other teams of representatives journeyed to Quebec in response to a Department of Labour report that there was a surplus of experienced beet workers there. Led by Sylvio Pinsonneault and a relatively new employee, Neil Shaw, they succeeded in attracting about forty men to work in the beet fields of Ontario. Even so, the needs of the beet farmers were still greater than the available supply of workers, and so a major programme of recruiting school children was begun once school had ended and resulted in 700 vitally needed pairs of hands to thin the crop.

Difficulties continued for the beet sector when the arrival was reported of the first in a series of refined sugar cargoes from Mexico at the Montreal docks, for subsequent trans-shipment and prospective sale in Ontario.

This led to an immediate outcry by the beet growers' lobby and C and D, for it was nothing less than a repetition of the earlier Cuban situation. Some senior corporate representatives were even reported as saying that unless the government took immediate counter-action, the Ontario sugar beet industry would be "dead" by the end of 1956. When no supportive steps were taken by the government, the company was forced to keep Wallaceburg closed for the season, while the poor prospects for the year's beet harvest indicated that the Chatham plant would run at less than 50% of its capacity.

In July, the Annual General Meeting for the company took place and revealed a number of mixed reviews for the year. On the negative side, it recorded the permanent closure of the Montreal Products and the seasonal suspension of production at Wallaceburg; in contrast, it stated that the modernization of the Montreal refinery was basically complete, with the result that daily output had been increased by almost 50%, while costs had fallen by over 21%. On top of this, the experiment with bulk deliveries of raw sugar were declared to be a success, and it was planned to expand deliveries of this type by the end of the year. In Toronto, reports showed that all preparations were now ready for the construction of the main refinery, commencing with the driving of long piles through the still relatively new landfill of the upper surface to the firm bedrock below. Financially, too, the year's report was somewhat of a mixture as the improved profits being accrued through technical improvements and astute raw sugar trading were offset by the yearly failure of the beet industry to add anything but a marginal sum to the company's bottom line.

The other major feature of this meeting was the intense questioning that arose from the shareholders over the purchase of shares by Tate & Lyle and its implications for a future full take-over. Many of these questions, it must be admitted, came from descendants of the Redpath and

Driving the piles for the new refinery at Toronto.

An accident during construction.

Drummond families who still held a substantial block of company shares. However, following an explanation of the background to the shares purchase and the financial and technological benefits that a closer association with Tate & Lyle would bring, the initial objections of the shareholders were withdrawn.

Towards the middle of September, the Chatham refinery was prepared for its year's campaign. Good weather favoured the harvest for once, but the poor start to the crop season had left its mark so that only 14,158 acres were actually harvested, a loss of 33.8% on the original contract acreage. The industry was now facing a major crisis of confidence, and everyone from the individual farmers to the company were in united voice that without direct government support or a miracle, the 1957 beet season would not take place.

Since it was proving almost impossible to obtain government support, it was perhaps something of a dubious miracle that the international crises of the Soviet invasion of Hungary and the political upheavals in Egypt (which resulted in the events at Suez) caused a sudden jump in the world price of raw sugar. This unexpected rise in the value of sugar now permitted the company to make an additional payment to farmers for their 1956 crops with the hope that it would encourage the growing of additional acres in 1957.

Bolstered by this sudden opportunity and determined not to let "his" industry go down without a fight, W.J. McGregor spearheaded a new drive to turn the Ontario beet industry around. First on his list of actions was the development of a joint venture with the H.J. Heinz Co. of Canada Ltd., McNeill & Libby of Canada Ltd., the Ontario Sugar Beet Growers Marketing Board, the Ontario Vegetable Growers Marketing Board, the Kent Peach Growers Association, the Essex County Associated Growers, and the Federation of Agriculture, who together formed the Southwestern Ontario Field Crops Employers Association (S.W.O.F.C.A.) under the presidency of Mr. Davidson of C and D. The expressed purpose of this new body was to co-ordinate recruitment and timetabling of teams of labourers to rotate between the various production areas as each crop season dictated. In direct support of this programme, Bev Easton and Neil Shaw were despatched to Europe to recruit families from northern Italy, the Netherlands, Belgium, Germany, France, and Portugal. Despite all these efforts by the company to obtain labour, many farmers remained sceptical and would not commit for an increased level of acreage, so that the 1957 season began with only 20,572 acres under contract. This naturally depressed Mr. McGregor but, not willing to surrender, he redoubled his efforts to obtain government support for the beet industry.

In a series of meetings, Mr. McGregor pressed such individuals as the Agricultural Prices Support Board Chairman, A.M. Shaw; the Ontario Premier, Mr. Frost; the Deputy Minister of Agriculture, Dr. Graham; and even his old nemesis, Trade Minister C.D. Howe for a guaranteed floor price of $14 per ton. Despite his appeals, each in turn and later collectively turned W.J. down and claimed they could not or would not do more than support the objectives of S.W.O.F.C.A. and seek to speed up the immigration of the recruited workers from Europe.

As the growing season progressed, the need for workers became increasingly more desperate and as well as the regular groups of immigrants, local workers, school groups, and company employees were called upon to join the labourers in the fields to thin the crops. In most instances, this help was both willingly given by the employees and gratefully received by the farmers, but in one reported case, when several office staff volunteered to help a farmer who had been repeatedly clamouring for workers, they arrived at the farm, were given directions to the fields in question, then were left on their own to do the work while the farmer took his family to the local cinema. Fortunately, this incident proved to be the exception rather than the rule in the relations between the farmers and company workers.

In August, following the general election and a change in the ruling party from Liberals to Conservatives, the beet lobby, led by W.J. McGregor, immediately sought the financial support refused by the previous government and the enacting of legislation to curb the imports of foreign refined sugar at dumping prices. This time they found a relatively sympathetic ear in the form of Prime Minister John Diefenbaker, who had spoken out several times during the election campaign in support of the sugar beet industry and now intimated he would seek to develop some system of assistance in co-operation with the provincial authorities.

By harvest time, although the crop acreage was only just over 19,000 acres, Chatham was worked for fifty-nine days and Wallaceburg processed beets for thirty-eight days.

December brought with it

At a beet workers camp in 1957.

Farmers trucks lined up to deliver beets.

both a sad loss and a major victory for the company. The loss occurred on December 9, 1957, when Huntly Redpath Drummond died at the age of ninety-three in his Montreal home on Drummond Street. This death broke the direct chain of family involvement in the company at senior management levels begun by John Redpath, Peter Redpath, and George Alexander Drummond back in 1854. The funeral took place a few days later and was reportedly attended by many of Canada's major business leaders, politicians, and a large contingent of senior employees and company retirees.

The victory came about a week later when on December 16 the Minister of Agriculture, the Hon. D.S. Harkness, rose in the House of Commons to state:

Mr. Speaker, I wish to announce that the Agricultural Prices Support Board has been authorized to support the price of sugar beets grown in 1957 on the basis of $13.00 per ton.

Elated by this supposed vindication of his policy of aggressive pressure, W.J. McGregor was reported to have responded:

This positive action by the Canadian Government demonstrates its intention of stabilizing this important cash crop and placing one of Canada's basic food industries on a more secure foundation ... the establishment of a floor price also enables the government to impose import controls on foreign refined sugar which has been flooding eastern Canadian markets.

In early January 1958, the Board met to discuss the prospects for the upcoming year. At Montreal, the new equipment was producing at desired levels with the result that four improved lines of sugar packaging were introduced into the market-place consisting of 2 and 5 pounds of golden yellow sugar in polyethylene bags and newly designed 5 and 10 pound paper bags for white granulated sugar. At Toronto, the building of the refinery was moving ahead smoothly with most of the structural steel in place, large tanks and equipment being installed, and the first courses of over 1 million specially manufactured bricks covered with a white glaze were being laid to create what would become a dramatic and clean look to the new refinery.

Sugar packaging in 1958.

On the beet side, although the government guarantee for price support had improved the confidence of farmers, there was still the unresolved question of what the level of support would be for 1958. Furthermore, the lack of definitive action on the Mexican sugar imports question had caused some farmers to delay or refuse to sign beet contracts. This action or rather non-action did not please the Board, as they also had to decide upon the capital investment to be made at the beet plants. Wallaceburg, for example, required a new steam boiler plant, evaporators, beet diffusor, turbines, and an extension of the concrete beet yard "runway." Chatham was scheduled for new weigh scales, mechanical beet pilers, a "runway" extension, and the installation of a bulk sugar system. On top of this, the labour

Construction at Toronto in 1958.

camps needed expansion and modernization, and new temporary ones would have to be established to accommodate an expected total of 270 men under the S.W.O.F.C.A. arrangement.

At the end of this meeting, W.J. McGregor brought a matter to the attention of the Board that had been bothering him for some time. This concerned the wartime measures originally imposed by the Sugar Administrator when all of the sugar industry was controlled by the government. This meant that customers had no choice of which brand of sugar they received, nor could each refiner choose its individual market area, for everything was stipulated by government decree. To C and D in 1958, the reasons for these wartime restrictions were now long past, but the decree that had prohibited *Redpath* sugar from being sent to the Maritime provinces still stood, while the similar restriction that had kept the Atlantic brand sugar from central Canada had long since been rescinded. Unhappy at this inequality, Mr. McGregor now wanted to have all inter-provincial restrictions removed and to compete on a pure market basis with the other Canadian refiners. In support of this position, Mr. McGregor sent company representatives to discuss matters with federal and provincial government agencies, newspaper publishers, and executives of the major sugar users across the region. Most of these contacts gave a warm and cordial reception to a prospective return of *Redpath*, but few actual orders were received, for it was later revealed that the Atlantic Provinces Economic Commission (A.P.E.C.) was pressuring the various companies not to allow their business to go to a central Canadian operation but rather to buy only from Maritime producers. As a result, something of a war of words developed between A.P.E.C. and McGregor over the issue, with the individual sugar users being caught in the middle. One unusual ally for C and D was the United Mine Workers Union. This support was due partially to the historical connection between the Maritimes coal industry and Sir George Alexander Drummond and also to the fact that the Atlantic Sugar Company refinery in Saint John had

Construction at Toronto in 1958.

recently disposed of its coal-fired boilers in favour of an oil-burning system. As a result, it was possible during this period to see union signs at various pitheads urging their members to ask for *Redpath* brand sugar in the grocery stores. Eventually, political pressures from Maritime interests persuaded the provincial governments to reverse their earlier support for C and D and through the federal government, the message was sent to W.J. McGregor to back down or face retribution in the form of a hardening of government policies towards beet support payments. This naturally rankled with Mr. McGregor, as it created a market where, from Manitoba westward, the B.C. Sugar Co. ruled virtually exclusively, while the Maritimes were the domain of Atlantic Sugar. In comparison, products from both these competitors and extensive volumes of foreign sugar were completely free to enter the Ontario and Quebec markets without any sign of comment from the government. Nevertheless, Mr. McGregor had no real choice in the matter and for the time being, the company had to defer its return to the Maritime provinces.

On a more positive note, the action taken by the government to provide a guaranteed floor price to beet farmers led to a substantial increase in the total acreage signed up for 1958, which amounted by April to 33,447 acres. The weather, too, co-operated, allowing much of the crop to be planted in March and April with very little loss being reported. With this substantial increase in acreage, the problem of obtaining sufficient labour surfaced once again. This time, the previous solution of recruiting skilled workers in Europe was not available as the Canadian government refused to allow additional immigration during the current period of slow economic growth and increasing unemployment. This forced the company to search the labour exchange offices of Hamilton and Toronto for general unemployed labourers and bring in native American Indians from across Ontario and Manitoba. Nor did the S.W.O.F.C.A. programme work out, for despite the fact that C and D representatives selected experienced men from the available pool of labour, those who arrived at the fields were often totally different individuals and ignorant of the proper techniques required to tend the beets. Worst of all, some were unwilling to put in more than a few hours a day and complained bitterly or quit if any form of comment was made on the generally poor quality of work that was being produced. The native Indian workers likewise proved unsatisfactory, as many quit after the first few days and left, leaving behind outstanding debts with the local merchants who supplied the camps; in addition, inter-tribal rivalries flared into violence at the work camp shared by the native workers, forcing the company to fire some workers and ship them back to their separate reserves.

Fortunately, the weather continued to favour the crop and predictions were made for a bountiful harvest in the autumn. The government then announced that its floor price for 1958 would remain at the same level as the previous year, which virtually guaranteed that the beet returns would be profitable for the first time in many years. This was just as well, as overall profits from raw sugar trading had been seriously undermined by an injudicious decision to purchase substantial quantities of raw sugar on a fixed-price basis over an extended period of time. Earlier trends had given the indication that there was to be a surge in world prices. Unfortunately, the surge turned into a major plunge and under its fixed contracts the company was required to pay a sum that was far above the open rate for raw sugar and suffer a financial loss on the deal. Such was the severity of these losses that consideration was given to eliminating the shareholders' dividend for the year and extending the corporate debentures in order to continue the financing of the Toronto refinery construction.

Meanwhile, despite the financial worries of the

New bulk granular sugar railcars in 1958.

company, the construction of the Toronto refinery continued at such a pace that the first shipment of raw sugar was scheduled for delivery in September. This was done so that if the St. Lawrence Seaway was not opened on time to coincide with the planned start-up of the refinery the following year, a stock of raw material would be on hand.

One week before the delivery was to take place, however, construction at the Toronto refinery came to a sudden halt when a strike of Toronto cement masons shut down all building work across the city. Some violence was reported at various other locations and it was feared that a picket line would be established to disrupt the arrival of the first cargo, but fortunately nothing happened, the strike was settled, and work resumed with only a minor delay.

The following month, the Ontario beet harvest began in favourable weather and for the first time over 50% of the

The arrival of the first load of raw sugar for the Toronto refinery.

One of the company's bulk granular trucks.

31,583 acres cropped was collected by mechanical harvesters. The good weather also aided the percentage of sugar content in the beets so that 114 million pounds of refined sugar were eventually produced from ninety-three days of production at Chatham and seventy-seven at Wallaceburg.

By the end of the campaign, such was the level of optimism within the company that the corner had been turned on the beet support question, that approval was quick in coming from the Board for a total modernization of the Wallaceburg facility at a cost of over $1 million, while Chatham received a lesser but still substantial $70,000 worth of new equipment to bring it up to par. Within weeks, this optimism was dampened by the public announcement that the Combines department for the Restrictive Trade Practices Commission was to initiate an inquiry into the manufacturing, purchase, sale, and supply of sugar in Canada, with particular emphasis on the stated suspicion that collusion had taken place between the sugar refiners to apportion sectors of the country for exclusive supplies by individual sugar companies. Reportedly Mr. McGregor was furious at this government attitude in view of the current price war being waged between the sugar companies in Quebec and Ontario and the ongoing policies of that self-same government that specifically prevented *Redpath* sugar gaining access to the Maritimes. Following due consultation with the remainder of the Board, W.J. was persuaded not to rush into a response but to take a wait-and-see attitude before initiating any decisive action on this issue.

In early January 1959, the company decided to move early in the season to ensure a prospective high return on its beet contracts and avoid the labour problems of the previous year by announcing the year's contract two weeks ahead of normal. In response, the farming community signed for 30,000 acres in the first seven days, and the remaining 10,000 acres to complete the company's stated requirements were forthcoming shortly thereafter. To obtain labour under the restrictions still imposed by the government, the bulk of the year's workers came from Quebec (although sixty-three family groups were eventually brought in from northern Italy) and were housed in the labour camps established at Chatham, Wallaceburg, Dover Centre, Comber, Wyoming, and Dresden.

By March 1959, the continuing losses incurred through raw sugar commitments, plus the cuts in margins forced upon the company by the high level of competition in the market were compounded by the political changes taking place in Cuba. There Dr. Manuel Urrutia and Fidel Castro had taken control of the island and subsequently dismissed nearly every official in the government, including those responsible for the sugar industry. This left the company wondering what would happen to its contracted deliveries and led Mr. McGregor to propose that C and D investigate the purchase of cane plantations in the West Indies to secure supplies in the event of the Cubans reneging on the signed contracts. He also proposed to lead a delegation to Cuba to initiate direct negotiations with the new authorities and determine what new policies were likely to be forthcoming on the matter of refined sugar shipments to Canada. Both proposals were readily agreed to by the Board, but his third proposal, which was to cut the shareholder dividend in order to retain corporate funds for the completion of the Toronto refinery and the ongoing modernization of the Wallaceburg plant, was not supported by the majority of the Board, especially by those Directors representing Tate & Lyle.

Good news for the whole industry came in April when the new federal budget announced the ending of the earlier imposition of an upper price limit under which the dumping

Aerial views of the completed Toronto refinery.

duties would be applied. This meant that importers of refined sugar from Mexico or Cuba would now have to pay duties that brought their prices up to the full Canadian market level, and no one was more pleased than W.J. McGregor, who saw in this change a vindication of his policy of "attacking" an unwelcome governmental policy. The happiness of the moment was soon lost, however, in view of the deteriorating financial reserves of the company. At the next Board meeting, it was decided to defer elements of the modernization at the Wallaceburg factory and to cut back on the proposed levels of output for the now complete Toronto refinery. More controversial was the decision to cut the corporate dividend, which as expected produced a strong negative response from the shareholders and perhaps contributed to the circumstances that were to occur at the end of the year.

On May 21, 1959, the new Toronto refinery began processing its first full-scale batch of raw sugar. Following the eight-hour production cycle and a thirty-hour "curing" time, the first bags of refined sugar emerged from the packaging machines to the general delight of all concerned.

The following month, on June 29, the official opening ceremonies for the refinery took place on a bright summer day when her Majesty Queen Elizabeth II and His Royal Highness Prince Philip, the Duke of Edinburgh, visited the plant. The refinery was selected for this prestigious visit because it was the first industrial facility constructed to coincide with the building of the St. Lawrence Seaway, and since the Queen had come to Canada to participate with U.S. President Eisenhower in the official opening of that waterway, it was considered appropriate to include the refinery in her itinerary.

Naturally, for some months previously, various representatives from the Canadian government, Scotland Yard, the R.C.M.P., and equerries of the royal household had visited the plant to prepare schedules, inspect the physical layout of the refinery, and check the records of all employees. On the day of the arrival of the Royal Yacht Britannia, police sharpshooters took up positions in the raw sugar weigh tower that overlooked the docking place of the vessel. Even the elevator that was to be used to take the distinguished visitors to the upper levels of the plant came in for minute scrutiny, and the police insisted that the operator not allow any other people to ride on the elevator for any reason.

On the day of the royal visit, hundreds of employees and their families gathered inside the gate of the refinery, while outside, over a thousand members of the public lined the newly named Queen's Quay East. Just before the scheduled arrival of the royal party, a bus load of media people arrived and demanded to be taken up in the elevator to the fifth floor of the refinery, which was 100 feet above ground level. True to his instructions, the elevator operator refused to allow them on board and they were directed to the adjacent stairwell for the ascent. Having just come from an air-conditioned Press Club and a substantial lunch, the prospect of climbing 253 steps in the heat of summer did not appeal to many of the reporters. Although a hardy few made the long climb, most stayed at ground level to report the visit or even returned to the press bus muttering against the company for being "denied their rights" to cover the story. This perhaps explains the following pure fiction that appeared in the columns of the *Toronto Daily Star* the next day.

Let Redpath Sweeten It

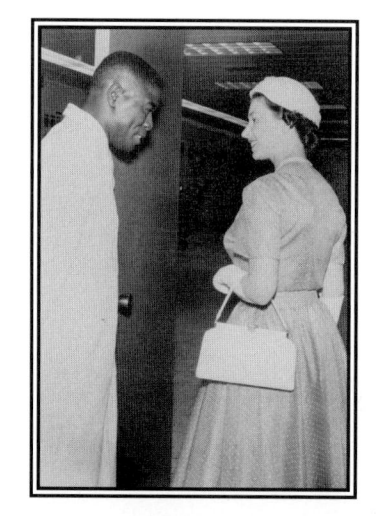

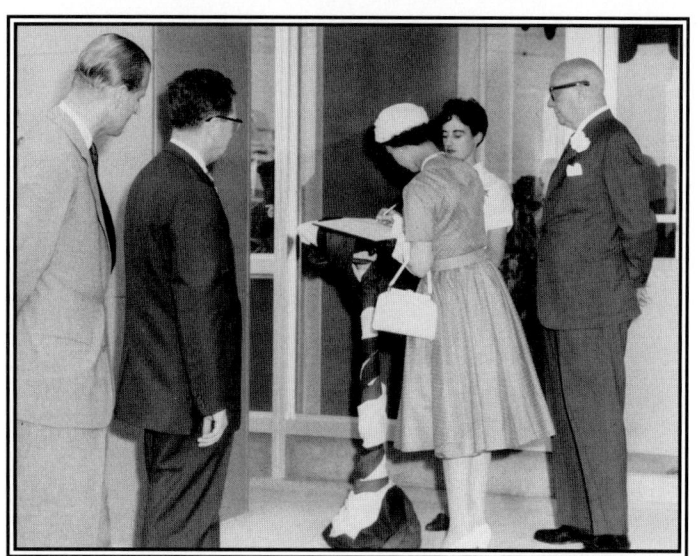

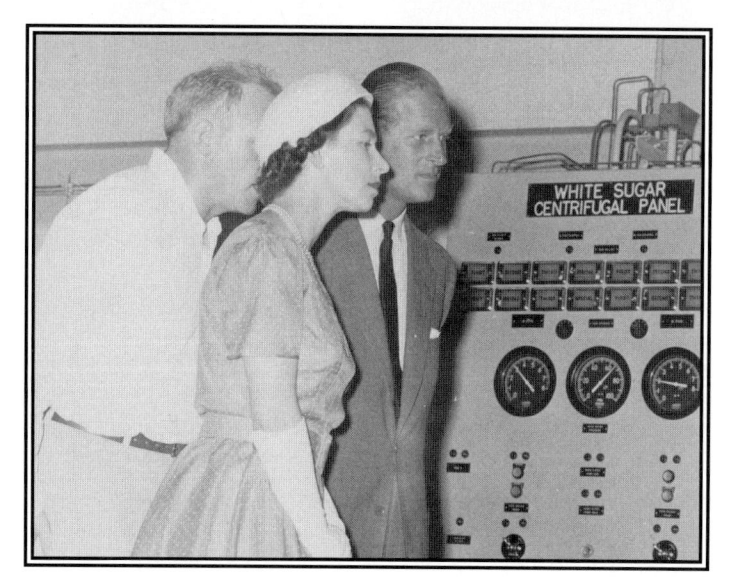

The official opening of the Toronto refinery.

Just a few minutes before the royal party arrived more than a dozen employees ... ran from machine to machine, from control panel to control panel. "We've got a bad batch ... we'll have to dump it on the floor." The royal couple carefully detoured around a portion of the floor made tacky by the spilt syrup. Photographers who used this portion of the floor for their picture taking had to use more than a little strength to free their feet.

Since no other paper reported anything of this supposed incident nor do any of the employees actually there at the time recall it, it can only be supposed that this version was concocted from the vantage of the Press bus.

At the appointed time, the Queen and Prince Philip were welcomed to the refinery by W.J. McGregor and M.W. Davidson. Accompanying the royal visitors were Premier Leslie Frost, Toronto Mayor Nathan Phillips, and Finance Minister Donald Fleming. The royal couple showed considerable interest and an informed understanding of the workings of the refinery and, much to the consternation of their aides, lingered well past the official time allotted. This surely must have been the crowning achievement to the career of W.J. McGregor, now aged seventy-one, and one he treasured for the remainder of his life. In a postscript to the day's events, it was realized that due to an oversight during the planning, the local Member of Parliament, Roland Michener, had been overlooked when issuing invitations. Fortunately, the gracious gentleman forgave the unintended slight but reportedly his wife, Norah, was somewhat less forgiving and refused to use *Redpath* sugar thereafter.

Following the official opening, mainstream production continued uninterrupted except for scheduled breaks until October 31, when the refinery was closed for the season. At Montreal, the added volume of sugar from Toronto allowed the opportunity to ease back on production and undertake some much-needed maintenance. On the beet sugar side, following a mixed season of heavy rains and periods of extreme heat, the harvest period began with over five inches of rain that rapidly turned the beet fields into lakes of mud. In such extreme conditions, neither machines nor even hand labour could salvage all the crop, and by the end of the harvest, 33,306 acres yielded 505,000 tons of beets (the largest volume in the company history) but with the lowest sugar content in forty years. Subsequent processing at both beet factories was therefore not as profitable as had been hoped, and the end result was a substantial operating loss on the season for the company and an unsatisfactory financial return for the growers.

Matters had now reached a point where current policies and conditions could not be continued indefinitely, and during the next Board meeting, the Tate & Lyle representatives made an offer to purchase 51% of the shares of Canada and Dominion in order to bail the company out of its current financial difficulties. Following some intense discussions, the Board decided to recommend the acceptance of this offer and the matter was placed before the shareholders for ratification. Almost immediately, a substantial outcry arose from one group of shareholders headed by Guy Drummond, who forced the Board to call a Special General meeting on December 4, 1959, to discuss the issue.

During the period immediately prior to this meeting, the Drummond faction had used advertisements and circulars to argue their case that the proposed take-over at the price offered was bad for the company and should be rejected, while on the other side, W.J. McGregor spent many hours on the telephone, campaigning to deliver enough proxy votes to support the recommendations of the Board. On the day of the "showdown," according to the recollections of M. Davidson:

The dissenting shareholders and their legal counsels occupied space in front of the table occupied by President McGregor. W.J. was flanked by the corporate Secretary Jack Wood on one side, and Don Pringle Q.C. on the other. W.J.'s speech was slurred and his mental processes cumbersome. To those who knew him it was evident that he had been awake all the night before ... The success of the Tate & Lyle offer depended on overcoming the dissenters, so Sir Ian Lyle was in attendance, accompanied by ... J.O. Whitmee. My impression is that Sir Ian and J.O. were surprised that most of the hundred shareholders and investment counsellors present had never heard of Tate & Lyle, and they had to be convinced of the advantages of the takeover.

Guy Drummond opened the argument by calling for the presentation of all background information on the Tate & Lyle shares bid, which was countered by Mr. McGregor, who claimed it was not wise to reveal details of correspondence and records unless required to do so under the Law of Companies Act. He then proposed that Sir Ian Lyle address the meeting, a suggestion that was immediately objected to by the dissenters. Eventually, Sir Ian gave his presentation and made a strong case for the Tate & Lyle position by revealing that while the effective control of C and D could have been obtained with less than 51% of the shares, the Bank of England was required to approve the purchase of the required dollars and would not do so unless Tate & Lyle acquired a majority shareholding. Furthermore, Sir Ian stated that the policy of Tate & Lyle was to have C and D run as an autonomous corporation and had no plans to reorganize the Board or import Tate & Lyle staff to replace experienced local personnel.

Following a considerable amount of very heated debate and the continued objections of Guy Drummond and his supporters, the final vote passed by a slim majority for acceptance of the Tate & Lyle offer, which to some measure can be credited to the many sleepless hours put in by W.J. McGregor.

Thus the small company that had been started by the vision of one man in 1854 had, just over 100 years later, become an international player in the world of sugar production. It was also to lead the way for a new series of developments by Tate & Lyle in the North American market during the decade ahead.

Branching Out

The cavernous interior of the raw sugar shed.

Technicians monitor the entire refining process in the control room.

Icing sugar being packaged in 1 pound cartons.

Stockpiles of refined sugar wait for distribution in the refined sugar warehouse.

Part of the fleet of company delivery trucks at Toronto in 1961.

CHAPTER NINE

For the Times They Are a-Changing

With the acquisition of the Canada and Dominion Sugar Co. Ltd. by the Tate & Lyle group and despite the commitments by Sir Ian Lyle to the contrary, everyone within the company lived on tenterhooks for the first few weeks of 1960 waiting to see if any sweeping changes would occur. When things continued as they had before the meeting of the previous December, the employees began to relax and concentrate on their jobs once again.

At Board level, initially W.J. McGregor continued as President but he made it clear to everyone that having successfully passed on the financial control of the company, he intended to do the same with the office of President and retire from the Board.

This resulted in a corporate restructuring with the appointment of George B. Foster, Q.C., as President, and J.O. Whitmee (of Tate & Lyle) as Managing Director. To these gentlemen fell the unpleasant duty of having to deal with the fact that the company was losing money; nevertheless, the business of the company had to continue and there was certainly plenty to do.

At Montreal, the refinery was currently closed for the winter due to the emptying of the Lachine Canal, and much work was underway to revitalize elements of the production.

George B. Foster

James O. Whitmee

The older method of manufacturing sugar cubes by cooking the sugar in large slabs and then slicing the slabs into cubes was totally obsolete, therefore approval was given for the installation of a new moulding system of production which, it was hoped, would significantly cut both production costs and wastage of sugar on this product. Similarly, the icing sugar and golden yellow packaging systems were located in separate areas of the plant, increasing production costs. Under a new proposal, they were now to be relocated in a new central packaging department, leaving a much-needed space into which new I.S.E. machines could be installed.

Toronto, too, was temporarily shut down as the low volume of current sales had made continuous production through the winter of 1959-60 uneconomic, although it was planned to re-open production in March to coincide with the opening of navigation on the St. Lawrence Seaway and continue until the close of shipping in November.

For both refineries it was decided that due to the expanded requirements of obtaining raw sugar, the concept of each plant buying its own stocks would be wasteful, and so a centralized purchasing department was located in the new office wing alongside the Montreal refinery. On the marketing side, the popularity of liquid sugar as an industrial food ingredient had increased sales from an initial 2.5 million pounds in 1952 to the current 20.4 million pounds, which required the addition of new specialized tanker trucks to the fleet of delivery vehicles at both Montreal and Toronto.

For the beet sector, the high level of financial losses from the 1959 crop made a re-evaluation of the entire operation necessary, starting with a sizable cut in the price offered for the

Making sugar cubes on new machines at the Montreal refinery.

A bulk granular sugar tanker in 1959.

1960 crop. This resulted in an immediate refusal by farmers' representatives to sign up, and a deadlock was settled only through the use of an arbitrator who decreed the company's offer fair in light of the prevailing circumstances. This angered the farmers and as a result, the actual acreage signed up for 1960 was only 18,000 compared to over 41,000 the year before.

Once this figure was known, it was realized that the amount of labour required for the year would be substantially reduced but since there had already been a company commitment for 50 families to arrive from Trieste within the month, an attempt was made to place them on regional farms; the follow-up of 103 single men was cancelled. Similarly, those labourers who were initially signed up from across Ontario and Quebec were cancelled as the local labour force available from the ranks of the unemployed was more than sufficient to cover the work required.

All these factors led to the inevitable conclusion that despite the huge investment in modernization at the company's beet plants, both could not be operated economically on such a low prospective crop. Therefore it was decided to keep Wallaceburg closed for the year with the prospect of permanent closure if circumstances did not improve the following year.

When the Annual Report for the 1959 - 1960 financial year was released, it showed a net loss of $1.7 million compared to a $3.2 million profit for the previous year. Reaction to this news by those who had originally opposed the Tate & Lyle take-over was quick and blunt, as they attributed the loss to this event even though it was quite obvious that such a poor showing for the year was inevitable long before the take-over occurred. Also in the report was an address by the President, Mr. Foster, who outlined the Board's severe concerns for the continued viability of the beet sector by stating:

The vintage steam locomotive used by the company in its railyard.

> *The Company is conscious of its responsibility to the beet sugar industry of Ontario ... but the farmers cannot expect Canada and Dominion shareholders to continue indefinitely to subsidize what is proving to be an uneconomic industry [for] over the past seven years ... the operations resulted in a loss to the company. Your directors have instituted conversations with Government authorities in an endeavour to find a solution to this problem ... but if raw sugar prices remain at their present levels at or below the floor price established in the International Sugar Agreement, the Company cannot expect to do more than break even on the 1960 beet operations.*

Throughout the following summer, every effort was made to curb costs by deferring expenditures on equipment and cutting the level of staffing, but the major drain on the company's resources continued to be the maintenance of two beet refineries in the face of crop estimates that did not amount to enough to supply even one plant at full production; it was decided to run only the Chatham plant once again. This led to a series of meetings between company representatives and the Ministry of Agriculture. Also in attendance were several local members of Parliament and members of the provincial Parliament who supported the company's position that the provincial and/or federal governments must take immediate action to avoid the collapse of the beet industry by the end of the year. Under this combined pressure, the Ontario government eventually agreed to investigate the needs of the industry but made no promises to implement any significant support measures in the immediate future.

By September the company's restraint measures seemed to be producing results as the half-yearly report indicated a small profit. However, unforeseen costs were also incurred during the period at both Montreal and Toronto, but for different reasons. At Montreal, the previously agreed contract with the union for a pay rise had to be re-opened when a higher settlement by St. Lawrence Sugar and its own branch of the same union caused the C and D union to demand parity or face a major strike. Unwilling to suffer disruption, the company subsequently agreed to a higher base rate for the next year and an interim payment to the workers to cover the remainder of the year.

At Toronto, although the labour situation remained stable, the fact that raw sugar supplies were being stockpiled for extended periods led to a high level of spoilage that was valued at over $50,000 with an expected further financial loss of $25,000 in the next few months.

The next month, the year's beet campaign was begun under good weather conditions, no shortage of labour, and no difficulties of delivery or storage. Despite these positive circumstances, however, the fact that only 14,000 acres were available for harvesting meant that the Chatham refinery ran for only sixty-six days, which left no one in any doubt that things were in a very bad way for the future of the beet sugar industry of southern Ontario.

Beginning in November 1960 and through until February of 1961, the Ontario Minister of Agriculture was reported to have held several meetings with his federal counterpart on the specific question of financial support for the beet industry, but little news and even less support actually emerged to encourage the company or the farmers for the contracting of the 1961 crop. This led the company to review its position, and the company offer that emerged was only $9.75 per ton.

Naturally the farmers complained bitterly and refused to sign up. This refusal finally provoked the personal intervention of the Minister of Finance, who pressured the company to raise its offered price and lose money in the short term in order to allow the government time to investigate the needs of the industry and work out a national sugar beet policy. To this ridiculous request, the company responded that the government had been requested for years by the sugar industry to establish a national policy. Furthermore, the company contended that it had lost money on its beet operations in most of the past ten years of contracting and the current offered price only reflected the conditions prevailing in the industry as a whole. Ignoring these facts, the government continued its pressure tactics with warnings of other unspecified retaliation if the company did not comply with the government's "request." In the end, the company succumbed and raised its offer by another 50 cents per ton to which the Ontario government agreed to contribute a special one-year-only payment of another 50 cents per ton.

Following these commitments, the federal authorities finally made their own contribution on March 2, 1961, by stating they would guarantee a similar one-year payment to bring the farmers' returns up to a minimum of $13 per ton and would implement a national sugar policy by the end of the year.

With this backing, the company was now able to settle a contract with the members of the Ontario Sugar Beet Growers Marketing Board on March 9, with the clear understanding that due to the Board of Directors' views that the additional funding provided by the company was in contradiction of prevailing market conditions, only 20,000 acres would be contracted out and only the Chatham plant would be operated for the year.

In April 1960, the U.S. government instituted a change in its foreign policy that was to have a major impact upon Canadian businesses, and especially the sugar industry, when it was declared that any country purchasing sugar from Cuba would be specifically excluded from shipping refined sugar into the United States under its already restrictive quota system. This created a mild panic for the Canadian refiners in general and C and D in particular as it had already accumulated large stocks of Cuban raw sugar and processed sugar derived from Cuban raw which had been shipped across the U.S. border under bond awaiting sale or delivery. Now due to these restrictions, virtually all the American customers refused to accept these deliveries and equally refused to pay for them. It left the company with little choice but to return the stock to Canada and attempt to dispose of it elsewhere. Neither was the company able to elicit support from the Canadian government to try to change the American judgement and re-open the lucrative export market. Therefore the Board immediately issued an order to curb raw sugar purchases generally until the excess refined stock was disposed of and specifically to cease buying Cuban raw sugar for the remainder of the year or for however long the current American attitude prevailed.

In retaliation, the Cubans reacted swiftly by ignoring the earlier agreements with the Canadian sugar industry over refined sugar shipments to Canada and despatched a cargo of 2,000 tons to Montreal. When it heard of this, the company immediately notified the customs authorities. Unfortunately, this warning was ignored and the ship was able to arrive, unload its cargo, and offer it for sale at bargain-basement prices around the city despite, and in direct contravention of, a court order forbidding the unloading of the vessel pending payment of an $80,000 bond.

In a lighthearted break from the almost continuous stream of bad news for the company, it is pleasant to note that three positive events occurred for the company in July 1961.

First was the establishment of a special division within the company for the transportation of the sugar under R.R. Porteous with depots at both the Montreal and Toronto sites.

Second was the setting up of a scholarship fund for children of employees attending university. The value of the fund was set at $1,000 per annum for each student up to a maximum of five years. Third was the publication of a new form of in-house magazine for distribution amongst the company employees called *Canada and Dominion Crystals*. Produced in both English and French versions, the newsletter carried articles not only about company business or reports on matters that affected company policies but also recent social events, sporting activities, and personal profiles on various employees. In the first edition alone, for example, there were announcements on the University Scholarship Fund, and the progress of the national sugar beet policy programme; reports on visits to the Chatham refinery by delegates of the U.S. Farmers and Manufacturers Beet Sugar Association and the arrival of the largest single cargo of raw sugar ever to be unloaded at the Port of Montreal; notes on retirements, promotions, transfers, the Toronto workers' club spring dance, and the results of company sports teams in such fields as bowling, soccer, ice hockey, golf, and softball. Published quarterly, the newsletter continued in this and later forms right up to the present day, revealing many glimpses of life within the company which otherwise would have been lost.

The following month, circumstances took a more serious turn when a strike developed in the shipping industry involving the longshoremen's union. As a result, raw sugar vessels were delayed in docking and unloading. Although the company initially attempted to use other union and non-union labour to get the job done, once picket lines were set up, the crane operators refused to cross the line and attempts were made by the strikers to interfere with the free passage of refinery staff and customers' trucks. This led to some rapid negotiations with the longshoremen's union and the pickets were withdrawn pending further talks. Fortunately, the strike was settled shortly thereafter, and operations returned to normal just in time to coincide with a new business opportunity contained in an approach by the Canada Starch Co. By this proposal, the Canada and Dominion Sugar Co. Ltd. was to prepare and ship blends of Canada Starch glucose syrups with the C and D liquid sugars for sale to various industrial manufacturers.

Almost immediately afterwards, the company received another offer for a similar deal with Canada Starch's main competitor, the St. Lawrence Starch Co. This left the company in something of a dilemma as it could not accept both bids. Following extensive discussions with both parties and a market analysis, an agreement was eventually signed between C and D and the St. Lawrence Starch Co. This deal was to bring in $100,000 of badly needed revenue in the first year of production alone.

In September the company was surprised to hear that another cargo of refined Cuban sugar had arrived at the Montreal docks, and once again the federal authorities were immediately notified. Fortunately the government moved more quickly on this occasion and although the cargo was eventually off-loaded for sale, the Minister of National Revenue placed a dumping duty on it, which made the Cuban refined no more attractive financially than the Canadian product. The time had now come when the Ontario beet crop was ready to be harvested. Thanks to good summer weather, the beet yield had been high, and with the extensive use of mechanical harvesters, the crop from 16,353 acres was gathered quickly and delivered to Chatham. Here a new mechanical loader with a specially designed seven-ton scoop was used to transfer the beets from the storage piles to the factory flumes, doing in a single journey what had previously taken several trips for a small fleet of trucks. The plant ran for eighty-eight days and yielded 62.5 million pounds of refined sugar. Finally at the end of the year, in fulfilment of its earlier promise to devise an official policy on sugar beet, the federal government announced on December 15 that a support programme would be implemented for 1962 in the form of a deficiency payment to beet growers if the average declared value of imported raw sugar during the crop year fell below a set rate. This was welcome news for both the farmers and the company, but it still did not address the long-term problem of the industry and left the company considering its policies for the future.

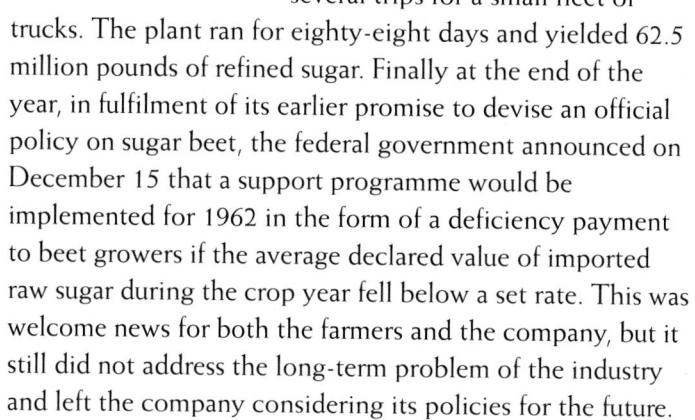

Early in 1962, several situations began to develop that would linger on and have extensive repercussions upon the company for some considerable time. One of these was the

A bulk liquid sugar tanker in 1962.

pressure being applied by U.S. refiners on their own government to restrict or even ban Canadian-made sugar from entering the United States on the publicly declared reason that it contained Cuban content. In reality it was because they recognized that the Canadian refiners were substantially more efficient in their production methods and could easily sell their sugar in the United States at lower prices due to the reduction of costs accrued though modern methods.

Another matter with serious implications was the ongoing investigation of the sugar industry by the Combines Department, which had now led to a charge being laid on Atlantic, St. Lawrence, and the Canada and Dominion Sugar Co. Ltd. of "arranging to lessen unduly competition with respect to refined sugar in various Provinces of Canada."

It was expected that if matters came to a head, the company would be prosecuted on the specific offence of having entered into an arrangement in 1954 with official representatives of the Cuban sugar industry for the purchase of Cuban raw sugar in return for the Cubans ending their flood of refined sugar into Canada (which, it should be remembered, was done mainly by W.J. McGregor in response to the failure of C.D. Howe to safeguard Canadian interests.)

According to the company's legal counsel, it was felt that a plea of guilty could be safely entered with the argument of mitigating circumstances as it was simply following the specific example set by the Canadian government in its trade arrangements with Cuba from 1951 - 1953. Further-more, payment of the maximum fine under the current legislation would be less expensive than fighting the

The new beet loader at the Chatham factory.

case and incurring all the subsequent legal costs. Suddenly circumstances changed as the government prosecutors recognized the gaping hole in their case, and the charges were altered to claim that between January 1, 1954, and January 1955 the combined group of Atlantic Sugar Refineries Ltd., St. Lawrence Sugar Refining Co. Ltd., and the Canada and Dominion Sugar Co. Ltd. had arranged to:

> *lessen unduly competition in the production, manufacture, purchase, barter, sale, transportation or supply of refined sugar throughout the Provinces of Ontario, Quebec, New Brunswick, Nova Scotia and Prince Edward Island.*

To C and D, these new charges smelled even more of government hypocrisy, as it was specific government legislation that had prevented *Redpath* selling in the Maritimes. Furthermore, it was interesting to note that the

Quebec Sugar Beet Refinery owned by the provincial government was specifically excluded from these charges, although during the period in question they had equally been part of all trading and selling of sugar. This led to some strong comments being made at the company's Board meetings about the obvious double standard being applied to private companies as opposed to government-owned facilities. Despite these facts, the legal advice still stood and the company agreed to plead guilty and simply take the bad medicine of the fine.

In February, a cargo of raw sugar that had been originally scheduled to arrive at Montreal the previous December finally arrived, not by the vessel chartered to deliver it but by railcar. This was due to the fact that the M.V. *Senator Hagelson* had been damaged by a severe storm during her trip to Canada and required towing into the port of Halifax. By the time repairs were made, the shipping season at Montreal was over and the only way to complete the delivery was to use railcars, which made this cargo particularly expensive to buy. Also at Montreal, construction was begun on an extension to the office wing to provide additional facilities for the staff, and an expansion was made to the transport division with the purchase of eight new trucks. At the Toronto refinery, despite the relatively new nature of the plant, it was realized that storage space was running out, so a new building was erected to house expanded storage space for bags and packaging supplies as well as an enlarged garage while the "old" garage was converted into a liquid sugar truck-loading facility.

In the beet division, despite the announcement of a support price by the government the previous December, many farmers had now given up entirely on beets as an economic crop, so only 17,198 acres were signed up for in 1962 despite intense efforts by company representatives to elicit more. Planting began in ideal weather but a subsequent period of dry weather reduced some acreage and necessitated re-planting.

One of the highlights for the season was the first international spring demonstration, held on June 6 at the company's experimental farm in Dover. Nearly 600 sugar beet growers from Michigan, Ohio, and Ontario, as well as representatives from the European beet industry, arrived to see demonstrations of the company's determination to push for increased mechanization of all aspects of beet farming as the answer to the problem of cutting costs and reviving the industry.

The problem still remained that it was now just too expensive to attempt to maintain two refineries when the acreage grown had required only one. This led to an announcement being made on July 9, 1962, that the Wallaceburg plant would be closed permanently. The new and entirely unused machinery installed just a few years earlier would be dismantled for transfer to Chatham and the majority of the lands of the Wallaceburg plant would be sold off.

This raised a storm of protest from local newspapers, but even those in the agricultural field admitted that there was little else that could be done in the prevailing circumstances, and the matter gradually died down.

Meanwhile, back in Montreal, the company was given an opportunity to make some much-needed revenue when the U.S. Sugar Act expired on June 3 and the amended replacement Act was not signed into law until July 13. During the interim, all restrictive quotas were automatically

An aerial view of the Wallaceburg plant in 1962 shortly before its permanent closure.

suspended, and C and D took the initiative by immediately shipping 40,000 bags of refined sugar into the United States, where it was then stored in bond until the details of the new Act were clarified. In reaction, the U.S. refiners made unsuccessful attempts to blockade the railway lines and pressure the railway companies to refuse C and D access to shipping facilities. Eventually, following clarification of the new Sugar Act, the sugar was released for sale and was disposed of, yielding a small but much-needed profit for the company.

Late in the summer, the world political situation once again turned ugly as tensions increased in Europe due to the deaths of several East Germans trying to escape across the Berlin Wall in August. This was then followed in September by an announcement from the Soviet Union that it would be arming and training Cuban military forces. In quick succession, prices for goods began to rise and sugar was no exception. But with the peak of the crisis in the week of October 21, which has become known as the Cuban Missile Crisis, prices soared and there was an immediate run on food commodities as a possible nuclear war was feared. Even the usually prominent story of the year's sugar beet crop was pushed off the front page of the Chatham press as the world held its breath. Fortunately, the situation was resolved and tensions eased, leading to a corresponding fall in the price of most commodities, except sugar, which now maintained its high levels as the volume of Cuban sugar normally sold on the world open market was severely reduced due to its diversion to the Soviet Union as payment for the proffered military aid.

As to the beet crop itself, the weather co-operated and almost 90% of the crop was mechanically harvested. However, losses in acreage from the original contracted area were more than 26%, leaving only 12,653 acres, an amount generally considered to be insufficient to yield any profit unless the prices for raw sugar continued to stay high or even increase.

By December, the Board was pleased to find that sales were generally increasing, especially in the export field, with sales being recorded for refined sugar to Antigua, Barbados, Bermuda, Bahamas, St. Lucia, St. Kitts, St. Vincent, the Dominican Republic, Aruba, St. Pierre Miquelon, and the United States. On a negative note, however, the judge from the combines case deferred judgement on the grounds that he did not have sufficient data to decide what penalties should be applied. This left the corporate executives wondering what new twist was to come from the Crown, as the penalties normally applied in cases of this kind were clearly established.

Harvesting beets in 1962.

In January 1963, at a time when most prices were falling, sugar began to steadily rise in value so that even the small beet harvest of the previous year could be sold at a sizable profit for both the company and its farmers, who now received additional payments for their efforts. This encouraged farmers for the new contract year and just under 20,000 acres was contracted and planted in good springtime conditions.

Within the rest of the company, a new co-operative agreement was signed between St. Lawrence Starch and Canada and Dominion whereby glucose produced by St. Lawrence Starch would be delivered to the Montreal C and D refinery for blending and subsequent delivery by C and D to Quebec customers of both companies. In the Ontario market, the process was inverted by having C and D liquid sucrose delivered to the Port Credit facility of St. Lawrence Starch for blending and distribution by St. Lawrence Starch.

Competitive factors also made their mark at this time as C and D sought to match new packaging lines produced by Atlantic with the introduction of I.S.E.s in 5 pound packages instead of the earlier bulk volumes and the wrapping of 1 pound icing sugar boxes in twenty-five-unit parcels instead of the bulkier fifty-unit bundles.

In March, a new programme of plant alterations was considered. Chatham was still in the process of receiving machinery removed from Wallaceburg and would continue to do so for some considerable time; in addition, the plant was approved for installation of a liquid sugar system and a transportation division similar to those already in operation at Montreal and Toronto.

Toronto itself was not scheduled for any additional production machinery but its transport division received several new tractors and trailers. It was, however, at Montreal that the main investment of capital was made with the inclusion of:

- a new computer control system,
- palletizing equipment,
- new conveyor systems for raw and refined sugar,
- two new conditioning silos for sugar,
- additional packaging equipment,
- a totally new automatic refined sugar warehouse on the south side of St. Patrick Street,
- a complete self-contained water coolant system in order to eliminate the reliance of the refinery upon water drawn from the Lachine Canal.

These improvements were estimated to cost in excess of $5.5 million and would increase the output of the plant by nearly 20%.

Outside the bounds of the physical requirements at the company facilities, the Board also realized that a closer co-operation between Canada and Dominion and Tate & Lyle in staff training and informational exchanges would benefit both companies. Therefore in the first of what was to become a series of corporate exchanges, the Export Sales Manager at Montreal, Neil Shaw, was seconded to Tate & Lyle in London while in return Michael Kitchin joined C and D.

At the end of the month, the Combines case came to the fore as the sentence on the sugar industry was handed down. An additional and unwelcome surprise came on the day of the hearing when the prosecuting counsel submitted an addendum to their earlier specification of penalties. This took the form of an Order of Prohibition, which outlined specific business and trading practices that would be considered illegal from that point onwards. This meant that if at any future date a case were brought against the sugar refiners of Canada, the company in question if found guilty would be deemed not only to have broken the law but to have been in contempt of court. The judge immediately accepted the additional penalty and applied it on top of the set fine of $25,000 on each sugar company. It must also be noted that at no time was the defending counsel either allowed to see the Order of Prohibition prior to its submission or allowed to appeal its implementation. Realizing they had made a bad judgemental error in pleading guilty in the vain hope of simply paying a fine and getting back to business, the cited sugar companies decided to appeal the sentence as a whole and additionally to unite in their determination that if they were put into the same position in the future, it would be a no-holds-barred fight to ensure that their defence was argued as strongly as possible. Pleased with its easy victory, the government now changed the rules on fines by first raising the limit and then abolishing it altogether, following which they immediately began to start investigations once again on the activities of the privately owned sugar companies while ignoring the provincially owned Quebec Sugar Refinery.

Also at this time the price of raw sugar on the world market had risen to such an extent that it now caused the list price for refined sugar to escalate to a new high of $17.65 per 100 pounds compared to the $7 per 100 pounds of only one year earlier.

Packaging Dominion brand sugar.

Newspaper and media editorials made strong condemnations of the "corporate bums" who were supposedly siphoning off money and making obscene profits from the "suffering" of the Canadian consumers without once acknowledging that the sugar refiners were totally at the mercy of the world market fluctuations. Fortunately, at more official levels, namely in the government and the courts, it was recognized that there was no blame to be attached to the Canadian sugar refiners and the Minister of Justice, Lionel Chevrier, went so far as to state:

> *Price advances have not been out of line with the increased costs for the basic and essential raw materials, ... and in fact Canadian refinery prices have gone up less than the price for raw sugar.*

Fortunately by June, the prices began to fall and continued to do so until mid-August. During this time the company was busy with its plans for the Montreal refinery modernization. Unfortunately, quotations on the expected cost of these alterations were rising steeply and led to a reconsideration of some elements in order to reduce the overall cost. Likewise in Chatham, the plans for the new transportation unit were put on hold, not because of costs but because the local union was blocking its implementation unless the company paid higher rates for its drivers.

In August, sugar prices began to rise once again and continued to do so throughout September and October until they exceeded the levels reached in May and eventually peaked on November 21, 1963, at $18.65 per 100 pounds. Normally this fact would have been the cause of more media outcry, but the following day, news of the tragic events at Dallas dominated the thoughts of everyone and relegated all other news to relative obscurity.

Within the company, this high price for sugar held some unwelcome consequences that had an impact on the entire processing sequence. First, at the raw sugar level, the purchase of replacement stocks would now entail a larger outlay of funds. Secondly, the current policy of maintaining a large supply of raw sugar on hand meant holding a substantially higher monetary value of stock, without it providing any financial return to the company. Third, during the stages of refining, any accidental loss or wastage of sugar would represent a larger financial sum to be deducted from potential revenues. Finally, higher sugar prices would inevitably cause customers to cut back on orders and either use less sugar or find cheaper substitutes. The only people who really benefited from this unexpected high price were the beet farmers who had contracted to produce beet in 1963. Their harvest began in October and totalled 16,811 acres, but processing at the Chatham factory was delayed for a couple of days when a fire broke out on the roof of the main process building. Fortunately, quick action by the employees and the city's fire department prevented the fire spreading beyond the roof and repairs were undertaken during the "campaign" period, which lasted from October 10, 1963, to January 2, 1964, and yielded 71.6 million pounds of sugar. This harvest was subsequently sold at a good price, resulting in good returns to both the company and farmers.

Two additional consequences of this series of price fluctuations was, first, the increased attentions of the Combines Department, who made a number of unannounced visits to the offices of the various sugar companies to obtain up-to-date information; and second, at the Department of Trade and Commerce where it was decided the interests of the consumer would be served if extended or long-term contracts were developed between producing countries and the Canadian refiners. In support of this new policy, the Assistant Deputy Minister of Trade and Commerce, D. Harvey, notified a delegation of representatives of the Commonwealth Sugar Producers Group that the Canadian government would welcome longer term contracts but did not wish to interfere with normal business activities. He therefore directed the representatives to negotiate directly with the refiners. Following these directions, the refiners and producers came to a mutually acceptable agreement which guaranteed the Commonwealth signatory countries 75% of the Canadian raw sugar supplies with a stipulated floor and ceiling price for the next twelve months. When this was placed before Mr. Harvey for ratification, he approved it, but Mr. Henry of the Combines Investigation Branch vetoed the deal as being illegal under the terms of the Order of Prohibition. This now led to an interdepartmental conflict between the Trade Department and the Combines officials as each department pressed to gain the solution it wanted leaving the producers and refiners caught in the middle. Eventually it was decided by the government that in the interests of the consumer, the refiners should buy their immediate requirements of raw sugar at the higher world prices and sell it as refined at a loss, with the old familiar promise of protection in the future when world prices fell.

Not believing for a moment that by some miracle the government had changed its nature, the company countered with the statement that if these government promises were meant to apply to all of Canada's requirements for sugar, then provision must be made in writing indicating that the companies were acting upon government instructions and would not be subject to any action by the Combines Department. Furthermore, restrictions needed to be applied to refined sugar imports to prevent outside interests not signatory to the agreement importing refined sugar once prices fell and undercutting the refiners. To these requests the government adamantly refused and the meeting broke up without an agreement.

Subsequently, Mr. Harvey advised the refiners to proceed with their future purchases for 1964 as the government was no longer going to press the issue, but within a week a memorandum was received by C and D stating that the government wanted an increase in Canadian sugar beet production and longer term raw cane sugar contracts. These contradictory statements led the company to notify the government that although increased beet production was highly desirable to the company it would require long-term government incentives and support to change the prevailing attitudes of the beet farmers. Furthermore, while an increase in long-term cane contracts might result in short-term lower prices, in the longer term, once world supplies caught up with demand and the rest of the world got lower prices, Canada would be trapped into paying more due to its long-term contract obligations. After considering these facts, another memorandum was received from the authorities indicating that it was no longer governmental policy to call for long-term contracts and there the matter was dropped, for the time being.

As predicted by the company, once the new cane season came into effect and supplies began to increase, raw sugar prices and consequently refined prices began to drop. However, this period of extreme price increases had some long-term effects as many third-world countries decided to begin or expand their own sugar growing capabilities. In Canada, one individual, Robin Austin, decided to enter the sugar refining business in order to make what he assumed would be a quick profit, by starting his own refinery using second-hand machinery put together in a building leased from the Canada Car Company in Lachine, Quebec. To the other sugar companies, the prospect of making a success from this kind of hodge-podge of a business was remote at best, especially when the provincially funded Quebec Sugar Refinery was unable to prevent itself suffering continual losses and the other sugar companies were in tight financial straits. What they did not anticipate was the amount of trouble and deliberate aggravation this new sugar maker would cause in the years ahead.

For the Times They Are a-Changing

An aerial view of the Montreal refinery in 1963.

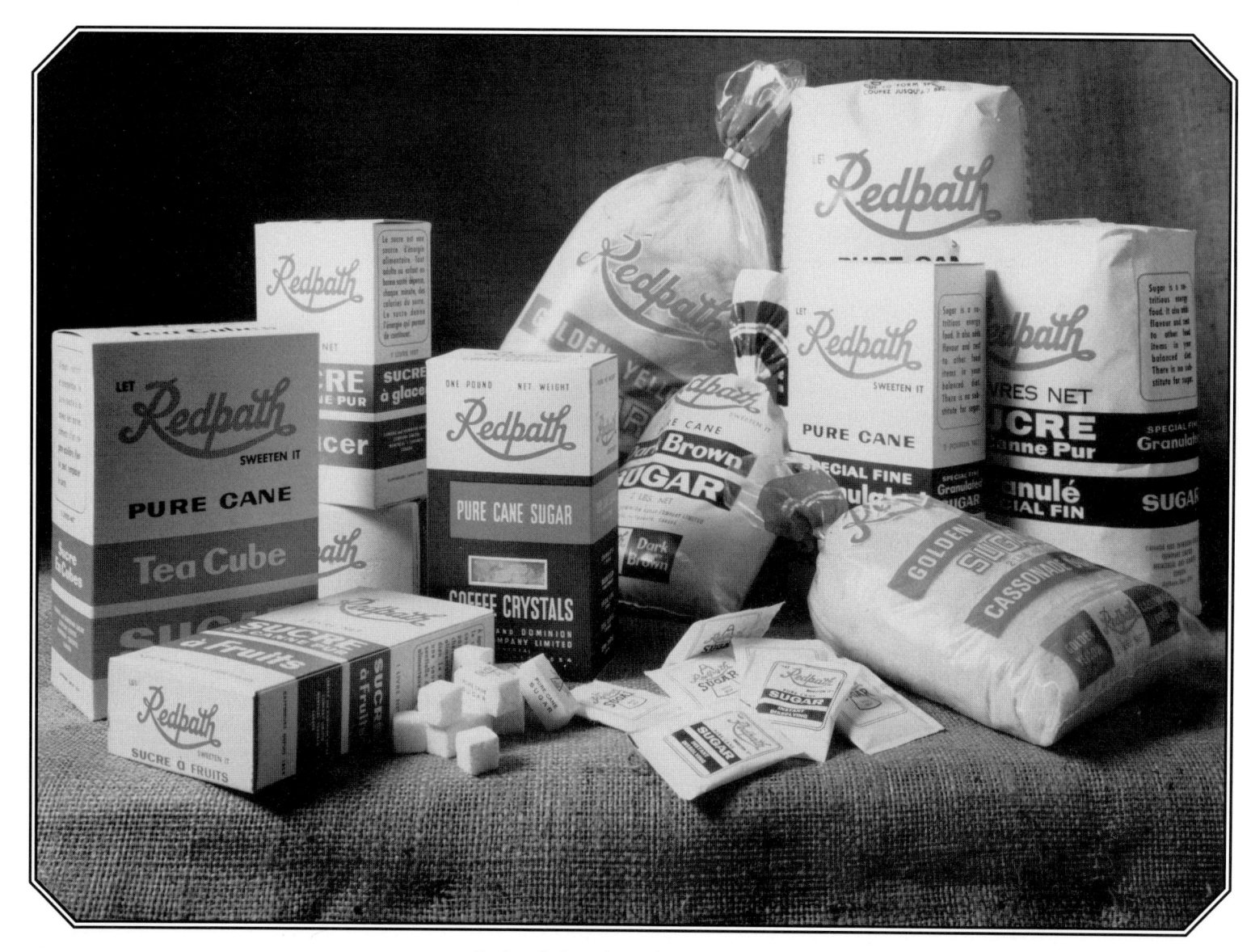

Redpath brand products in 1965.

CHAPTER TEN

Hard Times, and Even Harder Choices

When the company began its contracting for the new beet season in January 1964, it was – not surprisingly – inundated with requests from its long-standing growers who wished to increase their acreage and from new farmers who wanted to begin planting for the company. As there was an upper limit for the capacity of the Chatham plant, first choice was given to the existing growers and the full quota for the year was achieved without difficulty. The company also recognized that a new plan for the Chatham plant had to be implemented, with priority being given to the environmental improvement of the water that was used in the processing of the beets and then dumped into a large settling pond adjacent to the factory.

At Montreal there was notification that the current raw sugar dock might be expropriated for use by the forthcoming Expo 67, which led to an immediate search for alternative sites in case the location was lost. In the refinery itself, a successful programme of sales resulted in large export orders to West Germany and Tunisia on top of the previous staples to Bermuda, Nassau, and the West Indies.

Also at this time, the two new sugar conditioning silos were put into operation, giving the Montreal refinery the distinction of being the first sugar refinery in the world to condition all of its output. Unfortunately, the use of the silos had to be curtailed when small particles of paint were discovered in the sugar during regular quality control tests. Enquiries revealed that the problem was caused by newly developed epoxy resin paint that did not adhere properly to the concrete sides of the structure and the decision was made to revert to the older, but more reliable, method of lining the silos with wood. By the early summer, although the general price of sugar had fallen substantially from the previous year's high point, sales

Installation of the framework for the new conveyor bridge at the Montreal refinery, April, 1964.

in eastern Canada did not improve due to the introduction of large volumes of sugar from Robin Austin's new Cartier Sugar refinery. These were offered to customers at extravagant discounts, thus undercutting all of the other refiners and forcing a price war across the province of Quebec for the maintenance of market shares.

Subsequent testing of the new Cartier product by the C and D laboratories revealed, as suspected, that the overall colour and quality of the sugar being produced was below the standards set by the other sugar companies, but the prices being offered still drew away some C and D customers.

Another point that emerged about the Cartier plant was that it continually suffered mechanical breakdowns, reportedly caused by pieces of cord that blocked the filters it used. Similar cords were also found in the raw sugar delivered to C and D but they did not have the same impact on production due to the better quality of filters being used. Subsequent enquiries revealed that the pieces of cord in the raw sugar were the result of the loading methods employed in several Caribbean countries. There the local governments had blocked the development of deep-water, bulk-loading port facilities in the hopes of maintaining employment for their unskilled labour force. As a consequence, the larger cargo vessels had to anchor off-shore and be loaded from barges filled with sacks of raw sugar. Once on board the ocean vessel, the labourers had to cut the cords on the neck of each sack and dump the contents into the open hold. This, of course, resulted in hundreds of pieces of cord being found inside the sugar. For sugar refiners such as C and D, these pieces of extraneous material were no different from the other pieces of unwanted solid matter regularly removed from raw sugar cargoes. However, when these items began to interfere with the production at Cartier Sugar, instead of improving the filtration methods, Mr. Austin sent a stream of telegrams to the Canadian government accusing the other sugar companies of deliberate sabotage. Unfortunately, there were those in the corridors of power who were all too ready to believe these wild accusations and to use them against the sugar companies in the future.

At the end of the summer, the company prepared its Chatham refinery for the new season with hopes that all the additional equipment brought from Wallaceburg and the regular improvements made to the delivery systems would reduce both the level of beet spoilage and the costs of production and allow a good financial return for all concerned. Harvesting began on October 5 with the factory starting the following day. The crop for the year totalled in excess of 18,700 acres and the plant ran for 105 days, resulting in the production of more than 76.6 million pounds of sugar, which as hoped did lead to a profit being made for the year.

Unfortunately, the news from Montreal was not so good as the conversion of the warehouse to an automatic system would now be delayed until May or June 1965 due to the overly optimistic schedule of production for the computer by Canadian General Electric. Therefore it was decided to run the system manually until the computer was ready and installed.

Another problem that developed shortly afterwards concerned the conditioning silos, where the replacement wood linings had collapsed under the weight of sugar. The problem was again traced to the epoxy resin paint, which prevented the proper adhesion of the wood lining. The

Hard Times, and Even Harder Choices

An aerial view of the Montreal refinery in 1965.

costs of repair were estimated to be more than $25,000 and discussions were held with the contracting company to determine the levels of responsibility and compensation involved.

By the end of 1964, the price of sugar had fallen back to its earlier "normal" levels. Even so, the period of high prices had forced some food manufacturers to switch their use of sweeteners away from sugar to other products, especially the artificial chemical sweeteners of saccharine and cyclamates. This had further been aggravated by the huge advertising campaign mounted by the artificial sweetener companies to undermine the confidence of consumers in regular sugar. Stung to respond to this challenge, the sugar industry as a whole instituted a campaign of its own with the stated aim of "spreading knowledge of the facts about the role of sugar as a source of food energy in a properly balanced diet." Thus began a war of words that continues between these two competitors right up to the present day.

In concluding the year, it should be noted that a restructuring of the Corporate Board took place on December 16. The President, G.B. Foster, now became Chairman of the Board and the current Managing Director, J.O. Whitmee, became the new President. The following day both gentlemen represented the company as they participated in the official ceremonies to present McGill University with a set of stained glass windows decorated to represent the crests of the senior universities in Canada, the United Kingdom, and Eire. The ceremony took place within the old Redpath Hall originally presented to the university by Peter Redpath in 1892 and was held in commemoration of the 110th anniversary of the founding of the original Canada Sugar Refinery and the long-standing connection between the Redpath company and McGill. Early in 1965, the Board met to discuss the current state of the sugar industry in eastern Canada. With the continued aggressive marketing and discounting campaign being mounted by Cartier Sugar, the sales of the other sugar companies were dropping rapidly. This had led to discussions between Canada and Dominion, Atlantic, and St. Lawrence on the prospects for a merger between two or even all three. Unfortunately, when Mr. Henry of the Combines Department was approached for his opinion on the matter, he stated categorically that any such acquisition or merger would be viewed with hostility by the government and would lead to an immediate enquiry under the Combines Investigations Act. Furthermore, he warned C and D in particular that any acquisition of shares in other sugar companies by Tate & Lyle would initiate investigations with an aim of prosecution.

Obviously, since it was impossible to consider an internal re-structuring of the company or a streamlining of the sugar industry, the Board was forced to consider alternative ways to increase the overall corporate profitability by looking at diversification into non-sugar-related fields. This move was to have significant and long-term effects on the pattern of corporate development for the future.

Meanwhile on the beet sugar front, it was hoped that the profits made from the previous year's crop would indicate a change in fortune for this troubled industry. However, with the fall in value of sugar prices in early 1965, farmers again began to get "cold feet" and after several days of canvassing by company field representatives it was obvious that the full capacity acreage would not be achieved. In fact, in the

Hard Times, and Even Harder Choices

An aerial view of the Chatham plant in 1965.

coming month only 16,878 acres were eventually signed up despite the strenuous efforts of the field representatives and an earlier than normal announcement of the government stabilization plan, which increased the guaranteed price for beets to the farmers for 1965.

April proved to be a difficult month for the company as poor weather conditions in Ontario caused extensive damage to the budding beet crop; in Toronto, contract negotiations with the union broke down and a strike was called. Fortunately, the strike lasted for only four days before the contract was settled and work resumed. Montreal, too, suffered setbacks as the market situation was now so grave, due to the exorbitant discounts being given by Cartier, that a full three-shift production level was no longer justified. It was decided to switch the refinery to a temporary two-shift basis and lay off the extra staff usually required for the third shift.

The cycle of disruption continued later in the summer when the installation of a new tower-type beet diffusor was delayed by the simultaneous action of a strike by millwrights across Ontario and a more local grievance by the electricians' union for the construction company hired to do the installation of the diffusor. The union picketed the plant in order to press their demands for Canada and Dominion to employ only contractors' union electricians in the installation of the machinery instead of C and D plant electricians. Not wishing to concede these demands, the company filed for an injunction with the courts while it continued negotiations that eventually led to a settlement whereby both sets of electricians would work on the project but in separate areas.

In September, which seems to have been a small period

Installation of the tower-type beet diffusor.

of respite from the ongoing litany of problems for the company, a request was received from Tate & Lyle for Canada and Dominion to undertake an experiment in production automation at its Toronto refinery in an attempt to significantly improve production efficiencies. As additional staff and office space would be required, questions were raised about the capacity of the Toronto office to accommodate the new Tate & Lyle personnel who would be supervising the experiment. Also joining C and D at this time from Tate & Lyle was a new Director, Saxon Tate, who was appointed to fill the unexpired term of a retiring Director, H.F. Smith, Jr.

The cycle of bad news returned in October, beginning with the year's beet crop which was gathered under extremely wet and muddy conditions; fewer than 11,000 acres were recorded as harvested, yielding only 196,000 tons of beets. These figures, it was argued, showed that the time had come for a major decision by the company on whether to close down its beet operations entirely. After much discussion it was decided that a new cyclical plan would be presented to the farmers in the hopes that it would provide encouragement and leadership for beet farmers in the future.

Next on the list of bad news was the continued delay in the completion of the Montreal automatic warehouse, which was now proposed for implementation early in 1966.

Finally for the month, the recent unilateral declaration of independence from Great Britain issued by the Rhodesian white minority government had led to an international boycott of sales or purchases involving Rhodesia. This decision affected the company, as it had three cargoes contracted for delivery, which were now effectively banned. Fortunately, some immediate behind-the-scenes negotiations between the government and the company permitted the single cargo already at sea when the ban was imposed to be allowed into Canada. At the end of the year, the Annual Report revealed that the net profit for the corporation was $3,420,449 compared to the previous year's $3,433,636, a surprising result in view of all the negative events during the year.

After the Annual General Meeting, the Board met to discuss the future plans for the company. It was decided that a Managing Director was required and the position was given to Saxon Tate.

One of Mr. Tate's first tests of office began with a series of meetings between the company and the Ontario Beet Growers Association. This meeting led to a co-operative arrangement that would see Canada and Dominion develop a series of yearly plans for a progressive five-year span that would cover investments, crop requirements, and production. In return, the beet growers were to grow sufficient beets to allow the refinery to run at capacity. Almost immediately, this programme ran into difficulties as many farmers refused to grow sugar beets without knowing the extent of the government stabilization plan. The company was left with only 13,000 acres confirmed for 1965 and had to face the stark alternatives of either abandoning the season or coming up with more beets. After discussions between the

Saxon Tate

company's Agricultural Superintendent, B.E. Easton, and Mr. Tate, it was decided to use the company experimental farms as well as rented land to grow full-scale crops of beet, using company fieldmen and plant workers to tend the fields. They would then include this added volume to the main harvest for processing. This emergency solution added another 1,600 acres to the projected year's crop and allowed the Board to agree to keep Chatham open for another year. However, the subsequent comments made by one member of the Ontario Sugar Beet Marketing Board to the effect that "I never expected them [C and D] to reach their goal" did not lend encouragement for the future.

Next, Mr. Tate began to investigate prospects for corporate diversification; the areas he looked at included grain elevator companies, copper and brass foundries, an ice-cream carton packaging company, and various agricultural projects in southwestern Ontario. Although initial advances to specific companies were not overly successful, the idea was deemed strong enough to justify the hiring of an outside company to compile a list of prospective acquisitions that would benefit the company. Mr. Tate and the Board also decided to re-examine the prospects for a merger between the sugar companies of Canada, with special emphasis on the acquisition of the troublesome and now financially troubled Cartier Sugar, which was estimated to have lost nearly half a million dollars in its first year of production. Surprisingly, after some investigation, the Combines officials recognized that the current surplus of capacity in the Montreal refinery would be eliminated with the acquisition of the sales volume from Cartier and made no strong objections to the new merger proposal.

With this tentative approval to continue, Canada and Dominion approached the new major shareholder of Cartier Sugar, Steinberg's Ltd., for negotiations on an eventual purchase. During subsequent talks, it was made clear that Steinberg's was not interested in selling its refinery unless it received in return a full partnership with Canada and Dominion for the company's Montreal facility. Obviously such a development was out of the question and so negotiations were concluded without an agreement.

This left the company needing to review its marketing strategies to acquire more sales, and it was decided that the best way to achieve these goals would be to re-organize the sales department into two distinct divisions under the general supervision of E.J. Faust. The new Western Division was to concentrate on the Ontario market under John Morrison while the Eastern or Quebec Division would be supervised by Neil Shaw, who had recently returned from the United Kingdom.

In early May 1966, Canada and Dominion signed an agreement with St. Lawrence Sugar and Atlantic Sugar to participate at the Quebec pavilion of Expo 67 under the joint banner of the newly formed Canadian Sugar Institute. Separately the company was also negotiating for participation in the agricultural pavilion, "Man the Provider," by sponsoring a guidebook and providing copies of a new movie made by the company entitled "Crystal from the Sun."

Through the early part of the summer, the main attention of the Board was centred on several submissions made by the diversification consultants. Some prospective areas of new business included biscuit, confectionery, and candy production; wine making; house renovation products;

and synthetic resins. Each was examined by the Board with a general agreement that a definite decision would be made by the end of the year on the direction the company would take.

Also during this period, trade talks between the Canadian and West Indies government delegations led to a tacit agreement for the granting of preferential treatment to West Indies sugar in return for similar treatment for Canadian finished goods.

When this matter was put before the Canadian refiners, it was argued that it was not possible to grant one country such a specific benefit without equally regulating the quotas currently applied to other nations and the production of beets domestically. The industry also felt that

Installation of the computer system at the Montreal refinery.

such an arrangement could not work without specific legislation to define the new levels of "control" being imposed upon it. In response, the Trade Minister stated that although he did not wish to implement legislation, he still expected the refiners to support the government by favouring contracts with the West Indies. This led the refiners to point out that the Minister was, in effect, telling the sugar companies to purchase their sugar by methods that would be in direct contradiction of the court Order of Prohibition and could lead to prosecution against the companies involved. After some thought, the Minister replied that he had expected there would be some "technical" hurdles, but that he expected the refiners to comply with his wishes and avoid the "inconveniences" of the court order without contravening it in any way.

To the refiners, it was obvious that the Minister and his staff either did not understand or care about the magnitude of the problem they had just dumped onto the refiners. Even if a legal way of implementing the Minister's directive could be found, it would not be in the financial interests of the industry to purchase the more expensive raw sugar from the West Indies when other cheaper sources were readily available. Determined not to be made the scapegoats, the refiners took the whole question before the Combines Division and received an immediate confirmation that any joint purchase or preference agreement scheme would be regarded as illegal and would bring forth charges under the Order of Prohibition.

The sugar refiners were now certain that their best course of action was to do nothing and let the two government departments fight it out.

By September, the anticipated inter-departmental fight was well underway. The Minister of Trade and Commerce stated that he considered the proposal between the two countries to be a definite commitment; as such, he had instructed his staff to prepare by September 26 a schedule of how the plan would be applied. On the other side, the Combines Department held the matter to be illegal if it forced the refiners into a joint purchasing position, backed by the additional fact that the representatives of G.A.T.T. and other Commonwealth sugar-producing companies were now protesting the favouritism being granted to the West Indies.

After the September 26 deadline had passed without the appearance of new regulations, the sugar industry began to relax. However, shortly thereafter a telephone call was received by the company from the Director of the Agriculture Branch of the Department of Trade and Commerce "requesting" that the company refrain from ordering any raw sugar for 1967 until the question of the international pact had been clarified. Stunned by this call, the company immediately rejected any such policy for it knew that the other Canadian refiners had almost completed their 1967 quotas and contracts without any inclusion of West Indies cargoes. No immediate response to this refusal was forthcoming from the government, but it is interesting to note that shortly afterwards, the annual announcement by the Federal Stabilization Board on the year's payments to beet growers specifically excluded the acreage planted and tended by the company in direct contravention of the recommendation made by the Beet Growers Marketing Board earlier in the season.

The company immediately appealed this exclusion, and eventually some 400 acres of the original 1,600 were

Hard Times, and Even Harder Choices

admitted for payment. But the concept of self-grown beet on a large scale for 1967 had been effectively killed as far as the company was concerned and it determined that unless circumstances changed considerably for the better after the current harvest was gathered, little hope remained for the continuation of beet growing in Ontario.

The harvest of 1966 began in early October with excellent prospects and good weather but on November 1, a freak early snowstorm followed by two weeks of continual rain made the balance of the harvest increasingly difficult. Nearly 150 acres were abandoned to the sea of mud, leaving the total acreage for the year at under 12,000 acres. The refinery processed beets for sixty-three days and yielded 60 million pounds of sugar, a volume far below the stated level required to run the plant at a break-even level.

On a more pleasant note for this late-year period, the Toronto and Montreal plants were running well and brought out two specialized product lines for consumer use. First was a special series of I.S.E.s depicting pavilions in the upcoming Expo 67. These were eagerly collected by many people in commemoration of the show and have since become collectors items. Additionally, a new container was developed for the fruit powdered grade of sugar, using a heavy-duty cardboard tube sealed by plastic ends. This subsequently won a number of packaging awards for the company.

At the end of the year, the corporate annual statement showed that net profits were down once again. It also included a comment that the ongoing situation of a pact between Canada and the West Indies was in "some difficulties."

SUCRE

Redpath

SUGAR

CANADA AND DOMINION SUGAR CO. LTD.
MONTREAL · TORONTO

161

In fact, matters had reached such an impasse between the various ministries and the outside pressures from other countries that the Department of Trade and Commerce finally conceded the failure of its "deal" and made alternative arrangements for a system of direct payments based on the tonnages of raw sugar exported to Canada from the West Indies. The Minister was still determined not to "lose face," however, and declared that he would carry through on his commitment to the Commonwealth Caribbean countries in a meeting with the refiners, held in January 1967.

At that time, the Minister informed the refiners' representatives that they would be "obliged" to purchase 275,000 tons of raw sugar from government-designated sources at undiscounted rates. When the refiners protested at this draconian attitude and again raised the conflict such a policy would bring with the Order of Prohibition, the Minister replied that if the refiners were unwilling to co-operate then legislation could be introduced to force their compliance. He did not indicate how the industry was to solve the problem imposed upon it.

Things were not much better for the company in its beet operations, where the farmers had reacted angrily to the announcement by the company that due to market conditions the year's contract price would be marginally below that of the previous year. This was then compounded by the government's notice that the stabilization payments would also be cut for 1967. In response many farmers decided that the beet industry was all but dead and refused to grow any beets when asked to do so. This resulted in a series of emergency meetings between the company and representatives of the Ontario Beet Growers Association. At these sessions the company warned that unless 20,000 acres of beets were contracted by March 31, the Chatham refinery would not be operated that year. The growers' representatives countered with the claim that the company announcement two years previously of a five-year plan was, in effect, a guarantee that the plant would be run for the full five-year term regardless of growing conditions or acreage. This interpretation was vehemently denied by the company, who reiterated its stand by stating that the scheme was merely a plan of action developed for a five-year period but with annual re-evaluations as circumstances dictated. Furthermore it would make no sense for the company to guarantee production without regard to the volume of raw material. In the end, no agreement was reached on prices, but it was recognized that immediate action needed to be taken to secure the backing of the government once more. As a result, the growers' representatives approached the government with a series of demands that included that the stabilization payment for 1967 be increased to $15.50 per ton. That interim stabilization payments be made to secure additional acreage, and that Canada and Dominion be made eligible for inclusion in the payments scheme for any acreage grown by the company to supplement the total.

In response to these calls, company Vice-President Mel Davidson was summoned to Ottawa to meet with Agriculture Minister J.J. Greene, External Affairs Minister Paul Martin, and Mr. Williams of the Stabilization Board.

Mr. Davidson was informed that the claims by the farmers were too high to be acceptable and no change would be made in the government position. Furthermore, it was revealed that the Stabilization Board had taken a survey of beet growers that showed that sufficient beets to run the Chatham factory at capacity could never be grown regardless of future government support; it was not the intention of the authorities to maintain industries which could not be economically justified in their own right. After some discussion, the government then proposed that if the company agreed to run the Chatham plant, it would stabilize the financial returns from the company's beet division for the year's efforts. The company reluctantly agreed, upon the express condition that the government's details for the stabilization be drafted and announced by the following week and that the farmers contracted a minimum of 20,000 acres by March 31, 1967.

By the stipulated deadline no announcement had been made by the government, and the beet growers were trying to get the company to guarantee production at Chatham with only 15,000 acres under contract. When the company stated that it was not prepared to lower its demand for 20,000 acres, it led to a rumour that the company had decided to close Chatham. The next day Mr. Davidson received a telephone call from Mr. Martin, who "suggested" that the company reconsider its attitude in the light of "other advantages" the company enjoyed.

This message was repeated by Mr. Martin on February 21, in an interview with the company's Managing Director, Saxon Tate. Mr. Martin stipulated that the government was "reluctant to permit" the Chatham plant to be closed and if the company did not do as it was told it would be necessary for the government to re-examine "certain advantages currently enjoyed by the company." As if to force home this point, that afternoon Mr. Williams of the Stabilization Board telephoned the company to notify it that the year's payment for 1967 had been reset to $15 per ton, that there would be an interim payment to beet growers as requested, but that C and D would not be considered as an equal recipient if it grew beets of its own.

Having received the government's decision on stabilization, the farmers had to live up to their part of the bargain and contract at least 20,000 acres by March 31. Some farmers were still not willing to believe that the company would follow through with its oft-repeated warning about closing the Chatham plant, and by March 10, only 11,000 acres had been signed. This led to the most intensive day-and-night contracting effort ever seen in the beet industry, dedicated to the single aim of persuading enough farmers to change their minds and grow sugar beet. Personal farm-to-farm visits by field representatives were backed by promotional advertisements in magazines, newspapers, radio, and television. As a result, the desperately needed acres were added, one contract at a time, causing many sleepless nights for company representatives. Finally, only twenty-fours hours before the deadline, the sum of 20,882 acres were on paper as contracted for the year. At the Board level, much discussion now took place as the stipulated minimum had been reached; but, as experience showed, there was bound to be some loss of acreage during the year. The question was, how much could be tolerated before the financial losses became too much for the company to bear.

Within the rest of the company, despite the overwhelming predominance of attention given to the beet sector, business continued as normal until April. At that time the Minister of trade and Commerce, Robert Winters, let it be known to the company's president, J. O. Whitmee, that due to a new trade agreement between Canada and the West Indies, the whole of the Canadian preferential duty for sugar was committed to the Commonwealth Caribbean sugar-producing countries. This announcement was no surprise to Mr. Whitmee, considering the attitude of the government the year before. Fortunately, with sufficient low-priced sugar available from elsewhere, it would not be a problem, but it was equally recognized that it could have a serious impact on the company in the future.

At the end of the month, production was temporarily disrupted at the Montreal refinery when a strike was called by the union; it lasted till May 5 and resulted in a settlement that gave the Montreal employees wage rates substantially higher than their counterparts in Toronto. It was certain that when the time came for similar negotiations at Toronto, the union would call for parity. On a slightly lighter and happier note, many of the Montreal staff took either an official or unofficial day's holiday on April 27, when Prime Minister Lester B. Pearson officially opened the Expo 67 fair located only a mile or so from the refinery. Throughout the summer, groups of individuals from all the other company sites took the opportunity, with the co-operation of and hosted by the Montreal personnel, to visit this extravaganza and enjoy the celebrations connected with Canada's one-hundredth birthday.

Back on the beet front, however, things were going from bad to worse as continual periods of rain throughout the seeding period reduced the planted acreage to 16.604 acres. This left the Board in something of a quandary, as more losses could be expected before the harvest was complete. It was suggested that the season be abandoned but the English directors felt that a commitment had been made and they were concerned about the company's image if the commitment was withdrawn for the year so despite the lower acreage, it was decided that the harvest would take place. It was also agreed that once the final figures were assessed, a decision would be made about the 1968 season.

In August, the Board met to discuss the final choices for the proposed diversification outside of sugar refining. The decision was to proceed with the acquisition of the Daymond Co. Ltd. This company had been formed in 1939 and manufactured aluminium extrusion products such as window and door frames, siding, soffit fixtures, kitchen and bathroom mouldings; another part of Daymond concentrated on plastic extrusion products for domestic and industrial-grade pipe fittings. This was to prove to be the first in a chain of new enterprises acquired over the following years and would change the face of the company entirely. October 1967 proved to be a time of major corporate development all round. The Montreal refinery, for example, brought onto line its new water-cooling towers. This released the plant from the unreliable water supply of the Lachine Canal for coolant, and plans were developed to continue

A view of the Montreal refinery following the installation of the new cooling towers.

production throughout the winter instead of shutting down once the canal was drained and the water supply was cut off.

At Toronto, improvements to the distribution department included the purchase of new tanker vehicles to cope with the growth in bulk sugar sales. Also, tests were done for the Carnation Company on the packaging of instant coffee creamer powder in I.S.E.s.

At Chatham, the beet harvest suffered yet another period of disastrous wet conditions with the result that 929 acres were lost, despite desperate attempts to recover them. The final yield was reduced to only 14,123 acres which were processed in eighty-four days for an output of 70 million pounds of sugar. Few people celebrated at the end of the campaign as normally would have happened; they were waiting to hear the verdict of the company for the 1968 season – that is if there was to be a 1968 season.

Beet harvesting alongside the Chatham refinery in 1967.

Hard Times, and Even Harder Choices

An aerial view of the Chatham refinery in 1967, shortly before its permanent closure.

A new bulk liquid sugar tanker railcar in 1969.

CHAPTER ELEVEN

A New Direction

Following the Annual General Meeting of the company in January 1968, the members of the Board met to decide the fate of its beet sugar operations. Figures on the harvest indicated that a small net gain would be made if sales continued on an upwards trend but before next year's campaign more than $1 million of new equipment would be needed to bring the Chatham plant up to a compatible level of efficiency compared to the Toronto plant. Furthermore, assuming that the harvests for the next five years yielded enough beets to run Chatham at its full capacity, the prospective earnings from beets would total only $2.5 million for the company. In comparison, a similar volume of production at Toronto, without any expenditures on machinery and in only three years, would generate $6.9 million.

Finally, and most telling, were the series of statistics revealing that since 1960 the only year in which the minimum required contract of 20,000 acres had been achieved was 1967, and that had been obtained only by extreme methods and efforts on the part of company representatives. In the same period, the crop losses between the contracted acreage on paper and the reality of acreage finally harvested had amounted to the following:

1960	22.6%
1961	13.8%
1962	26.2%
1963	12.0%
1964	6.8%
1965	34.5%
1966	22.2%
1967	33.0%

Based on the average loss rate for the above period, the company recognized that the required contract for 1968 would have to be set at a minimum of 24,888 acres in order to ensure 20,000 acres. Furthermore, informal surveys of the farmers growing beets indicated that even with another publicity blitz like last year, only around 11,000 acres would be contracted. In the end, the fact remained that trying to maintain the beet industry in southern Ontario was akin to "flogging a dead horse, it just wouldn't get up and run." The decision was therefore reluctantly made to close the Chatham refinery for beet production and to attempt to convert it to some alternative agricultural use. Current plant employees would be either transferred to the Toronto plant or given generous severance packages related to age and years of service. In addition, those farmers who had invested in automated beet machinery during the previous two years, in support of the company's five-year plan, would be eligible to sell the equipment back to the company at current market rates for second-hand equipment.

The public disclosure was made on January 29, 1968, and as expected released a torrent of criticism and condemnation at both the company and its executives. Newspaper articles in regional papers called for a public enquiry of this "abandonment" of the farmers in the region. The Sugar Beet Growers Marketing Board went one step further and claimed that the company had acted in "a complete breach of faith with the growers and the government" and in co-ordination with the Farmers Union established picket lines at the Chatham and Toronto refineries.

It was the politicians, however, who reacted most outspokenly to the closure. In the forefront was the Member of Parliament for South Essex, Eugene Whelan, who began his attacks against the company with a statement to the effect that the company should either be forced to stay open or be expropriated and run as a Crown corporation. He followed this up with a letter to Mr. Davidson in which he stated:

The unloading of the M. V. Sugar Crystal in May, 1968, following her maiden voyage to Montreal with 17,700 tons of raw sugar from Trinidad.

> *I think you have known my feelings and suspicions for a long time in this regard, that I do not think this company was sincere in its intentions ... I am still deeply disappointed ... and it has aroused my suspicions more than ever on what we [the government] can do to control foreign ownership of companies in Canada ... I have stated my opinion that if this company does not intend to operate at Chatham the Provincial Government should immediately expropriate it ... and if they do not act, the Federal Government should take whatever action they can. I would also ... establish a sugar policy that would make it nearly impossible for Tate & Lyle to ship raw sugar into Canada to be refined.*

Mr. Davidson drafted a reply on February 16, which stated in part:

> *I thought your comments in your letter ... were based upon assumptions not related to fact. There are no external forces involved in the decision which has been made solely*

by Canadian Management and the Canadian board on the basis of economics.

This led to a further letter from Mr. Whelan who replied:

I have not changed my opinion ... My sugar policy if I was in charge of this country would not allow this to happen, you can rest assured ...

It is interesting to speculate that Mr. Whelan might have been more cautious in his claims if he had known that only a few years later he would become Federal Minister of Agriculture and would try unsuccessfully to find any company or government agency willing to finance a new beet sugar industry in Ontario. Mr. Whelan also did not know that seven months prior to the company's announcement, three agricultural economists from the Guelph Agricultural College had been retained by the Federal Department of Forestry and Rural Development to make a confidential report on the prospects of the Ontario sugar beet industry. This report emphasized the uncertainty of the future for beet growing and its susceptibility to world price fluctuations in raw sugar. Its conclusions were that the industry was economically doomed to failure as a self-supporting entity and in the long run it would be cheaper for the government to pay the farmers a severance package of $60 per acre to ease transition to other crops.

Meanwhile, at the Chatham and Toronto refineries, the Farmers Union picketers (most of whom had never grown beets for the company) began to take violent action to back up their demands for the re-opening of the plant. Sporadic acts of vandalism against the cars of certain employees escalated to threats and intimidation of the employees themselves and culminated in violence against supervising police officers. This led to the arrest of several of the picketers at the Chatham plant.

During the next month, matters continued to fester as the company was repeatedly vilified in various editorials while calls reverberated around the Ontario Provincial Legislature for an immediate take-over of the corporate property and its re-opening under government supervision. Eventually on March 14, the Provincial Agriculture Minister the Hon. William Stewart ruled out the possibility of a government expropriation on the grounds that it would be a misuse of public funds and held no justification on economic grounds.

By June, much of the original outcry had died away as the federal government announced its intention to pay a one-time severance fee to farmers, while the company continued to buy back farmers' agricultural equipment that could not be converted to other agricultural uses. But at the end of the month, the situation flared up again when a group of beet growers decided to take legal action over the closure by issuing writs against Canada and Dominion, Tate & Lyle, and most surprisingly against the English members of the C and D Board for an alleged breach of contract, claiming a total of $7.2 million in damages. The company lawyers immediately lodged an appeal against the inclusion of individuals, and following consultations, the Supreme Court of Ontario struck down those elements of the writ against both Tate & Lyle and the English directors. In response, the plaintiffs re-defined their position by bringing in more farmers and increasing their claims for damage to over $9 million.

Later in the year, the Annual General Meeting took

An illustration from the 1969 Annual Report.

place in Montreal and revealed that the year's earnings had been improved without the constant drain imposed by the beet refining. Furthermore, although it was taking longer than anticipated, the integration of Daymond Ltd. and a new enterprise called Albion Co. Ltd. (which was involved in chartering ships for the movement of raw sugar cargoes and cargo insurance) had proved to be beneficial to the company's bottom line, yielding an increase in earnings by 25%. This news heartened the company's shareholders who credited the success to Saxon Tate, but it also brought forth increased activity by the government, who saw in this economic turnaround a cause to investigate allegations made by Robin Austin, the original owner of Cartier Sugar, that the three major eastern refiners had been acting in breach of the earlier Order of Prohibition. As a result, on November 26, 1968, government investigators descended upon the head offices of each of the companies and seized various papers, files, and business records related to raw sugar purchases; these records were held until the following February, interfering with the normal running of business.

In March of 1969, several product innovations were introduced to the market. For the domestic consumers, the sugar by-product, molasses, was now sold in two varieties of container, a 1 pound glass jar for table molasses and a 3 pound plastic pouring bottle for cooking purposes. For the industrial user, a new liquid tanker railcar capable of holding 197,000 pounds was brought on line.

At the corporate level, Sir Ian Lyle retired from the Board of Canada and Dominion as did two Vice-Presidents, W.H. Punchard and G.E. Hrudka. In the Daymond sector, its President, F.R. Daymond, had decided to step down. These changes created a sizable gap in the business that needed to be filled. Since there were now two distinct elements to the corporate business interests, discussion began on the prospect of completely restructuring the company into two divisions as of May 1969. This was subsequently carried through with Neil Shaw taking up the post of Chief Executive in the new

Daymond Division; his counterpart for the Redpath Sugars Division was John H. Magee.

Almost immediately, Mr. Magee had to deal with a serious problem as negotiations with the Montreal union had broken down and it was feared that a strike could be called at any time. Anxious to bring matters to a decisive conclusion, Mr. Magee ordered the company to initiate a lock-out of the employees. This was immediately copied by St. Lawrence Sugar, who were at exactly the same point of negotiations with their branch of the same union. Following a six-week period of disruption, a final settlement was reached with a two-year contract at Canada and Dominion, but at St. Lawrence the dispute continued for a considerable time longer. To make up for the lost production, it was decided to accelerate the re-introduction of a three-shift system at the Montreal refinery, which further pleased the employees.

On July 11, 1969, the federal government decided to initiate a complete re-evaluation of its current duties, quotas, and tariffs on sugar in order to develop a Canadian sugar policy. This was to be only the beginning of a series of reviews, hearings, and reports that dragged on for the next several years and involved the company in countless hours of manpower and tens of thousands of dollars in expenses, as it provided information for the enquiry, and as before, representatives from the Combines Department sat taking notes for their own investigation.

During the remainder of the summer, the Board continued its policy of developing new prospects for the business of the company. It began by using the skilled expertise of the company's former beet agricultural workers and technicians in a new field by forming an Agricultural Consulting Services Division. It also acquired the Canadian rights to a newly designed pipe-laying system that could mechanically cut a furrow up to five feet deep, lay the pipe and then fill in behind leaving an intact surface.

In September, a new opportunity arose when an agreement was signed between Redpath Sugars and the Quebec Sugar Refinery for Redpath technicians to act as advisers for the modernization of Q.S.R.; in return Redpath would purchase semi-processed beet sugar and complete its refining for sale alongside the regular cane sugar product.

By the end of the year, the financial accounts indicated that the net income for the corporation was up slightly over the previous year, but the results were still disappointing as it was felt that more could have been achieved had it not been for the federal government policy of imposing price restraints to curb the current high level of inflation. Another negative effect was found in the terms of the International Sugar Agreement, which had been implemented at the beginning of the year; this agreement restricted the choice of suppliers available to Canadian refiners and reduced the raw sugar trading department's profit from $2.3 million in 1968 to only $750,000 in 1969.

In January 1970, the first of the hearings ordered by the Minister of Finance to re-examine the question of duties and other matters were held in Ottawa and lasted for three weeks.

John H. Magee

Apart from representatives of the individual Canadian sugar refiners and the Department of Finance, there were also delegations from the Canadian Beet Growers Association, the syndicate of Quebec Beet Growers, the Consumers Association of Canada, and sugar brokers from around the world. At each session, investigators from the Restrictive Trade Practices Commission not only made extensive notes but attempted to pressure the Tariff Board to hand over documents previously supplied by the sugar refiners to the Tariff Board under a guarantee of confidentiality and security.

Simultaneous translation of the hearings was attempted, but was abandoned after only a day because the translators could not comprehend the jargon of the sugar industry, while subsequent official transcripts of testimonies were a morass of errors.

During the proceedings, each submission and brief had to be duplicated seventy-five times for distribution among the various parties. C and D submitted an eighty-page brief, which the Chairman of the Tariff Board complimented for its clarity in explaining the current state of the Canadian sugar industry and referred to it as his "bible" for the hearings, which were, in his words, "one of the most complicated ... I have ever encountered in my years in the Tariff Board or elsewhere."

Overall the refiners were given a fair hearing, the company being cross-examined on its brief for three days. But one fatal weakness in the case presented by the refiners was the lack of a single set of recommendations; instead each brief ended up making different and sometimes contradictory proposals. This lack of inter-industry collaboration perhaps contributed to the unsatisfactory report that eventually appeared in November and which will

A bulk granular sugar tanker in 1970.

be referred to later.

During the next three months, discussions took place at Board level on the mixed results of its diversification policy. On the positive side, negotiations were progressing to acquire the rights to a new line of non-toxic windshield washer fluid that was already being successfully test-marketed in the United States, and the Badger trenchless pipe-laying system was generating significant interest in the agricultural and construction sector. Also under discussion was a future acquisition called Cello Bags Ltd., which produced polyethylene film for the manufacturing of plastic carrier bags, wrapping material, package wrappers, and associated products.

A New Direction

In opposition to this upbeat series of developments was the fact that the Daymond Division was losing money. This led to a question of whether certain segments of Daymond should be rationalized or the entire operation should be sold off to cut the ongoing financial losses.

Meanwhile in the core sector of the corporate business, a co-operative arrangement had been developed with the Package Research Corporation to produce a new line of containers called tubelets, which could be used not only for sugar but also salt, pepper, and coffee creamer powders. Additionally, sections of the Chatham property were re-zoned for housing and were being developed by the company for a new estate of some 100 houses under the collective name of "Crystal Estates."

The final piece of good news for this time came in June 1970, when the lawsuit initiated against the company by the farmers' group over the closing of the Chatham plant was dropped on the advice of their legal counsel.

Through the remaining summer months and into the autumn, negotiations and arrangements continued so that by October, the President's report recorded that in the non-sugar sector, Cello Bags Ltd. had been acquired, that rationalization of certain facilities within the Daymond Division had taken place, and finally that there had been several sales of the Badger pipe-laying system to various farming groups. In the Redpath Division, little was stated beyond its renaming under the new title of Redpath Sugars Ltd. and the successful introduction of sugar tubelets. Overall these developments allowed the company to record a modest increase in its profits and a subsequent rise in its dividend to shareholders. But it now reflected an increasing degree of interest in non-sugar related products.

In December 1970, having earlier sold off most of his interests in Cartier Sugar, Robin Austin now re-appeared on the sugar scene by sending letters to the boards of Canada and Dominion, Tate & Lyle Ltd., St. Lawrence Sugar Ltd., Atlantic Sugar Refineries Co. Ltd., Czarnikow Montreal Ltd., Hodgson (Sugar Ltd.), and Mansugar Ltd. In his letter, Mr. Austin listed a tirade of accusations blaming everyone in the trade for his business losses and he demanded compensation of $1.4 million to be paid within a week. As might be expected, the Board of Canada and Dominion rejected these intimidation tactics and no record of any response, let alone any payment, is recorded to have taken place.

Early in 1971, Redpath Sugars Ltd. received an enquiry from the Canadian government about whether the company could supply technicians to work with the Canadian and Congo governments in a developmental aid package for the African nation. Although this project was not developed beyond the initial study, it proved to be the first of a number of foreign projects that involved Redpath personnel and provided some much-needed revenue for the corporation. Domestically, the intense competition caused by the excess capacity of the Canadian sugar industry continued to reduce the profitability of sugar refining in Canada as a whole and led the Board of C and D to increase its pace of diversification into non-sugar-related fields. This included the expansion of Daymond into the U.S. market through a joint venture under the name Certain-Teed/Daymond Co. and the acquisition of two new companies, Anvil Plastics Ltd. and Gienow Sash & Door Co. Ltd., whose product lines were destined to complement the equivalent ranges in the Daymond Division.

Despite this turn of higher corporate attention away from its sugar base, Redpath Sugars Ltd. continued to develop in its own right as plans were made to re-equip elements of the production system at both the Montreal and Toronto plants. Simultaneously, negotiations for a new set of contracts were underway with the local unions. Unfortunately, in August 1971, the discussions with its Toronto union broke down and a strike was called that subsequently lasted right through until November. This was perhaps one of the lowest points in management-union relationships within the company, as it appears from the newspaper reports of the time and the comments of those involved that matters got somewhat out of hand on both sides. Tempers flared, leading to accusations by the union of company strike-breaking tactics, telephone tampering, and subversion of union members. In return, the company accused the union of picket- line violence upon company employees, sabotage of company equipment and vehicles, and even vandalism of employee cars and private homes. None of this made for good relations once the strike was finally settled, and it still remains something of a sore point in the memories of some of the company's longer-serving employees.

Outside of the refineries proper, but still within the sugar field, other concerns began to come to the company's attention as Robin Austin made public his intention to establish a new sugar refining company at Kingston. It was supposedly backed by federal funding and had guarantees of government dredgers deepening the harbour to accommodate ocean-going vessels. Coincidentally, the George Weston Co. Ltd., whose interests were in bakeries and other related industries, announced its own plans to erect a refinery in the Toronto area to compete directly with Redpath Sugars Ltd. With the distinct overcapacity being suffered in the industry, Mr. Magee and his management team were concerned about the possible fragmentation of the already strained market. Discussions were held with Weston's on the prospect of Redpath Sugars Ltd. refining sugar on behalf of Weston at a discounted toll basis in order to persuade Weston's not to proceed with its planned construction. Fortunately for the company, they were soon able to discount the Robin Austin project, which fell apart when no government funding was given to subsidize the much-publicized venture.

At the end of the year, the long-awaited Tariff Board report was finally issued, and with the amount of time and expense expended, it was hoped that it would reflect a balanced and definitive statement on the future of the industry. In reality, this document, produced by so-called government experts, must stand as one of the most contradictory and faulty pieces of work ever issued by an official bureaucracy. Almost all of the proposals and recommendations made by the sugar industry that had been given verbal support during the hearings were either omitted from the report or contradicted by the written conclusions. Statistical information compiled from incompatible sources was presented in a multitude of tables, graphs, and appendixes, revealing a plethora of glaring inaccuracies, mathematical errors, and downright contradictions. For example, it claimed in one paragraph that the sugar industry was benefiting from rising profits, while in another it clearly stated that profits were falling. It proposed that there should be more competition within Canada by increasing the number of sugar companies, while at the same time, it noted the overcapacity in the industry and called for rationalization of the number of producers. Most incredibly, however, it stated that it was both inconceivable and suspicious that there had been "no failures for decades." This would indicate that the government determined that an industry was competitive and thriving based upon the number of businesses that closed down. In conclusion, the report subsequently proposed that protection for Canadian sugar refineries be effectively eliminated. This proposal was eagerly seized upon by the government and implemented with such zeal that in the end rates were restructured so that it was more advantageous to import refined sugar from sources in the United States and abroad, while Canadian refiners were penalized for every pound of sugar they made.

The reaction of the corporation to this report was not long in coming, nor was it complimentary, as can be seen in the statement of Mr. Tate to the shareholders at the Annual General Meeting on January 25, 1972.

The thesis upon which the report is written is that there should be greater competition and that the industry has excess capacity which dictates that rationalization should take place ... [but] under the existing combines legislation rationalization through acquisition is not acceptable to Ottawa, at least not if it is brought about by Redpath ... acquiring a competitor. This can only mean that the tariff board is recommending rationalization by failure with its subsequent plant closures and loss of employment. It even singles out Montreal where there are three refineries for particular attention in this respect.

As a result of this publication and the company reaction, it is not surprising that the corporate directors were even more convinced of the need to diversify into non-sugar fields. This trend was spearheaded by Saxon Tate when, shortly after the Annual General Meeting, J.O. Whitmee stepped down as the Canada and Dominion President due to ill health, to be replaced by Mr. Tate. Following an intensive review of current conditions and future projections, it was decided that development would be concentrated in the construction materials sector, while the sweeteners branch would expand if significant opportunities presented themselves. This was not particularly good news for Mr. Magee and his staff at Redpath Sugars Ltd., but it was not entirely unexpected in the light of the prevailing circumstances, which included:

– plans by the Quebec government to invest $6 million to modernize its beet refinery;
– the announcement of the commitment by the Weston Corporation to build its proposed refinery at a site in Oshawa outside of Toronto with a capacity of 75,000 tons per year;
– newspaper articles reporting that Robin Austin was touting the future establishment of his new attempt for a sugar refinery under the name Austin Sugar Refineries Ltd., with prospects for a location at Cornwall, Ontario;
– rumours that the National Farmers Union and the federal government Agriculture Minister Eugene Whelan were proposing to revive the sugar beet industry in Ontario as a Crown corporation to combat the current world price increases for raw sugar;
– the continuing uncertainty and restrictive boundaries placed upon the Canadian sugar industry under the current Combines legislation.

Responding to these features of the industry, Mr. Magee attempted one last time to persuade the Weston Corporation to defer the building of its Oshawa refinery in exchange for a shares interest in Canada and Dominion. When Weston's responded that it would consider such an arrangement only if it owned 50% of C and D, the whole idea was dropped. Instead the company turned its attention to its long-time competitor, St. Lawrence Sugar. In return, the management at St. Lawrence indicated that they were also interested in a merger. This led to a joint approach to the Combines Department in mid-June 1972, for its official pronouncement. By August, no definite conclusion had been made by the Combines Department and the Redpath negotiators were becoming agitated as approaches for a merger had also been made by Atlantic Sugar. In order to get a resolution to the issue, Saxon Tate visited Ottawa. Upon his return, he was pleased to report that contrary to expectations, the director of the Combines investigation had recognized that some decision had to be made and that current conditions in both the Canadian and world markets were vastly different from those of the period when the initial investigation was begun. He even went so far as to say that some form of rationalization of the sugar industry could be in the interest of consumers. This left Redpath Sugars Ltd. with a strong incentive to carry through the considered merger, and negotiations were therefore immediately resumed with St. Lawrence.

At the same time, Redpath Sugars Ltd. also continued with its negotiations with the Quebec Sugar Refinery for technical and management services to be provided by Redpath during the Q.S.R. modernization. A new facet of the discussions included the prospect of selling some of the surplus equipment from Chatham to Q.S.R. in return for Redpath's purchasing Quebec Sugar Refinery beet raw sugar. All of this activity was looked on with interest by the Quebec government, who were under some pressure to dispose of this money-losing enterprise, which had suffered an annual deficit of over $600,000 for the previous twenty-eight years.

In October, one sticky situation that developed for the staff at the Toronto refinery came about when a delivery truck accidentally clipped a main pipe carrying molasses to one of the site's molasses tanks, splitting the pipe. The pipe discharged some 400 gallons of black strap molasses into the truck yard before the flow was cut off. Fortunately, the cold weather and the thickness of the grade of molasses combined to restrict the gooey mess from spreading and it was speedily cleaned up, although the smell took somewhat longer to disperse.

By the end of the company's financial year, the continuing development of the corporation away from sugar-based production led to the recognition that the current title of Canada and Dominion Sugar Co. Ltd. did not properly reflect the multi-faceted interests of the group. Therefore a major decision was made to completely restructure the corporation under a new title of Redpath

Neil M. Shaw

Industries Ltd. (also referred to as R.I.L.), which would now consist of the following divisions, subsidiaries, and affiliates.

    Redpath Sugars Ltd.
    Cello Bags Ltd.
    Chatham and Wallaceburg Land Development Division.
    Gienow Ltd.
    Trenchless Pipe Systems Division.
    Daymond Ltd.
    Multi Fittings Ltd. (formally Anvil Plastics)
    Agricultural Consulting Services Division.
    Albion Co. Ltd.
    Certain-Teed/Daymond Co.
    Crystal Estates.

Simultaneously, Saxon Tate was given new responsibilities within the Tate & Lyle corporate structure, which made it impossible for him to remain as President of the Corporation. As a result, the corporate executive structure was also re-organized with the appointment of the new Chief Executive Officer, Neil M. Shaw.

The way of the future, metric packaging.

CHAPTER TWELVE

Lawyers and Judges and Shares, Oh My!

Almost immediately after taking office as President of Redpath Industries Ltd., Mr. Shaw and Vice-Presidents R. Porteous and M. Davidson were summoned to meet with the Director of the Combines investigation, Mr. Henry. At the meeting they were informed that the government had changed its mind once again, and that if the proposed merger with St. Lawrence went ahead, the department would either initiate an investigation with an aim towards prosecution or veto the merger entirely. This sudden reversal effectively killed the St. Lawrence proposal and as no similar merger would be likely approved between Cartier Sugar and Redpath Sugars Ltd., it left the company with very little manoeuvring room for the future.

At the next meeting of the R.I.L. Board, Mr. Magee and his Managing Director, P.S. Stachenko, were called upon to make a presentation evaluating the current and future prospects for sugar refining within Canada and its impact upon Redpath Sugars Ltd. The report was presented by Mr. Stachenko and made gloomy reading; it revealed that domestically Redpath Sugars Ltd. was facing a market expanding at only 1% per annum, while Canadian production was expected to increase by 10% once the now complete Oshawa Westcane refinery went into production.

As the only refiner running two plants, Redpath Sugars Ltd. would likely take the brunt of any market splintering and could be expected to lose up to 45 million pounds of sales annually, the equivalent of seven years of normal market growth. Furthermore, recent budget changes had reduced the refiners' margins by first allowing more imports of foreign refined sugar and second by slashing the basic value of current inventories.

In the international sphere, likewise, the company was experiencing some difficulties as raw sugar exporters were agitating for a retroactive increase in the official supply commitment price previously agreed to under the International Sugar Agreement. If this change were granted, it would leave Redpath Sugars Ltd. in a position where it was forced to pay more for its raw material while being unable to increase its price for refined sugar due to long-term contracts and Canadian government anti-inflation regulations. With all these prevailing conditions, the R.I.L. Board now had to decide whether to close one of its refineries, either temporarily or even permanently, and try to ride out the current difficulties using only one refinery. Following a long period of evaluating the various options, it was decided to maintain production at both facilities but review the question if circumstances did not improve in the near future. One other decision made at this time was to officially relocate the company's head office from Chatham to Montreal, reflecting the switch away from the earlier beet dominance of the company's sugar operations.

In the midst of this already difficult period, matters took a significantly more serious turn when on February 22, 1973, special investigators from the department of National Revenue, accompanied by plainclothes R.C.M.P. officers, made what can only be described as a simultaneous "raid" upon the corporation offices at Montreal, Toronto, and Chatham with a court order to seize any documents that related to the Albion Co. Ltd. and its operations in Bermuda. Searches were also made at the offices of Clarkson Gordon & Co., Czarnikow Canada Ltd., the Bank of Montreal, the Canadian Imperial Bank of Commerce, and Lash, Johnston, Sheard and Pringle. More alarmingly, other teams of investigators descended upon the private residences of corporate executives and conducted detailed searches under furniture, behind book shelves, and in basement storage areas; spouses were questioned about whether they or their husbands had spent time in Bermuda. At the Toronto office, the receptionist at the time, Evelyn Irving, remembered the arrival of several large individuals who demanded to see Mr. Davidson, without stating either their identities or the nature of their business. When she told them that they would have to explain the reason for their visit, the men barged past the reception desk, ran up the main flight of stairs to the office level, and proceeded to enter Mr. Davidson's office by kicking open the door. Mr. Davidson later recorded what happened next:

The leader had been sent from Montreal, and appeared anxious to show his Toronto colleagues how these operations were executed in Quebec. After reading the court order which empowered the team to carry out a search, he indicated he had some questions he wished answered. When the Vice-President refused to answer anything without the presence of a lawyer, the leader complained that would put him behind schedule ... The Vice-President had never been to Bermuda, Albion operations were not within his responsibilities, and there were no files pertaining to Redpath's subsidiary in Bermuda. Never-the-less the team rifled through files in the Toronto office all day and carried away a truck-load of documents.

Stunned by this totally unexpected and overbearing menace by their own government, the company executives were even more surprised to learn from one of the "visitors" that raids of this type were now a daily event for the investigators and that many companies were being treated to exactly the same kind of search-and-seize tactics to "fish" for information about offshore subsidiaries and taxation returns. The reasons for these drastic activities can be linked to the Income Tax authorities disputing the legal right of companies to exclude the patronage of any profits made abroad from its declared taxable income. In the case of Redpath Industries, declaring these profits would result in an assessment of some $3.5 million, which could be appealed but must be paid first.

Disagreements in such cases would normally be resolved by negotiated settlement or even in a civil court action, but in a follow-up to these bully-boy tactics, the government chose to apply criminal proceedings against the company.

In the midst of all this disruption, normal daily

business had to be maintained. This included the incorporation of a new element in the R.I.L. portfolio under the title Redpath Home Improvements Ltd. Daymond Ltd. expanded its production facilities with a new plant being constructed in Clarkson on the outskirts of Toronto. Likewise, Redpath Sugars Ltd. was involved in negotiations with Laing Engineering of Miami, Florida, to provide technical services for the construction of a small refinery in the African nation of Mauritania under the overall sponsorship of the International Development Association.

Closer to home, Redpath Sugars Ltd. was continuing to lose substantial amounts of money in its raw sugar trading as the International Sugar Council approved a retroactive increase in the supply commitment price, despite objections by the Canadian government. As Redpath Sugars had 100 million pounds of refined sugar already sold by long-term contracts on the earlier lower supply commitment price, the company was left in the position of having to pay more for its already received cargoes of raw material without any possibility of recouping it through a similar increase in the price of its refined product.

In June 1973, the ongoing matter of the Combines case came up again, as once more the government chose to charge the eastern Canadian group of sugar refiners with the same charges that had gained the government such an easy victory some years before. But this time the companies were not prepared to simply roll over and play dead. Instead, counsel was retained to prepare a strong and vigorous defence against what was seen by the industry as victimization.

Ironically, while the Combines Department was pressing ahead with its attack on the eastern sugar refiners and the Taxation Department still had not returned the seized documents, the Finance Department was actively co-operating with the sugar industry in developing a new system of tariffs for sugar in order to cope with the recent and continuing rise of world sugar prices.

Late in the summer, export sales for Redpath Sugars began to improve dramatically when special orders were despatched to Greece and Cyprus, and negotiations were started with representatives from Yugoslavia and Trinidad. Domestically, the company's sales improved, buoyed by a rail strike that left Redpath's Toronto refinery as the only operational facility to serve the requirements of southern Ontario, as the Westcane plant had suffered some pre-production delays. By October, the overall sales for the financial year were higher than the planned objectives, helping to offset the $1 million losses incurred by the raw sugar purchasing department and the absorption of huge interest-rate charges arising from the current higher cost of raw sugar.

As the year drew to a close, Redpath Sugars Ltd. was busy coping with several situations of importance that affected the company's operations. First was the ongoing taxation question, which was likely to go to court for a judgement. Second came the collapse of the International Sugar Agreement and a significant rise in prices of world sugar supplies. Third was the Combines investigation, which was rapidly proceeding towards public hearings at which Robin Austin was billed as the star witness for the prosecution. Fourth, the financial losses in raw sugar trading had continued to escalate and now dominated company discussions. Finally, the internal finances of Redpath Industries Ltd. were being strained by losses in many of the newer subsidiaries, leading the Board to consider disposing of money losers and acquiring new businesses.

With the start of 1974, Redpath Sugars Ltd. acquired a new President when J.H. Magee retired, to be succeeded by the Managing Director, P.S. Stachenko. Unfortunately, this was not the best of times for the company, as raw sugar losses were continuing to escalate without any realistic way of improving matters as long as current methods of purchasing were maintained. Therefore it was decided that, in future, Redpath would operate on the lowest possible inventory of raw sugar, even to the extent of shutting down production for short periods while waiting for raw sugar cargoes.

During the following months, Redpath Sugars Ltd. had to cope with a substantial jump in world sugar prices. The reason for this price rise can be traced to a vast increase in demand for cane sugar by the Soviet Union and its satellite countries due to crop failures in the Soviet bloc beet harvests over the previous three years. This now caused several problems for the company, not the least of which was the increased level of blame that consumers mistakenly heaped upon the Canadian sugar refiners as being the cause of the resultant sugar price increases. Even the Food Prices Review Board carried out an investigation, which completely cleared the refiners of any responsibility for the continuing escalation of prices. More immediately, however, the spiral of rising raw sugar prices created severe difficulties for the raw sugar trading department, which subsequently lost $10 million in the first eight months of 1974. As a result, consideration was given to

P. S. Stachenko

transferring all raw sugar purchasing to the Tate & Lyle raw depart-ment in London but upon reflection it was decided to retain control of purchasing in Canada.

By the beginning of October 1974, the company was taking stock of its financial options for future development. It was seen that for the first time, the level of earnings for the corporation from non-sugar interests would exceed 50% despite the failure of the Badger pipe-laying system and Redpath Home Improvements Ltd., both of which had by now been abandoned. Sugar had now slipped firmly into second place in the consideration of the Board as a subject for future investment, which was not helped by the ongoing harassment from the taxation inspectors, who were demanding additional details of the Albion business for a prospective addition to the government claim for taxes. Of more immediate seriousness was the Combines accusation, which was coming up for trial.

During the course of this trial, Robin Austin was a strong witness for the prosecution's case, claiming that the accused refiners had tried to prevent him from running his sugar business at Cartier. However, once the defence counsel rose to cross-examine Mr. Austin, new information involving Mr. Austin and a meeting that had taken place in London during April 1974 was revealed.

It was reported by the defence counsel that early in 1974, Mr. Austin had approached Tate & Lyle, calling for a meeting to discuss his willingness to remain outside Canada and not appear for the court case if he were paid to do so.

Recognizing the illegality of such a proposal, Tate & Lyle immediately contacted the police who fitted Saxon Tate with a small microphone and remote-recording equipment. When the meeting took place between Robin Austin, who was accompanied by his brother, and Saxon Tate, who was in turn supported by D.A. Tate, Robin Austin once again proposed that for $750,000 he would not testify at the Combines hearings although he openly admitted he was the instigating force behind the original accusations. Inside the court, this revelation was devastating to the case of the prosecution when it was further confirmed that Austin's proposal had been immediately rejected by the parties on the other side. Buoyed by this addition to their case, the company was shocked to read in the newspapers erroneous reports that the proposed bribe had originated with Tate & Lyle. Legal notices were immediately sent to the offending papers and appropriate retractions were made. Regrettably, the retractions did not appear before the damage had been done, and in future complaints against the sugar industry, government officials continued to refer to this erroneous report as a fact.

In concluding this all too extraordinary year, which one executive described as a period during which "we were all uncertain whether we were in Canada, or the land of Oz" the fact must be recorded that the price of sugar continued to climb until it peaked on November 21 at the astronomical value of $77.40 per 100 pounds for refined sugar before dropping back to $59.05 by the end of the year. This caused a major outcry by householders against the sugar companies, and in its defence Redpath Sugars Ltd. went so far as to put an advertisement in virtually every newspaper across its sales area to explain the realities of the situation. On the industrial

One of a series of advertisements explaining the cause of high prices in November, 1974.

consumers' part, while their reaction was less vocal, it was nonetheless damaging in the long term as they increasingly moved into the alternative sweeteners market for their supplies, reducing the overall demand for sugar by around 27%.

In February 1975, the corporate President of R.I.L., N.M. Shaw, addressed the shareholders of the company and outlined both the current and prospective state of the sugar industry.

Principal among the current problems mentioned was the recent period of high prices, which had led to inevitable criticism and reductions in consumption, while the government had reacted with increased pressure on the industry to accept less protection. Furthermore, U.S. refiners were now able to ship refined sugar into Canada at almost the same level of duty as the Canadian refiners paid for their raw materials. Fortunately, in a counterbalance to this negative factor it was shown that for the first time in forty years, the United States had become an open market for sugar with the expiry of its Sugar Act. This legislation had previously closely controlled imports of both raw and refined sugar into the American market and its termination allowed Redpath Sugars Ltd. to engage in some increased exports, thus raising the overall sales volume.

Another problem with the government was its refusal to accept the accounting methods used by the company in determining the tax to be paid on its raw sugar inventory; this refusal forced the company to pay vastly increased tax rates compared to its competitors, leaving it at a distinct disadvantage for future growth. Finally, the government was restricting the activities of the company through its Foreign Investment Review Agency, which required Redpath Industries, as a majority-owned part of the British firm of Tate & Lyle, to satisfy F.I.R.A. that any merger or corporate purchase would significantly benefit Canada before it could be completed. However, its other sugar competitors were under no such restraint, having their majority share holdings inside Canada. In response to this overwhelming number of restrictions the management of Redpath Sugars Ltd. began to condider various cost-cutting measures, including:
— reducing the number of shifts at the Montreal refinery back to two instead of three,
— laying off employees on a rotational basis,
— reducing production at the Toronto refinery from its present four-day week,
— eliminating all overtime,
— closing the Toronto refinery or converting it to a corn sweetener facility.

On the other hand, in comparison to the other Canadian refining companies, Redpath Sugars Ltd. was in a relatively good position through its increased level of export sales, the successful turnaround of its raw sugar purchasing department into a profit-making effort and the technical assistance contracts for foreign refineries. In March, this success in technical assistance was augmented by the signing of a new contract for $130 million with representatives of a new scheme for development in the African nation of the Ivory Coast. The following month, the success of the raw sugar department warranted its separation into a division of its own within the R.I.L. structure under the name of Comtrad Ltd. Less welcomed was the renewed media interest in the lengthy Combines case, which was continuing to drag on. In its own defence, the sugar industry had introduced several features of world trading in sugar, as well as expert testimony from foreign sources. This required the court to hold several sessions as far abroad as England, Belgium, and India. As a result of this worldwide independent testimony, it was shown that the consensus of opinion by the Canadian sugar refiners on certain international issues and their pricing and purchasing policies were no more than a natural reflection of the nature of the business – each company bought the same types of raw material, in similar quantities, from the same sources, transported and processed it in an identical manner, and then sold it to the same customers. In return, these customers were then quite free to switch to another company if its prices were not immediately competitive with its rivals.

Even some of the major food processors were called to testify and completely refuted the charges made by the Crown that the sugar companies had tried to stop the food processors from buying foreign sugar directly. By July, the case was completed and the judge retired to render his verdict, but this took some time, in fact until December.

In the meantime, Redpath Sugars Ltd. business continued as usual on several fronts. One was the investigation of co-operative ventures for the production and blending of a new variety of sweetener called High Fructose Corn Syrup or H.F.C.S. A second was the placing of complaints over the government's Prices and Incomes Controls, which restricted any price increases to no more than once every three months and reduced the company's ability to react to outside market forces.

At Redpath Industries Ltd. the policy of diversification continued to be developed with the offering of bids for Merry Packaging Ltd. and Holway Paper Box Manufacturing Co. Ltd., followed soon afterwards by investigations for other acquisitions in the oil and gas exploration industry.

In November 1975, Redpath Sugars applied for a tax refund of more than $8 million. This unusual event was due to the Taxation Department's refusal to recognize the base stock system for its raw sugar used by the company and its insistence on a First In, First Out inventory valuation. As a result, the amount of profit declarable for taxation had been difficult to determine in advance. Therefore, in order to avoid penalties for under-payment, the tax instalments had been paid on the basis of the prior year's sugar values. Now, because of the significantly lower values in 1975 compared to 1974, the company had overpaid by $8 million and wanted it back.

The following month, the R.I.L. Board decided that as the overall year had been generally successful, it would increase the dividend to its shareholders. To its surprise, the government's Anti-Inflation Board refused the application, even though the financial year ended on September 30, 1975, before the October 14 announcement of the imposition of Price and Wage Controls.

The final news for the year came in late December when Mr. Justice Kenneth Mackay rendered his verdict on the Combines case by finding the sugar companies not guilty on both charges. Although this naturally pleased the sugar companies, the Crown applied for an appeal which was subsequently granted, and so the matter began all over again, resulting in more expense and diversion of valuable manpower away from the business at hand. As an unusual sideline to this event, it was recorded that when he was notified of the acquittal, the Minister of Consumer and Corporate Affairs, André Oullet, reacted with extreme anger, calling the decision "a complete disgrace and completely unacceptable." He then went further and publicly questioned

Let Redpath Sweeten It

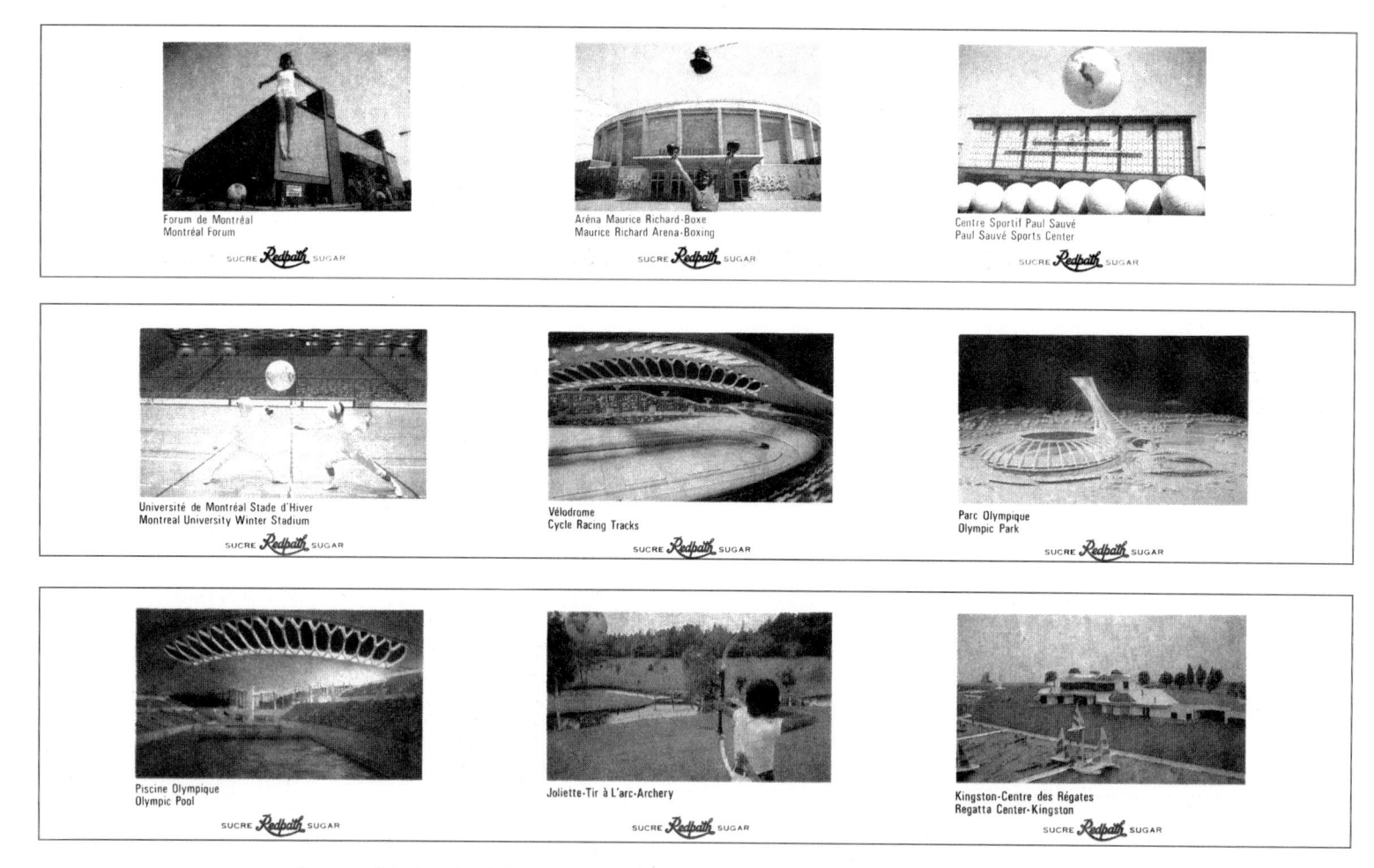

Strips of Individual Serving Envelopes produced for the 1976 Olympic Games.

the mental competence of the judge, for which he was quickly charged with contempt of Court, found guilty, fined, and ordered to send an apology to the judge.

In January 1976, Redpath Sugars Ltd. made a change in its packaging, a seemingly small event but one that had entailed months of preparation and untold expense in the mechanical alteration of the packaging machinery. The change was made to comply with the government's metrication policy, and from now on, the old ounce, pound, and ton were replaced by the gram, kilogram, and tonne as all packaging was converted to the metric system. Also involved with the packaging was a new series of I.S.E.s to coincide with the upcoming Summer Olympic Games in Montreal, for which Redpath had been awarded the contract for supplying sugar.

In March the company was able to secure the services of a new executive, Murray McEwen from St. Lawrence Sugar. He now replaced Mr. Stachenko as President of Redpath Sugars Ltd. when Mr. Stachenko moved to become Vice-President of Redpath Industries Ltd. and took on the supervision of the new Ivory Coast project. Unfortunately for Mr. McEwen, he fell foul of the ill luck that seemed to dog virtually all the presidents of the company; almost immediately following his appointment, the government demanded alterations to the company's methods of doing business and recording its selling prices under the terms of the government's anti-inflation legislation. These included the fact that the government wanted each grade and type of sugar listed separately, while Redpath claimed they should be grouped together as the base product was the same. Secondly, corporate expenses were to be restricted in such fields as advertising, research, and development to a percentage of the sales dollar figure in a base period. The company responded by arguing that this would not work for sugar due to the extreme fluctuations in raw material prices. Finally, the authorities demanded that the Comtrad Division for purchasing the raw sugar should be included within the allowances for Redpath Sugars Ltd.; if

Murray McEwen

applied, this change would completely unbalance the financial figures for Redpath Sugars Ltd. (figures that had been carefully controlled to ensure compliance with governmental regulations). Moreover this inclusion could lead to a governmental charge of making excess profits over the base period and would lead to these profits being seized by the government.

In order to clarify these problems, Mr. McEwen and the management at Redpath Sugars Ltd. initiated discussions with the authorities in hopes of getting them to see the sense in the company's position.

On a slightly lighter and happier note, the Toronto refinery was host in April to the arrival of probably the most unusual vessel to berth at the refinery's quay. This was the 1891 Thames sailing barge *May* which had been obtained for the summer from her owners, Tate & Lyle, to ply the Great Lakes and act as a goodwill vessel for the company. Then on May 5, the refinery acted as hosts to the International Convention of Sugar Industry Technologists, who were given the opportunity to study the production facilities. Finally, in a gesture of employee-employer relations, the company approved the extension of this accessibility to the refinery by holding the first company family day, where employees had the opportunity to show their children, families, and friends the usually off-limits interior of the refinery.

In July 1976, talks were begun about the introduction of a blend of sugar and High Fructose Corn Syrup as an addition to the Redpath product line. It was proposed to purchase

Let Redpath Sweeten It

The arrival of the Thames sailing barge May at Toronto.

H.F.C.S. from A.E. Staley in the United States; transport it to the liquid stations at Montreal, Toronto, and Chatham; blend it with Redpath's own liquid sugar products; and supply the industrial market before Redpath's competitors were able to develop similar product lines. This was subsequently contracted for and the first deliveries went out to customers in August.

The following month, the lucrative sales into the United States were all but eliminated when the American government tripled its import duties overnight in response to the outcries of its beet farmers, who demanded and successfully lobbied for protection, clearly indicating the difference between the U.S. and Canadian governments in their attitudes towards their respective domestic sugar industries.

As the final quarter of the year began to wind down, the decision of the Anti-Inflation Board was rendered on the question of Comtrad being subject to controls as an integral part of Redpath Sugars Ltd. despite the fact that it was listed as a separate division of Redpath Industries Ltd. The result was not good news for the company as Comtrad was declared to be covered by the regulations and restrictions applicable to Redpath Sugars Ltd. , and as such, Redpath was declared in violation of the regulations by making excess profits through raw sugar trading. As feared, the company was forced to surrender its profits deemed to be in excess of official allowances directly to the government, and in addition, the authorities applied new controls and limitations for future business dealings in raw sugar. When the company objected to some of the new terms being imposed upon it as being unworkable in the real market, instead of discussing the matter to find an appropriate solution, the bureaucrats simply stood by their original

The May under sail near the Toronto refinery.

demands and threatened to use negative publicity against the company if it did not comply.

In October, another government decision was rendered, this time by F.I.R.A., who finally approved the purchase of Merry Packaging Ltd. and Holway Paper Box Manufacturing Ltd. after a full year of deliberations. While this was good news for the company, it still showed that due to the negative atmosphere created at government levels by even the arm's-length involvement of Tate & Lyle in Redpath Industries Ltd., any future acquisitions or mergers involving Redpath would be subject to excessive investigation and bureaucratic delays. These actions would inevitably sour any future prospects if other bidders were in the same market and could offer deals not subject to F.I.R.A. authorization.

As a result, much of the Board's attention focused on making future corporate development within the United States proper, where restrictions were not so onerous. First on the list came the purchase of 30% of the shares in the Yonkers, New York, sugar plant of Refined Syrups and Sugars Inc. (also referred to as R.S. & S.) This plant had a capacity of production equal to both the Toronto and Montreal facilities combined, but only in the form of industrial products such as liquid sugar. Therefore it was proposed to re-equip the new plant for the production of granulated sugars and the development of new packaging lines which would be sold in the northeastern United States.

By the end of the year, the overall corporate position for Redpath Sugars Ltd. was generally considered successful due to the current low prices for raw sugar and the increase of per-capita consumption as well as several major sales to the United States prior to its alteration of the tariffs. However, there was a clear warning in the Annual Report that in the view of the Board the continued over-capacity in the refining industry of eastern Canada would inhibit the long-term profitability of Redpath's sugar refining operations. Other points of interest from this report that shed light on the corporation as a whole included the disposal of Albion Co. Ltd. and the establishment of a new corporate sector under the title Agro-Industrial Division to oversee the interrelated activities of Redpath Sugars, the Ivory Coast project, and High Fructose Corn Sweeteners. In fact, the level of complexity within R.I.L. had now reached the point where its foundation of sugar refining had almost become lost in the long list of divisions, subsidiaries and affiliates, which included:

COMPANY NAME	LOCATION
C.B. Packaging Ltd.	Toronto, Ontario
Certain-Teed/Daymond Co.	Ann Arbor, Michigan
Chantecler Wines Ltd.	St. Augustin, Quebec
Comtrad Ltd.	Mississauga, Ontario
Daymond Ltd.	Mississauga, Ontario
Devonport Trading Ltd.	Hamilton, Bermuda
Gienow Ltd.	Calgary, Alberta
London Plastics Machinery Ltd.	London, Ontario
Multi Fittings (U.S.A.) Ltd.	London, Ontario
Redpath Consultants International Ltd.	Toronto, Ontario
Redpath Sugars Ltd.	Montreal, Quebec
Refined Syrups and Sugars Inc.	Yonkers, New York
Seaway Insurance Ltd.	Hamilton, Bermuda
Spraycool Systems Ltd.	Rexdale, Ontario

But perhaps the most telling fact of all from the Annual Report was the small paragraph that stated that additions to property, plant, and equipment in the 1976 fiscal year were divided, with $1.3 million going to the sugar sector, of which Refined Syrups and Sugars Inc. took the lion's share, while more than $4 million went to the construction materials and packaging operations.

In conclusion, the Annual Report mentioned in passing that a decision had been made to celebrate the upcoming 125th anniversary of the founding of the original Canada Sugar Refinery by establishing a museum that would be located in a converted section of the bag storage warehouse at the Toronto refinery.

In January of 1977, the company extended its shareholding in Refined Syrups and Sugars Inc. from 30% to 100%, although it was recognized that up to $13 million would have to be invested in the Yonkers plant in order to bring it up to the efficiency and range capacities for new products currently applicable at the Montreal and Toronto sites. Subsequently 50% was resold to Tate & Lyle so that in future both companies would run this large U.S. sugar operation. Also at this time, the team of Redpath Consultants International was awarded the contract to undertake a feasibility study for the Government of Cameroun, West Africa, on the construction of a new cane mill in that country. Closer to home, Redpath Sugars Ltd. was actively investigating the development of an H.F.C.S. production plant in co-operation with either the A.E. Staley Co. from the United States or the Canadian corporation of John Labatt Ltd. This product was now recognized as being the single largest competitor that sugar would be likely to face in the next few years as any future rise in sugar prices would inevitably make H.F.C.S. more competitive and take sales away from the sugar industry.

On February 15, the employees at the Toronto refinery were surprised to hear the fire alarms ringing and soon saw a fleet of fire trucks racing to the plant. Fortunately, the alarm was not caused by fire but by water. According to Jan Kuzmicz, the Process Manager, a team of men were cleaning the raw sugar weighing tower when a high pressure steam hose over-heated a sprinkler detector, setting the whole system off. The steam was quickly shut off, but by the time someone got to a phone to cancel the alarm, the fire department had already arrived. This small incident generally brought smiles to the faces of the refinery employees and resulted in the good-natured teasing of the cleaning crew involved in the incident.

But smiles did not last long when only a few days later the federal government made known its response to the taxation question raised around the income of Albion Ltd. The government not only cited the company for evading taxes and claimed more than $3 million in back taxes, plus interest and penalties of $2.2 million, but pressed the matter as a criminal investigation. This could have the effect of doubling the amount of payment applicable and result in the imprisonment of corporate executives. While Redpath Industries Ltd. vehemently denied the charges and began to gather its defence for presentation, it felt that there was more than just an economic issue at the bottom of this case and that in reality Redpath was being made the scapegoat of governmental scare tactics aimed at Canadian industries at large. Nor did it appear that the choice of Redpath was merely a coincidence of timing, as it was discovered that the lead counsel for the Crown was the same individual who had conducted the Combines case and lost. Should he now be able to gain a conviction in this case, it was conceivable that it would support the ongoing appeal by the government and result in the overturning of the not-guilty verdict. For all these reasons, Redpath Industries Ltd. was determined to mount the strongest possible defence, starting with the simple fact that the value of the tax assessment supposedly not paid exceeded the total net income of Albion for the years in question.

Throughout the following months, the dual cases of Combines and Taxation continued to divert both finances and manpower away from the proper business of the corporation. To some degree it also reduced the attractiveness of the company as an investment opportunity because the rate of shares being exchanged increased significantly in favour of sales. The only pleasant news for the period was the arrival of the *Ethel* sister ship to the *May* which had returned to Europe the previous year. This Thames sailing barge was also owned by Tate & Lyle and was loaned to R.I.L. for the summer for the purpose of customer relations trips.

By September 1977, although the corporate financial results set new records for both net earnings and earnings per share, most of this increase had come about from non-sugar developments and it was specifically decided and stated by the Board that it intended to further reduce its dependency on earnings from sugar refining in Canada. This seriously worried many of the employees at the Montreal refinery, especially when at the same time it was announced that the executive offices of Redpath Industries Ltd. were to be moved from Montreal to the Royal Bank Plaza in Toronto. Rumours now began circulating about the prospective closure of the Montreal refinery, and it was not until Mr. McEwen made the announcement that the head office of Redpath Sugars Ltd. was remaining at Montreal that matters returned to normal.

The following month, Steinberg's Ltd. approached Redpath Sugars Ltd. with the proposal that Redpath purchase the Cartier refinery. Obviously, the company was more than eager to secure its market through this rationalization, but it was instead forced to react coolly to the offer as everything was subject to review by F.I.R.A., which had already shown itself to be particularly prejudicial to any expansion by Redpath as long as Tate & Lyle were the majority shareholders in the company.

This was soon followed by the hearing for the appeal on the Combines case, which fortunately took nowhere near the length of time given to the initial case, although judgement in the matter was deferred until the New Year.

Completing the month's busy calendar, the new version of the International Sugar Agreement was signed in Geneva, establishing new upper and lower limits on the world price of raw sugar. This did not have an

The Ethel cruising in the Toronto harbour.

immediate effect on sugar prices in Canada but it was recognized that as the exporting countries used up their surplus stocks, prices under the International Sugar Agreement would begin to rise once again.

In November, two sugar ships destined for the Toronto refinery attracted the attention of the local media. The first was the *Federal Schelde*, which gained the distinction of being the largest single vessel ever to sail up the St. Lawrence River. It initially delivered 10,000 tonnes of raw sugar to the Montreal refinery in order to lighten its draught (as otherwise it could not fit into the locks of the St. Lawrence Seaway) before continuing on to Toronto with a full 25,000 tonnes for that site.

At a length of 729 feet and with a 75-foot beam, it completely filled even the largest locks in the Seaway system, leaving a mere matter of inches between the hull sides and the lock walls. Upon its arrival at Toronto, a special reception was held on board. Local newspaper and television reporters attended and were amazed by the scale of the vessel and astounded when they were told that during her entry to the harbour, there had been only 8½ inches of water between the keel and the harbour bottom.

Some two weeks later, another ship, the *Bolina*, gained some less pleasant notoriety when it delivered a shipment of 5,600 tonnes of Cuban sugar to the refinery. Upon inspection, it was found that more than 1,100 tonnes of the cargo were ruined by leakages of salt water into the hold. While the cause of the damage was under investigation, the ship's owners were requested to post a bond by the insurance company. The owners refused, resulting in the seizure of the vessel for possible sale in order to cover the losses incurred. Eventually, the required bond was posted

M. V. Federal Schelde.

and the vessel was allowed to leave, but the damaged cargo was totally unfit for refining and had to be taken away by trucks for off-site disposal.

In the final month of the year, the extensively considered and equally extensively delayed announcement of the initiation of an H.F.C.S. production facility at London, Ontario, was made on December 19, under the joint control of Redpath Sugars Ltd. and John Labatt Ltd. at an estimated cost of $60 million.

Although it was not officially given its new corporate name, Zymaize Inc., for some months, it was hoped this new venture would become a major source of income for the company and retain a large percentage of the market within the corporate group a portion that would otherwise be lost entirely if sugar prices escalated or competitors developed an H.F.C.S. facility first.

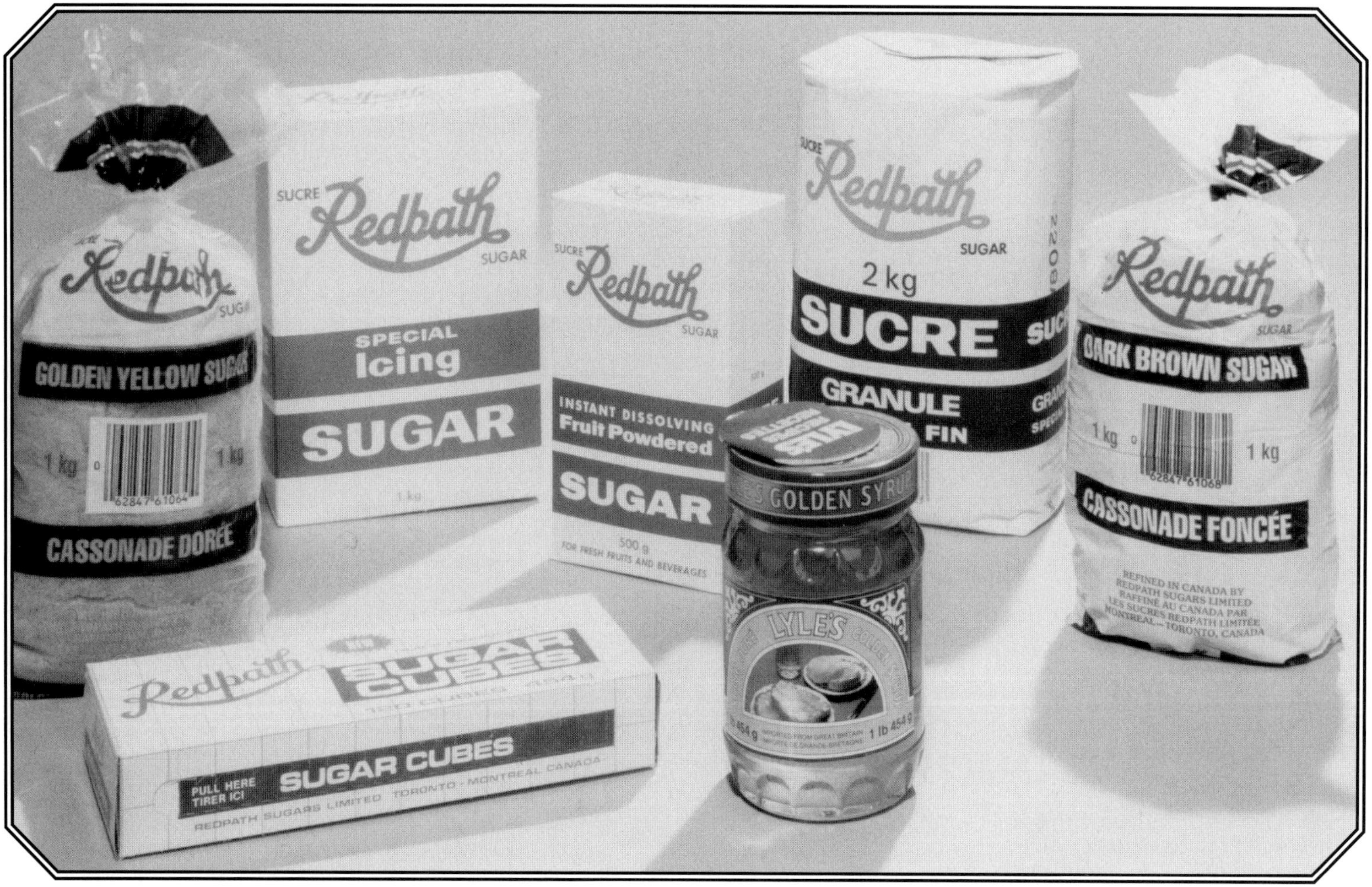
Redpath
1 kg
1 kg
CASSONADE DORÉE
SUCRE Redpath SUGAR
SPECIAL
Icing
SUGAR
SUCRE Redpath SUGAR
INSTANT DISSOLVING
Fruit Powdered
SUGAR
500 g
FOR FRESH FRUITS AND BEVERAGES
SUCRE Redpath SUGAR
2 kg
SUCRE
GRANULE
FIN
Redpath SUGAR
1 kg
1 kg
CASSONADE FONCÉE
REFINED IN CANADA BY
REDPATH SUGARS LIMITED
RAFFINÉ AU CANADA PAR
LES SUCRES REDPATH LIMITÉE
MONTREAL – TORONTO, CANADA
Redpath
SUGAR CUBES
PULL HERE
TIRER ICI
SUGAR CUBES
REDPATH SUGARS LIMITED TORONTO - MONTREAL CANADA
GOLDEN SYRU
LYLE'S
1 lb 454 g

CHAPTER THIRTEEN

Winners and Losers

The calendar year of 1978 began well for Redpath Sugars Ltd. on the technical side as a new system was brought on line at the Toronto refinery. This was the in-line liquid blending system, which was the first of its kind in Canada and represented a significant improvement for the mixing of various types of syrups to supply individual customer's orders. On the business side too, positive factors predominated as Cartier Sugar made known its willingness to merge with Redpath Sugars Ltd. The only remaining hurdle was the government and its Foreign Investment Review Agency followed by the Combines board, either of which could veto the proposed sale and force Redpath to reconsider its options regarding the continuation of production at its two refineries. It was perhaps on the legal side, however, that matters were somewhat less satisfactory, as on January 23, the Crown's argument in the long-awaited taxation case began with a lengthy and complicated dissertation of its version of events. It was fully expected that this case would require several sittings to complete, but no one had foreseen that the prosecution's case alone would be interspersed with a series of long adjournments that prevented the defence from presenting its case until the following year.

In March, the other outstanding legal question, the appeal of the Combines acquittal by the government, came to a head. The Court of Appeal confirmed the acquittal of the three sugar companies on charges of conspiring to enhance unreasonably the price of sugar but reversed the lower court's decision to acquit the companies on the second charge of conspiring to unduly lessen competition. The sugar companies were now left in grave danger of being held in breach of the Order of Prohibition issued in the 1960s and immediately decided to take the matter to its final conclusion in the Supreme Court of Canada.

At the larger corporate level, Redpath Industries Ltd. was experiencing a mixed financial year as revenues from its more successful corporate elements were drained by the high level of alteration costs and financial losses related to the R.S. & S. modernization in Yonkers, New York. This led to a discussion about the availability of funds to invest in the joint project for H.F.C.S. with John Labatt Ltd. By July, R.I.L. was on the point of withdrawing from the project but as the Labatt's group indicated its determination to proceed with or without Redpath involvement, it was realized that the choices were to risk a financial loss by investing in the project or be certain of future financial losses once the project came on line and began to attract business away from sugar. Therefore the approval was given for construction to begin in October with completion scheduled for August 1980.

Also in July 1979, the possibility of a merger with Cartier Sugar was brought forward in meetings with the F.I.R.A., who raised the question of Tate & Lyle's majority shareholding within R.I.L. as the main objection to approval of the merger. It was therefore suggested by the government that Tate & Lyle should reduce its holdings below 50%, at which time approval could be more easily granted. Cartier Sugar responded by calling for the proposed reduction to take place immediately, as it wanted to conclude a quick sale. But for Redpath and Tate & Lyle, the matter held more serious questions, and they called for a deferment of any final decision until the consequences of such an action were reviewed. This was approved and things were put on hold until September when Cartier advised the company that it no longer held itself committed to the agreement previously negotiated but that it was willing to re-open negotiations when the matter of the majority shareholding by Tate & Lyle was resolved. Redpath representatives now discussed the situation with the F.I.R.A. officials, who recognized the need for the merger and agreed to recommend to the Minister of Industry, Trade and Commerce that a final approval be granted as soon as possible.

In October, the Combines case took centre stage once again when the Superior Court implemented fines of $750,000 on each of the three sugar companies involved. This led to Atlantic, St. Lawrence, and Redpath Industries Ltd. expanding their appeal to the Supreme Court not only for the nature of the judgement but also for the size of the penalty. Fortunately, the Superior Court rendered a verdict that payment of the money in question would be deferred until the Supreme Court decision was finally made.

By the end of the year, the continuing level of expenditures linked to Refined Syrups and Sugars Inc. had reduced the net income for Redpath Industries Ltd. by almost 50%. However, the shareholders' dividends were maintained and even enlarged slightly due to the prior recognition of this drain during the conversion of the Yonkers refinery and the making of appropriate financial arrangements to avoid reducing the corporate dividend.

Meanwhile within Redpath Sugars Ltd., the increasing growth of industrial business in the Ontario market made it essential that a closer maintenance of company-customer relationships be established. Therefore a restructuring of the head office functions was decided upon with the establishment of a Western Division and an Eastern Division, each based upon its own refinery with its separate group of chemists, marketing specialists, personnel, staff, and production management. The Eastern Division was to be supervised by G. Bazinet, while E.V. Burgess took on the position of Vice-President and General Manager for the Western Division.

At the Annual General Meeting for R.I.L., which took place on February 27, 1979, the current state of the corporation was reviewed by Neil Shaw. It showed that each element of the corporate portfolio had worked well and achieved mechanically all that it was designed to do. Nevertheless, prevailing conditions of extreme competition in a depressed market had led to an overall fall in the economic indicators, prompting a considerable rethinking on the part of the organization to determine its plans for the future. For example, the realities facing Redpath Sugars Ltd. included:

- overcapacity within the sugar producing industry of eastern Canada,
- the virtual elimination of Canadian sugar exports to the U.S. market, while U.S. products still had easy access to the Canadian market,
- the certainty of a shrinking sugar market with the development of H.F.C.S. production,
- the negative connotations that the excess costs of modernization at R.S. & S. were causing on the Board, which spilled over to Redpath Sugar Ltd.,
- the ending of the Ivory Coast project with no significant or confirmed developments elsewhere,
- the negative attitude of the federal authorities towards Tate & Lyle's majority shareholding in R.I.L., and the subsequent objections raised in any proposal made by Redpath Sugars Ltd. to acquire other sugar interests.

Overall, therefore, this period represented a time for stringent cost-cutting measures; some within the company saw the funding of the nearly complete sugar museum at the Toronto refinery as a waste of space, time, and money. Fortunately (for this author at least), Mr. Shaw and a number of the senior executives recognized the role such a facility could have as a front-line representative to the public on behalf of the corporation. It would be a centre for the dissemination of information and facts to counter the growing flood of anti-sugar "health" publications that blamed sugar for causing everything from migraines to athlete's foot, from hyperactivity to criminal behaviour (all of which were later to be shown by proper independent scientific studies to be completely without foundation).

It was therefore decided to complete the museum, and on April 18, Neil Shaw and Toronto Mayor John Sewell officially declared the Redpath Sugar Museum open to the public by breaking a sugar loaf on the museum's loaf breaker in front of a crowd of employees, invited guests, and press. Also premiered at this event was the new corporate movie entitled "Raising Cane," which covered both the production technology of sugar refining and latest factual information on sugar and nutrition.

As a sideline, it might also be mentioned that since its opening the museum has served not only the local population but also has been visited by tourists from around the world; more importantly, it has become a standard element in the educational curriculum of many regional schools, who use its multifaceted tours to introduce a wide spectrum of topics to their students.

Meanwhile, for the corporation proper, the continuing drains upon the financial resources created a situation that necessitated a complete re-evaluation of all elements and divisions and their contributions to the common pool of investments. During the next few months, various propositions and plans were considered so that by September, certain definitive measures were concluded. Within the Construction Materials Division of R.I.L., most of the subsidiaries had rising revenues except for London Plastics Machinery, which was subsequently sold off. Likewise, the Packaging Division's returns were substantially better than in previous years, so it was slated for future investment.

For the Agro-Industrial Division, however, things were not so bright as the separate identities of Spraycool Systems Ltd., Comtrad Ltd., and Canadian Mouldings Ltd. were amalgamated on September 8 under a new title of Redpath

Holdings Ltd., which was designed to cut costs of administration.

At Redpath Sugars Ltd. the critical decision now had to be made about the attempt to maintain two refineries in the face of extreme market competition and projected shrinkage of market shares. Many hours of heated debate took place within the boardroom over which of the two plants should be sacrificed. Eventually the announcement was made on Thursday, September 27, 1979, that the company would close its sugar refining and packaging operations at the Montreal plant by January 1980.

The employees at all Redpath facilities were simultaneously notified of this decision at special meetings held at 9 a.m. on the twenty-seventh. At the Montreal session, the President, Mr. McEwen, had the difficult job of announcing the end of 125 years of production at the Lachine Canal site. As might be expected, there was a high level of emotion resulting from the meeting, but all the employees were given assurances that a co-ordinated campaign would be made to re-locate or re-employ within other occupations those employees made redundant. Sadly, the announcement of the closure was presented by elements of the provincial press as an anti-French exodus. Fortunately in the remainder of the media and in the business community at large, the realities of this unhappy measure were recognized as the natural consequence of the current economic climate and those who portrayed it otherwise were left to find other targets for their pens.

Shortly afterwards, company employees in Toronto were jolted out of their normal routines when on November 10, a massive freight train derailment occurred in the Toronto suburb of Mississauga. Fears of a toxic gas leak from

Views of the Montreal refinery in 1978, shortly before its permanent closure.

the de-railed tanker cars forced a widespread evacuation of the surrounding areas, disrupting social and business life for several days. Numerous employees of Redpath Sugars Ltd., Redpath Industries Ltd., and C.B. Packaging Ltd. were forced to leave their homes at a moment's notice and live with friends and relatives or in hotels with little in the way of extra clothes or even a spare toothbrush, creating a more casual appearance for some employees during the period of the emergency. For those employees of Daymond Ltd., this period also imposed an unexpected break from work as their office and plant were inside the off-limits area and were closed under police orders. Fortunately, the explosions and toxic clouds that were forecast by the media did not materialize and once the area was declared safe, life returned to normal.

The following month the protracted issue of the Combines case reached its jurisdictional climax on December 10, 1979, in a three-day hearing of the Supreme Court of Canada. Unfortunately, the court decided to defer its rendering of a verdict until after the Christmas recess and so the company was left once again to wait upon others to decide its future.

With the arrival of the New Year and the physical shutting down of production at the Montreal refinery as of January 27, 1980, plans were formulated for the removal of as much useable equipment as possible. It was then to be transferred to Toronto, where it would be either installed to increase the range and scope of production or held for use as spare parts. This naturally led to an increase in general activity at the Toronto refinery in preparation for the arrival of the machinery. In the office area, it was recognized that unless additional space were somehow created to house the influx of office personnel from Montreal, the working conditions would become distinctly crowded. As a result, plans were made for building an entirely new wing on the west side of the refinery that would accommodate both sets of staff comfortably as well as provide various business and social facilities more in keeping with the standards of the 1980s.

Back in Quebec, the costs of closing the refinery were totalled up and revealed the following:

Net book value of redundant refinery plant & equipment	$4.1 million
Related costs, including employee severance packages	$4.7 million
Less Income Tax recovery	$3.7 million
Total incurred losses from refinery closure	$5.1 million

Let Redpath Sweeten It

The demolition of the Montreal refinery.

This substantial figure, when applied to the year's accounts, resulted in R.I.L. recording a net loss for the year of $330,000 as opposed to the previous year's profit of $4.7 million. This naturally led to some strong questioning of the Board by the shareholders at the next Annual General Meeting. Mr. Shaw answered that this extraordinary loss was a singular occurrence that would not need to be repeated now that Redpath Sugars Ltd. was in the same position as its competitors regarding production facilities.

Following this public meeting, the Board met to discuss ways in which the company could be developed for the benefit of its shareholders without having to suffer the repeated scrutiny of F.I.R.A. and its possible veto of corporate purchases. After much discussion, it was agreed that the only reliable solution to the problem as long as the current restrictions remained was for Tate & Lyle to reduce its holdings in R.I.L. Therefore a plan was drawn up for a two-stage reduction, first by immediately dropping Tate & Lyle's portion from the current 56% to 50.99%, with a future drop to below 50% in the next few years to qualify Redpath Industries for re-classification under F.I.R.A. rules.

By March the economies resulting from the closure of the Montreal refinery were beginning to show up in the figures of the corporation. Likewise, the other sugar-related elements of the R.I.L. portfolio seemed to be striking an upbeat note, with Comtrad reporting substantial gains on raw sugar trading due to the escalation of prices since late 1979. Even Refined Syrups and Sugars Inc. showed a significant improvement on previous periods by recording a profit. It was therefore only around the Zymaize project that any uncertainty lay because of delays in construction due to labour and material problems and the significant level of cost over-runs for the project as a whole.

On June 16, 1980, an incident occurred that at the time caused some frayed nerves but that in retrospect had an amusing side. The circumstances involved the M.V. *Presidente Allende*, which was delivering a cargo of Cuban sugar to the Toronto refinery. During the period of unloading, it was common policy for the ship's crew to undertake housekeeping maintenance and painting of various parts of the vessel. In line with this custom, the vessel's captain ordered the tall derricks of the ship's cranes to be re-painted with marine grade canary yellow paint. All went well with the actual painting, using a combination of paint brushes and high-pressure spray guns. Unfortunately, no one took into account the direction of the wind blowing that day, which took the excess particles of yellow paint and drifted them over the bow of the ship, across the main road, and into the main parking lot of the vehicle maintenance department of the Ontario Provincial Police. As if this was not bad enough, the department had just taken delivery of nearly 200 brand-new black and white cruisers, which were parked throughout the vehicle maintenance yard alongside the private automobiles of the various police officers and staff of the division. Over all of them the fine particles of paint descended, firmly adhering to every surface and creating an unusual if not artistic effect, but one that was obviously not welcomed by the vehicles' owners. As one individual put it, "It looked like the cars had caught a dose of the dreaded Lurgi plague." As might be expected, there was a hue and cry over the incident and to ensure that the Cuban authorities would reimburse the O.P.P. for the complete stripping and repainting of the damaged vehicles, the Ontario Attorney General impounded the vessel until a

$150,000 bond was posted. Fortunately, while Redpath's was the scene of the incident, no actual responsibility or blame was attached to the company and the incident passed into the folklore of the site.

The following month on July 18, 1980, Mr. Justice Pigeon pronounced the verdict of the Supreme Court over the Combines case. Much to the joy of the sugar industry, it overturned the judgement of the Appeals court and declared the companies not guilty on both counts. Breathing a collective sigh of relief, the Atlantic, St. Lawrence, and Redpath sugar companies could now resume their business dealings without this particular black cloud hanging over them. However, it was also recognized that there was a definite need to develop a standards and procedures agreement to ensure that no such difficulties re-occurred.

Two weeks later, another major announcement was made that affected the corporation when Neil Shaw was made Group Managing Director of Tate & Lyle. This necessitated his moving to the United Kingdom to take up his new responsibilities. Although he retained the status of President of Redpath Industries Ltd. for a short time afterwards, it was recognized that a new President would be required in the longer term if the Tate & Lyle "arm's-length" corporate policy was to be properly maintained.

By October 1980, although the warehousing and trucking elements of the company's operations in Montreal had been maintained at the old Montreal refinery site, it was recognized that this was not the best location for either the maintenance of the company's vehicles nor for the efficient distribution of the various product lines. Therefore it was decided to initiate a detailed study to find the optimum location to which these facilities could be relocated within the Montreal area. The object was to serve the customers better while cutting the company's costs and freeing up the land occupied by the old refinery for future redevelopment or sale.

Later that same month, the world price of raw sugar, which had been steadily increasing since the latter part of the previous year, reached a peak of $1,140 per tonne. This was due to several factors which included:
- a major crop failure for sugar cane in Cuba,
- poor beet crops in the U.S.S.R. and China, which forced them to seek sources of sugar other than their usual main supplier, Cuba,
- major purchases of raw sugar by Mexico and India, countries which traditionally had been net exporters of raw sugar.

But most important and influential in this price rise was the concurrent period of extreme speculation on the world's gold markets. Gold prices had risen to such an extent that only the biggest "players" could afford to continue in that commodity, while the more moderate speculators turned to other commodities, including sugar, for investment. This excess demand, coupled with the reduced supplies of 1980, combined to elevate raw sugar prices to levels close to those experienced in 1974. In the refined sugar market, this was reflected in prices around $1,355 per metric tonne in October compared to $686 in January 1980 and $373 in January 1979.

With prices at this level, it was to be expected that some customers would cut back on their purchases or defer deliveries in hopes of better prices ahead. However, once the peak was past and prices fell as quickly as they had risen, a second effect was seen from customers who had signed long-term contracts when prices had begun to rise in 1980 and who had gained the advantages of fixed prices during the peak months. Some of these now repudiated their deals or refused to accept deliveries on their contracts as prices were now below their contracted rates. In most cases, while renegotiated purchasing arrangements were worked out, in one or two instances matters eventually had to be resolved by legal action.

At the conclusion of the year, the Annual Report showed that overall the financial status of the corporation had improved markedly and that, as predicted, the losses on the closure of Montreal had no significant effect, which left the company with a net income of $13.1 million. However, within each sector of the corporate portfolio, the individual returns and contributions varied substantially, beginning a new cycle of considerations by the Board of prospects for acquisition while reducing and selling off those elements that failed to measure up or provide a sufficient return.

High on the list of concerns for the group was the continued escalation of costs associated with the Zymaize project, which had now exceeded $76 million without any production having commenced. Nor was production likely to begin in the immediate future due to technical difficulties. In addition, the site development team indicated that a further investment might be required to allow for the installation of a system to produce a higher grade syrup that could be sold for use in soft drinks. These facts caused the Redpath leadership grave misgivings about the prospects for success, especially when sugar prices were falling from their previous year's peak, making H.F.C.S. a financially less attractive product to potential customers.

Meanwhile within the regular sugar market, Redpath Sugars' Toronto refinery was experiencing a period of intense activity as various pieces of machinery from Montreal were integrated into the production system. One area that was not being integrated, however, was the brown sugar making machinery, which had been specifically established and exclusively maintained at Montreal right up to the date of its closure. Now with Montreal closed, the initial promise of alterations to the Toronto refinery to allow brown sugar production in the manner of Montreal had met some technical difficulties. In the interim, a deal had been arranged with St. Lawrence Sugar to manufacture brown sugar for Redpath, but experience had shown that this was an unreliable source and so, spurred on by the calls of E.V. Burgess, experiments were conducted by a joint team of Jan Kuzmicz (the Toronto Process Manager), Theresa Balogh (Chief Chemist), and Ralph Tulloch (Engineering Manager) to develop a new system for making brown sugar without resorting to the methods used in Montreal. After several weeks of hand-mixed experiments and hundreds of taste tests, the team was still having difficulties finding the proper proportions of white sugar and syrups for blending when it was suggested that matters might be speeded up if they could use a blender. The next day and for some time afterwards, the refinery laboratory resembled something like a cross between a mad professor's laboratory and a hotel kitchen, as batch after batch of sugar was mixed using Theresa's blending machine. Once these initial trials were complete, the question was whether it could be duplicated at an industrial level. Fortunately, Ralph Tulloch had contacts with an outside company with equipment that could be used to finalize the experiment. Following the successful development of the new process, appropriate machinery was purchased and installed in the packaging building of the Toronto refinery for the future production of all the brown sugars sold by Redpath. Eventually, this new technology became something of an industry standard, and several companies in the United States picked up licences to repeat the Redpath success in their own plants. For once, it can truly be said that necessity was the mother of invention.

Meanwhile at the other end of the production line, the raw sugar purchasing department concluded that under the present system of always holding a base stock for refining, the quantity that had been established for the use of two refineries was far greater than that required for the one remaining refinery, even allowing for the expansion of production at Toronto to compensate for the closure of Montreal. Following consultation, the Board approved the reduction of the base stock by 7,000 metric tonnes, a move that subsequently added $2.9 million to the company's income.

In May 1981, Neil Shaw transferred fully to T & L and therefore officially resigned as President and Chief Executive Officer of Redpath Industries Ltd. in favour of L.R. (Red) Wilson, who had recently served as Deputy Minister of Industry and Tourism for Ontario. Mr. Wilson now joined the ranks of the company's presidents and learned very quickly what it was like to be back in the world of business, for the following month, news broke that Cartier Sugar was being bought out by Atlantic Sugar Ltd.

Lynton R. Wilson

and was scheduled for closure in the immediate future. In view of the repeated attempts by Redpath Sugars Ltd. to acquire Cartier Sugar and the equally repeated impediments applied by the government bureaucracy which prevented just such a merger, to see Cartier bought by Redpath's main competitor without let or hindrance was somewhat galling. However, in balance was the fact that Redpath Sugars had gained by the reduction of overcapacity in the eastern sugar market without having been forced to spend its own money to do so, while production at the Toronto refinery could be increased to reduce the per-unit costs of production.

Later in the summer months, the Zymaize project engineers confirmed their earlier call for additional capital to expand the production range of the still unfinished plant in London. Faced with the dilemma of either investing and hoping to recover the costs in the long term or bailing out of this expensive enterprise and guaranteeing to lose money on the deal, the Board agreed to press on with the plant. When the project finally did begin production in August 1981, the technology proved to be well up to expectations and the quality of the product was everything it was required to be. But the simple fact remained that the rising sugar prices that had encouraged the development of H.F.C.S. in the first place were no longer part of the Canadian market, and the current state of falling sugar values would act as a disincentive to major food manufacturers to switch to H.F.C.S. when sugar remained the cheaper sweetener.

At the end of the financial year, Zymaize was reported to have made a loss of $712,000 for its first month of active production.

The time had now come for a serious re-evaluation of this and all other elements of the Redpath Industries Ltd. group that were draining the corporation of its finances. Therefore, in October, R.I.L. re-aligned its corporate structure by amalgamating with its principal subsidiaries into one single company under the name of R.I.L., which now consisted of three major divisions:

SWEETENERS DIVISION made up of Redpath Sugars, Zymaize Co., and Refined Syrups & Sugars (now renamed Refined Sugars Inc. or R.S.I.).

CONSTRUCTION MATERIALS DIVISION consisting of Daymond, Certain-Teed/Daymond, Multi-Fittings, Multi-Fittings (U.S.A.), and Gienow.

PACKAGING DIVISION made up of C.B./Holway Packaging and Merry Packaging.

The remaining corporate element of Seaway Insurance Ltd. was absorbed into the structure of Redpath Industries Ltd.

Within the first three months of 1982, general raw sugar prices fell as world supplies increased. For Redpath Sugars, this was considered good news but for Zymaize it was nothing short of a disaster as major customers such as Coca-Cola and Pepsi-Cola put off their plans to switch from liquid sugar to H.F.C.S. Likewise in the non-sugar related sectors of the corporation, the ongoing national economic recession and high interest rates created a major downturn in the construction industry. This led to a reduced demand for products made by Daymond, Multi-Fittings, and especially Gienow, which had seen its sales figures plummet by more than 35% during the year. By April, the half-yearly report for the corporation showed an after-tax loss of $2.7 million. This bad news was then added to with the release of figures showing that an earlier joint agreement between Tate & Lyle and Redpath Sugars Ltd. for the purchase of set volumes from Swaziland over a five-year period had become a major financial loss. These facts forced the Board to reduce the dividend by 50%, much to the displeasure of the shareholders.

In early May, the U.S. government reacted to the current spate of falling prices by enacting legislation imposing new and reduced quotas for imports, while fees and duties were raised. This created an artificially high price for sugar and protected the U.S. domestic sugar-growing industry. Unfortunately for those sugar companies who relied upon imported raw sugar for their supplies, such as R.S.I., this new legislation produced significant additional costs for their production.

Nor was Redpath Sugars immune to this new legislation as it found its access to the U.S. market increasingly cut off. Anxious to find some alternative source of sales, a loophole was found to exist in the regulations allowing the importation of mixtures of sucrose and fructose or sucrose and dextrose as distinct new products outside the highly restrictive quota available for sucrose alone.

Steps were immediately taken to develop this new line and ship it into the United States, where it was eagerly received by food manufacturers because it was priced substantially below the U.S. statutory support price for regular sugar. Over the next few months, the Toronto refinery worked at or near its capacity output, producing both regular sugar and various blends for exports. This represented one of the few brighter elements of what was turning out to be a financially disastrous year for R.I.L. as losses were reported throughout the packaging and construction materials divisions, but above these was the ongoing drain of vital funds through the Zymaize plant. There, production breakdowns and technical difficulties were only part of the problem as the real operating costs turned out to be more than double those quoted in the original estimates.

All hopes of making a short-term or even mid-term profit from this project were now well and truly sunk, and the R.I.L. Board saw no possibility of continuing to pour money into the venture in the vague hope that some day in the future sugar prices would rise and remain high enough to allow a recovery of the investment. Therefore no other option seemed to be available to the Board but to reduce its losses by selling off its part ownership as soon as possible. Fortunately, its partner, John Labatt Ltd., did not raise any significant objections to the sale, and a search was begun to find a suitable buyer for the Redpath portion of Zymaize.

By the end of September, the corporate accounts revealed that Redpath Industries Ltd. had suffered a net loss of $448,000, although both Redpath Sugars and Refined Sugars Inc. had each made material improvements in their individual returns.

In the other sectors, however, matters remained serious if not grave, and rationalization was implemented for the group by selling off the corporation's 75% interest in MSV/Daymond Ltd. to the minority shareholder, while negotiations were begun for the disposal of Gienow by the end of the calendar year.

To conclude the year on a legal note – on December 14, 1982, the tax evasion case finally came to trial at the Court of Sessions of the Peace, District of Montreal, following months of written and verbal submissions, petitions, claims, and counter-claims. In the end, the corporation was found not guilty. Under normal circumstances this would have been the end of the issue. Surprisingly, and one might even say suspiciously, following consultation with higher authorities in Ottawa, the Crown prosecutor filed an appeal against the judgement forcing the company into yet more months of expenditures of manpower and legal costs in order to clear its name.

Fortunately for the corporation, the new year of 1983 brought with it an apparent turnaround in the Canadian economy that filtered its way down to the various elements of the corporate portfolio. Redpath Sugars, in particular, benefited, with its sales being recorded as well above projections due to the opportunity provided by the U.S. blends issue. It was recognized, however, that this situation was unlikely to last as the U.S. refiners were increasingly calling for closure of the U.S. border to Canadian-made sugar and blends of every type.

Domestically, too, competitive forces were on the increase as St. Lawrence and Atlantic Sugars responded to a new agreement between Redpath Sugars and the Quebec Sugar Refinery (for Redpath to accept raw beet sugar, refine it, and package it for Q.S.R. at a discounted price), by initiating a price war that lasted for some weeks and spread from Montreal to the adjacent sales regions of Ontario and the Maritimes.

As the year progressed, the financial state of R.I.L.

improved with the sale of Gienow and prospects of a similar agreement for the Holway Packaging facility in Toronto in the near future. However, the question of Zymaize still remained, and by now the debts of the facility exceeded $95 million, of which 50% was underwritten by R.I.L. This was a debt load that could not be maintained if the remainder of the corporation was to prosper. Fortunately it was agreed that John Labatt Ltd. would purchase the holdings of Redpath Industries in Zymaize and allow R.I.L. to bow out. Over the years since its inception, the total costs to Redpath Industries Ltd. were now estimated at over $62.5 million, and even allowing for returns on the sale plus a tax recovery, the bottom line still showed that there would be a net loss on the project in excess of $25 million, a sad end to what had appeared to be a bright prospect for the company.

In the sugar field, too, another bright prospect faded when U.S. President Ronald Reagan made a proclamation in which his government banned all imports of Canadian-made sugar blends and in addition removed all tariffs and quotas on sugar being imported into the United States for re-export. This immediately altered the whole complexion of the Canadian sugar market as the lucrative export sector into the United States was cut off except for the earlier highly restrictive quota system, while U.S. refiners were actively subsidized by their government to push sugar into Canada. At the insistence of the various refining interests in Canada, Mr. Thompson, the head of the Canadian Sugar Institute, was instructed to take the Canadian refiners' case that the restrictions were both unnecessary and unfair before the International Trade Commission in Washington and to bring the matter to the attention of the Canadian anti-dumping tribunal in Ottawa if the expected flood of U.S. sugar products into Canada took place.

By the end of the year, the various financial measures designed to achieve the consolidation of the corporation had been generally completed; as a result, the financial statements of R.I.L. showed the group to be in the black once again, due principally to the turnaround in the construction industry. Dividends were raised from 15 cents to 20 cents per share and a totally new employee benefit was introduced in the form of an employee stock purchase plan. While these reports appeared fine on paper, the fact remained that in its own environment Redpath Sugars was now in a position of fighting an economic battle on two fronts. The first was with the U.S. imports, which were growing at a disturbing rate and threatening the future margins for sales, and the second was with its main Canadian rival, Atlantic Sugar Ltd., who had just completed the purchase of the Oshawa Westcane refinery, thus shutting out Redpath from much of the retail grocery market held by that company.

Construction of the new office wing for the Toronto refinery.

210

CHAPTER FOURTEEN

Full Circle

By March 1984, the financial outlook for Redpath Industries Ltd. showed a sharp improvement over the previous year, due mainly to the elimination of losses from the Zymaize operations. This allowed the dividend to be raised and effectively signalled an end to the earlier disastrous period when revenues had been cut and shares had fallen from $17 to less than $7 per share. In fact, the current price was at $24 per share, reflecting the strong confidence of the investment market in the company's future and causing some behind-the-scenes discussion about the need for a shares split if the trend continued.

In May the Department of Revenue in Ottawa responded to the calls of the Canadian sugar industry for action against the flood of U.S. sugar. The department agreed that it would impose a dumping duty of 50% on the value of the sugar if it could be proved by the Canadian refiners that the dumping had caused "significant injury" to the domestic industry. This placed the burden of proof on the Canadian refiners and did nothing to curtail the current levels of imports or any future volumes until the case was "proved" to the government's satisfaction.

One event for the company during this month that had a distinctly more pleasant substance was the celebration held at the Toronto refinery to commemorate the 130th anniversary of the founding of the company and the 25th anniversary of the opening of the Toronto refinery. The main bag storage warehouse adjacent to the Redpath Sugar Museum was cleared and completely re-painted, then it was equipped with tables, a bar, seating, and a music sound system, to act as the main reception area for a six-day open-house celebration. Throughout the open house, customers, local dignitaries, employees, their families, and other invited guests were offered refreshments cooked by various members of the refinery staff and were given guided tours of the museum and the main refinery buildings. Entertainment

The 25th Anniversary celebrations at the Toronto refinery.

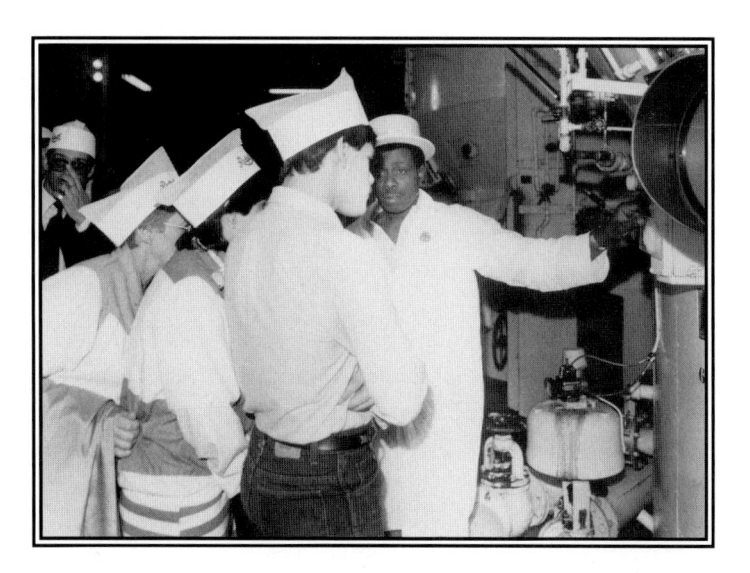

Views from the 25th Anniversary celebrations.

was provided by a troupe of jugglers and a military demonstration by a historical re-enactment group, the latter making the truck yard ring to the sound of marching feet and the crack of musket fire.

Shortly afterwards, a major sales opportunity arose for Redpath Sugars when the Quebec Sugar Refinery was unable to fulfil its commitments for sugar to the two largest grocery store chains in the province. This led to an immediate approach by Redpath sales and marketing representatives with offers to make up the Q.S.R. deficit, and, in the face of severe competition from the other Canadian sugar companies, acquired a substantial proportion of this windfall business for the company.

Legal matters came to the fore once again in June 1984, when the Crown's appeal of the lower court's verdict of not guilty in the taxation case was dismissed by the Superior Court and the government decided not to continue the matter in the Supreme Court. Over a decade had now passed since the original causes of this issue had been brought into question, and during that time several articles in various newspapers had erroneously pre-judged the issue and characterized the corporation as being guilty, prompting the company to demand retractions although the initial damage had already been done. Over half a million dollars had been spent in legal fees and countless hours of meetings and preparation of documents for submission had been required, none of which could be recovered.

While the motives behind the entire incident remained unidentified, some degree of suspicion now lay upon the governmental bureaucrats for their repeated and aggressive attacks upon the corporation. In fact, in his Annual Canada Tax Letter, Richard De Boo made the following independent pronouncement about the case:

That a prosecution was entertained in the first place is surprising. That it was actually pursued is astonishing. And having lost in the first instance, for the Crown to have appealed, in the face of the findings by the trial judge, is a matter which bears serious attention by both government and the public.

A second legal issue came up the following month when the anti-dumping tribunal in Ottawa ruled that despite the large volumes of U.S. sugar being pushed onto the Canadian market using U.S. government drawbacks to undercut the Canadian producers, it did not amount to a "significant" injury and so it disallowed the claim. Shocked by this judgement in the face of what was considered clear evidence to the contrary, the industry as a whole undertook an appeal of this decision.

The busy year continued in August when the Thames sailing barge *Ethel* returned to Toronto from an extended period of acting as a charter vessel in the Caribbean. The original plan had been to use her during the earlier summer months and participate in the tall ships celebration in June; however, her arrival had been delayed due to repair work on her hull. The company had been warned that since her sale by Tate & Lyle following her last visit, the S.B. *Ethel* had not been maintained in the manner of her previous owners, but no one was prepared for the virtual derelict that appeared out of the early morning mist and tied up alongside the refinery. I was made responsible for her preparation to receive guests for sailing tours only three days later and was initially at a loss to comprehend how this "scow" could be readied in time. Fortunately, with the total support and co-operation of the management and staff of several departments in the refinery, round-the-clock teams of workers scraped, de-bugged, sanded, painted, and polished every inch of the "old girl" until she once again appeared presentable. As scheduled, three days later, with paint still slightly tacky to the touch in some spots, the S.B. *Ethel* set sail with her first of several complements of guests — much to the relief and satisfaction of myself and all those who worked on her.

Another notable event of this time occurred in September when Redpath Sugars participated in the state visit to Toronto by Pope John Paul II. What was unusual was the fact that instead of providing sugar for the event as had been done for Expo 67 and the Montreal Olympics in 1976, Redpath Sugars provided hot water! The story behind this situation began earlier in the year when M. Davidson, the former Vice-President of Redpath Sugar and retired President of the Canadian Sugar Institute, approached the company with a request to use a number of the liquid sugar tankers as mobile hot water reservoirs for the making of hot beverages and first-aid services during the mass. Following discussions, approval was given and on the afternoon of September 14, thirteen liquid sugar tankers, filled with a total of 50,000 gallons of hot water, were escorted by police motorcycles in a convoy to the site of the mass at Downsview airfield in the north end of Toronto. As a result of this participation, the seventeen food concession tents were able to brew a total of 69,700 cups of tea and coffee every hour, which, on the cold and wet Saturday of the papal mass, was welcomed by the hundreds of thousands of people in the congregation.

Back on the business front, Redpath Sugars found itself in a position to achieve the purchase of St. Lawrence Sugar. Unfortunately, any prospective acquisition would require F.I.R.A. approval and therefore R.I.L. could only make a conditional offer subject to F.I.R.A. review. The owners of St. Lawrence Sugar found this conditional clause unacceptable as they wanted to conclude a sale as soon as possible. Despite negotiations, the St. Lawrence Sugar representatives would not relent in their position. This now allowed Atlantic Sugars Ltd. to place before St. Lawrence, a lower purchase offer but without the unwelcome pre-condition of obtaining F.I.R.A. approval. Deciding that "a bird (or a bid) in the hand etc." St. Lawrence Sugar accepted the Atlantic Sugars offer and so notified Redpath Sugars. This was a particularly difficult loss for Redpath for two reasons. First, it meant that in the eastern Canada market, the only two effective competitors were Redpath and Atlantic, with the latter holding substantially more of the regional production capacity and retail market share. Second, ever since the closure of the Redpath refinery in Montreal in 1980, the company had been obtaining sugar in an exchange agreement with St. Lawrence. With this new takeover, the opportunity to exchange was effectively ended and the need to have a main distribution centre for the Montreal area became a priority. As a result of earlier studies, a building was purchased in the northwestern end of the island of Montreal immediately adjacent to the main Trans-Canada Highway. The structure was then converted for use as a liquid and bulk granular sugar depot and distribution centre.

At the larger corporate level, Redpath Industries Ltd. undertook a major restructuring of its main non-sugar divisions by selling its holdings in the agricultural piping sector of Daymond in Canada and the assets of Certain-Teed/Daymond in the United States. It also disposed of its entire packaging capacity through the sale of C.B. Packaging and Merry Packaging.

Using the accumulated funds from its sales, R.I.L. now invested in two new purchases. The first was Krayloy Products Inc., a small electrical conduit fittings manufacturer in San Fernando, California. The second was substantially larger, however, and represented a major jump in the "league" of business acquisitions by R.I.L. The corporation in question was Donlee Manufacturing Industries Ltd., which was in itself a conglomerate of specialized companies spread across North America. For example, Donlee Manufacturing Industries Ltd. controlled Donlee Plastics (Toronto), Paramount Industries (Toronto), and Automotive Industries Inc. (Strasburg, Virginia), all of which produced fixtures for automobile manufacturers. It also consisted of Donlee Precision (Toronto), which specialized in precision

The new Montreal depot.

machined components for the Hydro, defence, nuclear, and aerospace industries; and General Gear Co. (Toronto), which produced gears and machined parts for various construction, forestry, mining, and machine tools industries.

At a cost of $44 million, this new venture represented a substantial change of direction for Redpath Industries Ltd. and confirmed the earlier decisions that the corporation would seek further diversification.

At the conclusion of this generally successful year, the Board was able to announce yet another raising of the dividend for shareholders. In addition, because of the formal acquisition of Donlee Manufacturing Industries Ltd. into the Construction Materials Division, this sector was re-classified as the Automotive, Industrial and Construction Products Division.

The year 1985 began badly for Redpath Sugars as negotiations between the company and its unions broke down and the unions called out their workers on strike. This stoppage eventually lasted five weeks, and although it did not reach the level of confrontation generated in the strike of 1971 there were strained moments on the picket line as non-unionized office staff and management were called upon to work in the refinery in an attempt to maintain a partial output of sugar.

Once the strike was settled, production quickly returned to normal and discussions now took place between R.I.L. and Tate & Lyle for future development plans. Attention was particularly given to the higher prices for sugar being maintained in the United States and the severe competition between various American sugar companies. Under these conditions, it was recognized that it might be possible to acquire refining capacity in the United States at a bargain price. Therefore it was agreed that together the two companies would make discreet enquiries for future purchases.

By the beginning of March, these enquiries had led to a proposal for the acquisition of Colonial Sugars Inc. in Mobile, Alabama. Similar negotiations were also underway for an entire series of sugar beet refineries run by the Great Western Sugar Co. of Dallas, Texas.

The story for this latter prospect had actually begun the previous year when Great Western was initially put up for sale by its owners, the silver speculators, Herbert and Nelson Hunt. They were desperately trying to liquidate assets in order to finance their main holdings, but no serious buyers took up the offer until Tate & Lyle made enquiries in February for the purchase of six Great Western beet processing plants located in Nebraska, Montana, and Wyoming. Since Redpath Industries Ltd. had experts in the beet industry still available, it was invited to provide a team of representatives to help assess the prospective acquisition. Following negotiations, a series of bids were made to acquire the assets of Great Western but each was met with rejection. Then suddenly, Great Western declared bankruptcy. When the R.I.L./Tate & Lyle negotiating team investigated this surprise move, they found that the bids made to Great Western had been withheld from its creditors for consideration. After some rapid negotiations, a new deal was struck and on March 28 a hearing was held before the bankruptcy court to authorize the sale of Great Western assets to Tate & Lyle/Redpath Industries Ltd. as a 50-50 joint venture. Following the approval of the courts, the final sale was formalized on April 3, 1985, and Redpath was back into beets.

During this same period, Redpath Sugars had been undergoing changes of its own, starting with the announcement by the U.S. government that food products containing even the smallest volume of sugar would now be classed under the established quotas applicable to sugar as a pure product. This not only effectively killed off the rising sales by Redpath to its major food manufacturing customers, but in addition reduced even further the time it would take to use up the annual quotas established for Canada to export to the United States.

On a more pleasant note, the company officially completed its new Montreal distribution centre in Ville St. Laurent and over the course of the next few months, various departments were transferred to this new location from the old refinery site while certain other functions were consolidated at the Toronto offices. This latter relocation also had the added result of precipitating a decision that had been pending for some time regarding the need to expand and modernize the office facilities at the Toronto refinery. Following approval, construction began on a completely new wing on the western side of the main refinery building to house executive offices, meeting rooms, a computer centre, various corporate departments and, most welcome of all, a new cafeteria to provide in-house freshly cooked meals instead of the pre-processed and ready-packed "food" available in the old cafeteria.

As the year progressed, Redpath Sugars continued as virtually the only sugar company in Canada able to claim it was running its refining operations at nearly full capacity. However, the growing volume of U.S. sugar being imported into Canada under the U.S. government's drawback and re-export scheme forced the Canadian refiners into an ever more constrained position, while appeals for Canadian government action to curb the clear damage to the domestic industry fell on deaf ears. It was now recognized that no help could be expected from that quarter, and the application to the Federal Court of Appeal was withdrawn pending a re-evaluation of action that could be taken under the current restrictions and one-way legislation applicable between Canada and the United States.

Meanwhile in the United States itself, the current significant difference between the U.S. support price of 20 cents per pound and the world market price of 3 cents per pound led to an unfortunate problem for Refined Sugars Inc. when certain other refiners and food processors were alleged to be engaged in the practice of purchasing raw sugar at the world price, ostensibly for processing and re-exportation, but in reality for the purpose of diverting it for sale within the United States at the higher U.S. support price; at the same time they were claiming the official export drawback payment using falsified papers. Because of this, the U.S. Customs authorities had initiated a general freeze on all drawbacks, without differentiating between those companies that had been involved in the dealings and those, like R.S.I., who were totally innocent of wrong-doing. Rumours now began to circulate that in retaliation and supposedly to offset the excess profit reaped by the illegal trading, the Customs authorities were planning to force all sugar refiners to export a volume equivalent to the falsified amounts out of their existing domestic stocks, thus incurring a huge financial loss. As this over-simplistic solution would penalize it, even though it was not implicated, R.S.I. went out of its way to offer the customs investigators every assistance, and it was hoped that Colonial Sugars would do the same. However, when U.S. government investigations relating to Colonial Sugars continued, both Redpath Industries Ltd.

and Tate & Lyle agreed to suspend negotiations until the matter was legally resolved one way or another.

At the end of the year, the 1985 Annual Report showed that net income was relatively unchanged from the year before but due to the high level of prices for the corporate shares prevailing for some time during 1984, it was decided to split the shares issue on a three-for-one basis. Other details included in the report were the fact that in October, Automotive Industries Inc., the U.S. subsidiary of Donlee, had acquired the operating assets of Texas Plastic Industries Inc. of Midland, Texas, a manufacturer of plastic injection moulded products. This now meant that the operating income from the Automotive, Industrial and Construction Products Division represented 56% of the year's total compared to only 17% the year before. To the shareholders, this figure showed clearly the determined direction the corporation was taking, and was confirmed by the statement of the Corporate President Mr. Wilson.

Redpath's basic objective is to provide its shareholders with sustainable growth and a consistent real return on their investment. As a result of ... restructuring, Redpath now has a base ... from its mature sugar business and internal growth potential from the remaining non-sugar operations.

In such an environment, it is not now surprising that the general accounts and minutes of various Board meetings show an increased tendency to be dominated by discussions over modernization and expansions for all of the automotive and machine parts facilities while, with the exception of two new silos for the Nebraska plant of the now renamed Western Sugar Co., few sugar-related expenditures are referenced throughout the remaining months of 1985 and into the first quarter of 1986.

On January 28, 1986, Quebec newspapers released a story that had been rumoured throughout the sugar industry for some time, concerning the sale of the provincially owned Quebec Sugar Refinery to Atlantic Sugar (now renamed Lantic Sugar Ltd.). Although this deal was not yet finalized, it was considered virtually assured, for Lantic had already stated its intention to close down the refining facility with the approval and co-operation of the provincial government. Meanwhile in western Canada, the beet growers of Manitoba and Alberta were calling for the establishment of a protectionist National Sugar Policy to boost Canadian sugar prices through subsidies to beet farmers and the imposition of strict quotas on the importing of cane sugar. All of this was a direct copy of legislation recently imposed by the U.S. authorities. Naturally this call was opposed by Redpath Sugars, as well as Lantic Sugar and to a lesser extent B.C. Sugar. Fortunately, the government was not overly keen to be seen as deliberately raising a staple food price to more than double its current rate or restricting the nation's consumers access to sugar supplies. Therefore in typical governmental fashion, a board of inquiry was set up to investigate the question and there the issue rested until later in the year.

April proved to be a busy month for the corporation as the Western Sugar Co. was able to negotiate a highly beneficial deal for the purchase of two more beet refineries at Greeley and Fort Morgan in Colorado. In Canada, Redpath Sugars entered into negotiations with two Canadian food companies for a prospective new blended product combining refined sugar with whole milk powder as an ingredient for chocolate and similar products. Finally for this period, the Quebec Sugar Refinery was officially acquired by Lantic, which gave them a total of 67% of the sugar market in eastern Canada.

In July, although business remained fairly uneventful in the Canadian market, south of the border, circumstances relating to Colonial Sugars required an immediate re-appraisal of the proposed purchase. The facts were that although the Grand Jury investigation had concluded it had insufficient evidence to indict Colonial Sugars on criminal charges, there was still the prospect of civil action outstanding. Furthermore financial changes in the U.S. sugar market and a new study of the assets of Colonial made its acquisition significantly less attractive. This led Tate & Lyle and Redpath Industries Ltd. to decide that unless Colonial Sugars accepted a lower offer for its facility, negotiations would be abandoned in favour of other possible options. In response Colonial Sugars did reject the new proposal and all consideration for its purchase was terminated.

At the conclusion of the year, the Annual Report outlined that a new purchase had just been included in the corporate structure. This was Arbour Plastic Products Inc. of Fremont, Ohio, a manufacturer of plastic fittings for automobiles. It also stated that the various oil and gas exploration projects that were no longer contributing significantly to the corporate bottom line had been disposed of.

With the start of 1987, Redpath Sugars received the unwelcome news that in order to finance its payments to the beet industry in western Canada, the federal government was unilaterally appropriating 50% of all premiums earned by the other Canadian sugar companies on exported sugar into the United States. This could certainly be called a situation of "robbing Peter to pay Paul" and led to some highly caustic responses from the majority of the Canadian refiners.

Meanwhile, Redpath Sugars continued with its programme of increasing the capacity and efficiency of its refinery to the point where it became the single most efficient plant for the production of sugar in North America. Redpath Industries Ltd., too, continued in its planned development of the corporation through acquisition and modernization at its individual locations, for a capital investment level on the year in excess of $36.5 million. These efforts yielded impressive returns, especially in those sectors related to the automobile industry, which recorded an increase in its revenues of almost 40%.

In the industrial and construction products area, the recent investments paid off with the development of new product lines, increased sales in the lucrative U.S. market, and the acquisition of a new company, H. & W. Building Products Inc. (renamed Heartland Building Products Inc.)

By the time of the publication of the 1987 Annual Report, Mr. Wilson was able to report to the shareholders satisfactory increases in revenues and incomes as well as the various acquisitions and expansions that had been undertaken throughout the year. However, one item that was deliberately not publicized was the ongoing development of a new and potentially revolutionary sugar-related product, which was to be called sucralose.

Discovered in 1976 through a joint research project run by Tate & Lyle and Queen Elizabeth College in London, England, sucralose was subsequently developed by Tate & Lyle's Research and Development branch as a non-calorie high-intensity sweetener achieved through modification of the natural sucrose molecule. This new substance had been submitted for governmental scrutiny to permit its future use in a wide range of foods and drinks and would represent a direct challenge to aspartame, which had dominated the low-calorie food market since the banning of saccharin and cyclamates earlier in the decade. Through a tri-partite arrangement involving Tate & Lyle, Johnson & Johnson, and Redpath Industries Ltd., this new product was to be brought into the market once various governmental approvals had been met. But until details were more advanced, this project retained something of a security blanket around it and so it was not included in this Annual Report.

Shortly afterwards, as part of the ongoing corporate development, it was recognized that the geographically dispersed facilities of sugar production within the group required some form of formalized co-ordination in their management systems. Therefore in addition to his responsibilities as President of Redpath Sugars and Vice-President of R.I.L., Murray McEwen was appointed to take responsibility for the corporation's sugar operations across North America.

In November 1987, the sugar cane refiners of Canada were again at the receiving end of discriminatory legislation when the U.S. Customs authorities ruled that for eligibility to qualify for the already restrictive quota for exports to the United States, the sugar product had to be derived from Canadian grown sources. This effectively eliminated all the cane refiners from supplying sugar into the United States, leaving only the two beet producing centres as technically eligible to sell to the U.S. market. But even there, things were not as opportune as might be supposed as the new United States Farm Bill reduced the proposed 1988 quota for imports by over 250,000 tonnes.

With the arrival of 1988, the three segments of sugar production within R.I.L. each had its own difficulties to contend with.

At Refined Sugars Inc. the recently completed alterations now permitted the production of a complete line of specialty sugars for the U.S. retail market. Unfortunately, it was also recognized that this extra production capacity would be wasted unless market conditions improved enough to allow R.S.I. to eliminate its current high levels of discounts in order to maintain its sales. Furthermore surveys had indicated that despite extensive promotion, the R.S.I. product lines were not achieving sufficient market recognition or brand loyalty from customers in the face of the competition posed by Amstar Sugar and its well-known Domino brand line.

Meanwhile in the mid-western United States, the Western Sugar Co. was contending with extremely dry weather conditions that adversely affected the seeding of the region's sugar beet crops; this in turn led to pessimistic forecasts for a successful financial year in this sector.

Within Canada, although Redpath Sugars continued to run its refinery at virtually full capacity and there were some successes in raw sugar trading, these were overshadowed by the development of negotiations for a Canada-United States free trade deal.

This prospective deal was seen as a distinct boon for the automotive and construction sectors of Redpath Industries Ltd. as well as Refined Sugars Inc. and to a lesser extent the Western Sugar Co. But for Redpath Sugars, it held no good omens due to the fixed and totally divergent policies towards sugar held by the Canadian and U.S. governments.

For the Canadian government, where sugar was

concerned, a completely open-door policy was in effect, whereby virtually any country could freely ship sugar into Canada for sale. On the other hand, the beet industry within the United States had successfully lobbied since 1982 for substantial pricing support levels, coupled with a systematic body of quotas to restrict or prevent foreign sugar from entering the United States. Having gained these powers, the American beet industry was determined to maintain its position, and it was supported by the corn growers across the United States who used the higher U.S. sugar prices as a means of pressing H.F.C.S. as a viable alternative sweetener. In fact, more than 45% of the U.S. liquid sweeteners market was now dedicated to H.F.C.S., causing six U.S. sugar refineries to close down.

For the export market, likewise, the U.S. refineries held a significant advantage compared to their Canadian competitors through the drawback system applicable to the American exports. But now the proposed free trade deal, if based upon a true equality of opportunity, would eliminate all of these American advantages and expose the less efficient U.S. cane and beet producers to the "lean and mean" Canadian refiners. Reports prepared by the beet processors and their allies used every conceivable argument, including the proposition that U.S. sugar production was a militarily strategic industry, in order to persuade the government to exclude sugar from the free trade talks. Unfortunately for the Canadians, these tactics worked. As a result, when the trade talks developed during the year, there was a basic refusal on the part of the U.S. negotiators to discuss any changes in the status quo. Nor did the Canadian negotiating team press the issue on its own merits but simply used the sugar situation as a disposable negotiating position to lever concessions from the Americans over American beer exports into Canada. In the end, due to the wording of the trade agreement eventually signed by both countries, the old status quo remained, with Canadian-made sugar being highly restricted in its entry to the United States while the U.S. refiners could pump sugar into the Canadian market not only without hindrance from the Canadian authorities but with the added bonus of obtaining U.S. duty drawbacks as an incentive for exporting. In other words, the theoretical free trade "highway" had become a one-way "street."

Throughout the summer, R.I.L. maintained its policy of capital investment for expansion and growth to the tune of $76.2 million, and for once Redpath Sugars was a major part of the action. Much attention was given to the new governmental legislation dealing with the use of chemicals and various substances in industry under the acronym W.H.M.I.S. In every department, studies and reports were made of each type of material, chemical, and process used within that jurisdiction. Even furniture polish, floor cleaning fluids, and toilet disinfectants were required to be listed alongside the more easily understandable acids, oils, and caustic substances found in the maintenance department and quality control laboratories. Overall, it was found that the current control measures did meet mandatory standards but in one particular area immediate alterations had to be made. This latter issue concerned the use of asbestos as an insulation material, for when construction of the refinery took place in the 1950s, asbestos had been an approved and acceptable insulation material. But under the more recent and restrictive legislation, asbestos had been declared a health hazard. It was therefore decided to remove and replace all the asbestos throughout the refinery. This plan of action would take several years to complete, as each individual designated area had to be sealed off from the rest of the refinery during the removal of the offending substance, while those employees involved directly in its removal were initially given seminars on its safe removal and then issued with special protective gear to prevent its absorption into the body.

In June 1988 one small but rewarding moment for the company came when it was announced that Redpath Sugars had been awarded the prestigious Presidents Award by the province's largest historical organization, the Ontario Historical Society. This was in recognition of the company's contribution to the province's cultural development by maintaining its own corporate museum and the more recent contribution of grants to a project on the Rideau Canal for the development of an interpretive programme at the Jones Falls dam which had originally been built by John Redpath in the 1830s.

In another area of interest, Redpath Sugars was also involved in the ongoing question of the changes occurring along the Toronto waterfront. For several years, the western end of the port had been losing its industrial base, which was being replaced by housing, recreational, and entertainment facilities. Now the eyes of certain politically active individuals had turned to the eastern end of the port, with a stated view of "cleansing the port of its dirty industries" and replacing them with parks and more housing. Obviously this posed a significant threat to the viability of Redpath Sugars on the Toronto waterfront as well as that of other similar industries around the area. As a result, talks were begun between several major industrial and commercial enterprises in the southeast Toronto area for the development of an information and lobbying group. They would argue the case for the valuable contribution to the local economy that industry did and could continue to make if it were not hemmed in by inappropriate development or even forced to move so that a small group of exclusive individuals could have a better view of the lake. Eventually this informal informational group became a formal association of industrial interests under the title of the South East Toronto Industrial Awareness Organization (S.E.T.I.A.O.). Its first President was Redpath's Vice-President Tom Chandler and under Mr. Chandler and his successor Peter Sharpe, also of Redpath Sugars, S.E.T.I.A.O. continues to voice the viewpoint of much of the Toronto waterfront industrial and commercial sector. In addition S.E.T.I.A.O. has actively participated in several studies made by all levels of government for the future development of the Port of Toronto.

In September 1988, Redpath Industries Ltd. underwent another major re-organization in its senior management when L.R. (Red) Wilson, the President and Chief Executive Officer of Redpath Industries Ltd. since 1981, was elected the Chairman of the Board of Directors as well as Managing Director of the North American holdings of Tate & Lyle. In his stead, W. Darcy McKeough, formerly the Chairman of Redpath Industries Ltd. and President of Union Gas Ltd., became the next President and Chief Executive Officer of Redpath Industries Ltd.

Together these gentlemen, along with Murray McEwen, took on a major opportunity that had developed in the United States where the owners of the Amstar Sugar Corporation were reported to be looking for a buyer. As the estimated cost of this prospective acquisition was reputed to be in excess of $300 million, there was no conceivable hope

W. Darcy McKeough

of R.I.L. going into negotiations alone and it was agreed between Redpath Industries Ltd. and Tate & Lyle to make a joint purchase approach. During the negotiations, however, it became clear that the acquisition of Amstar by R.I.L./Tate & Lyle would precipitate an investigation by the anti-trust bodies in the United States as long as the corporation also owned R.S.I. thus controlling a significant percentage of production capacity in the northeast United States. Despite the fact that so much had been invested in the R.S.I. facility over the years, the major advantages presented by the opportunity to acquire Amstar led to the unavoidable necessity of selling off the entire holdings of Refined Sugars Inc.

Negotiations continued throughout October and November for the purchase of Amstar, while simultaneously disposal of R.S.I. was completed by a sale to Lantic Sugar under its U.S. designation, Lantic America Inc.

Finally in December 1988, the Amstar deal was closed for a reported $305 million. This now made Redpath Industries Ltd., in conjunction with Tate & Lyle, the largest sugar and sweeteners company in North America, necessitating a reorganization of management responsibilities. As of January 1, 1989, Murray McEwen was appointed the Chairman of Tate & Lyle's North American sugar companies and relinquished his position as President of Redpath Sugars to Ed Makin who, at age thirty-eight, became the youngest President of Redpath Sugars in the history of the company.

Almost before they had made themselves comfortable in their new seats of responsibility, both Mr. Makin and Mr. McEwen were involved in yet another round of changes within the corporation, originating this time in the nature of the business activities of Tate & Lyle. In that corporation, the already substantial international holdings had been augmented by the major acquisitions of Amstar and A.E. Staley in the United States. These had absorbed liquid assets to such an extent that Tate & Lyle was having difficulty in supporting continued new investment in the non-sweetener sector of the T & L group. This was further compounded by the fact that in the near future Redpath Industries Ltd. was contemplating making substantial acquisitions of its own under its diversification programme. As a result, this would require T & L to make considerable financial commitments through further investment in Redpath Industries Ltd.

Faced with an extremely difficult decision, Tate & Lyle reviewed its options and following intense studies, reports and not a little argument amongst senior executives, the judgement was made that if only one type of business for the Tate & Lyle worldwide network could be supported properly, then it should be that which related to sweeteners and starches. At the larger world level this decision made perfect sense, but within the North American sector and for Redpath Industries Ltd., this new shift in the development of Tate & Lyle was not only a surprise, but also held many questions and challenges. These needed to be met and resolved if the previous policies of development in areas not related to sugar were now to be reversed successfully. One major

Ed Makin

consideration involved the prospective backlash of opinion from R.I.L. shareholders if the lucrative non-sugar elements were disposed of. Following discussions between T & L and R.I.L. it was recognized that such a radical retrenchment could be best achieved and current shareholders would be most equitably treated by means of the outright purchase of all outstanding minority shareholdings in R.I.L. by Tate & Lyle.

Within a short period of time planning teams were investigating the specifics of selling off such a major part of the R.I.L. portfolio, without causing detrimental effects upon the remaining sweeteners sector. At the R.I.L. Board, the Directors were also busy as they met to consider the bid by Tate & Lyle for the purchase of all the remaining minority shareholdings in Redpath Industries Ltd. On behalf of those minority shareholders, the R.I.L. Board rejected the initial T & L bid and subsequently negotiated a new price per share, substantially higher than the then current market value for R.I.L. shares. This was then accepted by the Board and passed on to the shareholders for ratification.

Between April and June 1989, the sales of Daymond, Heartland Building Products Inc., and Multi-Fittings were completed for a combined value of $67 million, while Donlee Precision, General Gear and the various elements of the Automotive Industries Division were under negotiation for future disposal that would be eventually completed in April 1990.

At the executive level, the various members of the Board of Directors for Redpath Industries Ltd. including Mr. Wilson, completed their terms and resigned as the Board was dissolved. Mr. Wilson went on to continue his career outside of Redpath Industries Ltd. first as Vice-Chairman of the Bank of Nova Scotia, and then as President and Chief Executive Officer of B.C.E. Inc. but he retained his post on the Board of Directors for Tate & Lyle. In October, Darcy McKeough reverted to his previous position as Chairman of the holding company, Redpath Industries Ltd. while Mr. McEwen became its President. At the end of 1989, Darcy McKeough also chose to retire as Chairman and left to continue his business interests as a director within several major Canadian corporations.

On January 1, 1990, Murray D. McEwen took up the joint position of President and Chief Executive Officer of Redpath Industries Ltd. which included: Redpath Sugars, Redpath Specialty Products, Staley Canada, Canada West Indies Molasses, and Comtrad. In addition, he had been appointed a member of the Tate & Lyle Board, sitting alongside other former Redpath executives including "Red" Wilson, Saxon Tate, and Neil Shaw.

In purely technical terms, it could now be argued that having become a fully owned division of a worldwide corporate entity, the independent history of Redpath Sugars had come to an end. This does not mean, however, that it ceased to function or develop, far from it in fact, as will be seen in the highlighting of some of the major events of the period since the end of 1989.

The Toronto refinery in 1992.

CHAPTER FIFTEEN

Something Old, Something New

With the disposal of the "non-core" elements of its portfolio, the head office of Redpath Industries Ltd. was wound down and most of its administrative functions were devolved upon various departments within its new divisions. At Redpath Sugars, life continued very much as before, with plans being drawn up for new installations and increased efficiencies of production that would ease the current problem of consistently running the refinery well beyond its rated capacity output.

In addition, new lines of retail sugars were introduced to the market during this period, continuing the history of innovation and leadership in product development established by earlier generations of Redpath sales personnel. These included "Raw Sugar from Natural Cane," a golden granulated sugar for coffee and tea and "Quickset", was a blend of sugar and pectin for use in the making of preserves and jam products.

On a larger scale, the Redpath Sugar's Toronto refinery was the site for some new developments when in April 1990 construction commenced on a special wing located adjacent to the charcoal filter house. This building was to act as a pilot plant for the experimental production of a low-calorie bulking agent called polydextrose for the A.E. Staley company, another subsidiary of Tate & Lyle.

Meanwhile, just across the main truck yard, the original building constructed in the early 1950s as distribution offices was modernized and converted into new offices, laboratories, and test kitchens for the ongoing development of the low-calorie high-intensity sweetener product, sucralose. This new product also required the establishment of new division, Redpath Specialty Products, that would be responsible for the successful completion of the regulatory hurdles remaining before sucralose could be made available for sale.

Over the following months, while Specialty Products continued in its development of sucralose and construction for the polydextrose or "Topaz" plant neared completion, Redpath Sugars itself was suffering the effects of rising world sugar prices which increased the attractiveness of H.F.C.S. as an alternative sweetener to some of Redpath's traditional customers. In the raw sugar trading department, the unpredictable fluctuations of the market reduced the profits from this facet below its previous levels. Despite this, however, the continued full – capacity usage of

Let Redpath Sweeten It

the refinery helped to maintain the financial viability of the company in the face of increased import competition from the United States. As a result, by the end of the fiscal year, Redpath Sugars was able to surpass its targeted profit level by 12%. At the end of the 1990 calendar year, yet another new product line was launched under the name "Golden Crystals."

The following month, a major change in the Canadian sugar industry occurred when it was announced that Redpath's prime competitor in eastern Canada, Lantic Sugar, would be sold to B.C. Sugar in an initial 50% shares purchase in February 1991 with the remaining 50% being held by its current owners, Jannock Inc. However, the deal also stipulated that B.C. Sugar would have the option to purchase the remaining 50% of shares in 1993. This now reduced the Canadian sugar industry to two separate companies with B.C. Sugar holding approximately 75% of the nation's refining capacity. On the other hand, due to the continued influx of U.S. imports plus the current level of efficiencies at the Redpath refinery, convinced Ed Makin and the Redpath Sugars management team of the necessity to improve the company's future competetive position by undertaking a new cycle of capital investments at the refinery. These were designed to increase its capacity output from the current 1,000 metric tonnes per day to 1,300 tonnes, through the installation of a new vacuum pan, centrifugal machines, granulator, holding tanks, pumps, and other associated equipment for an estimated cost of $9 million.

By February 1991, the initial stage of the new technical improvements for the refinery in the form of a decolorization plant was begun, while the Staley pilot plant for polydextrose initiated its production cycle suffering some setbacks as technical difficulties were ironed out. In April the Specialty Products Division received some good news on sucralose as it obtained the first stage of official clearance for general food use with the final release scheduled for the end of the year. Under tight security and, in the eyes of some Redpath personnel, not a little melodramatic secrecy, the sucralose marketing teams built upon the excellent customer relationships developed by the regular sugar sales and marketing department with several major food producers, to promote the advantages of sucralose. At the refinery proper, advertising agents held closed-door regular meetings with the Specialty Products management, finalizing details for the eventual market release and promotion of sucralose under its brand name "Splenda."

By September the final permission for the use of sucralose was granted and due to the high level of interest on the part of industrial customers who not only wanted to make use of sucralose for its material advantages over its main competitor aspartame but also to break the economic monopoly imposed upon the low-calorie sweetener market by the aspartame distributor, sales began almost immediately to several major food and soft drink producers while a retail product package line was scheduled for release in the spring of 1992.

Finally for the year and for this part of the story, it was announced in December 1991 that Ed Makin was about to relinquish his position as President of Redpath Sugars to

Robert F. Satola

take up a similar post at the sister company, Domino Sugar (formerly Amstar). Succeeding Mr. Makin as the new President was Robert F. Satola, previously the Vice-President of Grocery & Foodservice Products at Domino, who took office at the start of 1992, continuing the line and work of those gentlemen who preceded him as the leaders of Canada's oldest sugar company.

With this change in leadership, the story has reached its end point, and that which we call history has become the present. But what of the future? What does it hold for Redpath Sugars? In an interview with Mr. Satola, I asked this question, to which he replied:

It would be presumptuous of me to pretend to know the future. However, major trends developing today indicate more globalization. The Canada-U.S. Free Trade Agreement, NAFTA and a potential GATT Agreement all point to the importance of global competitiveness. Multinational customers will use simple economics to decide the most cost efficient location to manufacturer their products. In order to hold this base and make it grow, it is imperative that economics favour Canada and it is our job to make Redpath the choice for sugar within Canada... The future of the sugar business and of sweeteners in general is very encouraging and Redpath will continue to be a major contributor. The market place loudly proclaims that customers and consumers will be more and more demanding. We accept that challenge, not merely to meet their expectations but to exceed them. That is our tradition, that is our mission.

Postscript

In conclusion, to you the reader of this work, I leave this final thought. Redpath has been a name connected with the Canadian sugar industry for more than 138 years. During that time, it has had its ups and downs, tragedies and comic moments, successes and failures. But through it all, the simple substance that John Redpath set out to supply to the kitchens and industries of Canada has remained the firm foundation from which all the succeeding growth and development has evolved. Now as the new century and millennium approach, technological revolutions are beginning to appear that will make the current methods of refining as antiquated and "quaint" to future refiners as sugar loaf manufacturing seems to us. But whatever the future may hold economically and despite the constant trend towards automation and high technologies within the business of sugar refining, nature's own sweetener will continue to be needed. And unless something drastic happens to dictate otherwise, Redpath Sugars and its employees will continue to provide its customers in Canada and abroad with their daily sweetener needs.

Richard Feltoe
August 1992

Appendix 1

WHAT IS SUGAR?
Sugar as it is commonly known to the consumer is a complex natural chemical generally seen as crystals of natural sucrose. Sucrose is produced by every plant on this planet through the process of photosynthesis, which takes place within the green cells of chlorophyll throughout the plant. For photosynthesis to occur, the cells of chlorophyll use the sun's energy of light and heat to extract carbon from the carbon-dioxide gas in the atmosphere and combine it with hydrogen and oxygen taken from water to produce the "simple sugars" of glucose and fructose. These "simple" sugars are then bonded to produce the more complex molecules of sucrose.

Although all plants produce these sugars, only sugar cane and sugar beet produce enough to justify their use in the economic commercial production of "ordinary" sugar.

HOW IS SUGAR REFINED?
Sugar production at the Redpath Toronto refinery relies upon the importation of a partially processed sugar product, "raw sugar," which is derived from sugar cane. Sugar cane is a grasslike plant that grows best in tropical and sub-tropical countries lying like a fertile "belt" around the world. The sugar cane is grown in huge plantations and when it is ripe, the cane is stripped of its leaves and the stalk is cut into lengths that are transported immediately to a cane mill because fresh cut sugar cane does not keep.

At the mill, the cane stalks are shredded and pressed to extract the cane juice, this is then processed and boiled, whereupon the natural crystals of sugar begin to form. Following the boiling, the crystals are dried and produce what is termed "raw sugar," which is sold on the world market to supply the needs of Canada and other countries. Raw sugar is purchased by Redpath Sugars' "Comtrad" department and is transported in special bulk cargo ships from around the world up the St. Lawrence Seaway to the Toronto refinery where they dock at the company wharf alongside the main raw sugar shed. The volume of sugar in the ship can vary in quantity from 5,000 to 25,000 tonnes. (N.B. The upper limit of quantity is determined by the draft limits of the St. Lawrence Seaway.) The vessel is unloaded by two mobile cranes mounted on the dockside. These cranes are equipped with mechanical "grabs" that lift 3 tonnes of raw sugar out of the hold with every scoop. Later, as the cargo is removed from the centre of the hold, small bulldozers are lifted into the vessel to push the sugar remaining around the sides of the hold into mounds directly underneath the crane grab.

The unloaded raw sugar is transferred from the crane grab to wide conveyer belts that move it to the top of the raw sugar shed.

Once inside the raw sugar shed, the raw sugar is discharged from the conveyor belt, falls to the floor below, and slowly piles up to form huge conical mounds. The raw sugar shed has a floor area the size of almost two football fields and has a capacity of 65,000 metric tonnes. This huge capacity is necessary due to the closure, each winter, of the St. Lawrence Seaway. Redpath Sugars must bring in its entire winter supply of raw sugar before the close of the shipping season.

The sugar is removed from the shed by the use of a conveyor, located in a tunnel running the length of the building

Appendix 1

under the main shed floor. The sugar is fed onto the conveyor through a series of controlled openings set into the floor itself and is transferred to the top of the main refinery building through the covered conveyor "bridge," a distinctive feature of the refinery when viewed from the city.

The process of refining sugar commences when the raw sugar is automatically weighed into batches. It is then steadily fed into the "mingler" or mixing trough where the raw sugar is blended with a solution of molasses and water (affination syrup) in order to soften the thin coating of molasses around each raw sugar crystal. The blending of these elements produces a thick moist brown mixture, which is technically referred to as "magma."

After the mingler, the magma is fed into a centrifugal machine, resembling an oversized washing machine. The interior of centrifugal machine contains a large steel basket, the outer wall of which is perforated with small holes while an inner lining of copper wire mesh produce a screen. This screen holds the solid crystals of sugar in place while the high spped spinning action of the basket throws the liquid element of the magma through the mesh, to be collected separately. To ensure that the maximum amount of syrup and molasses is removed, hot water is then sprayed onto the sugar, completing this stage of the cleaning. The sugar remaining in the basket of the centrifugal is now termed washed raw sugar. Some of the spun-off syrup is recycled to the mingler as affination syrup, and the rest is separately boiled and re-processed to extract the maximum content of sugar.

At this point the washed raw sugar is as clean as can be achieved while remaining in a crystal form. Since this is not sufficient for refined sugar, the washed raw sugar passes into a "melter" where, as the name suggests, the sugar is heated with hot water and steam until it dissolves the crystals into a brown-coloured "liquor" around 72°C. (162°F).

The liquor of melted sugar is filtered through a mechanical strainer to extract as much of the solid particles and matter as possible from the sugar syrup. This solid matter consists of residue from the sugar cane plant and other natural and man-made contaminants and must be removed before further refining can take place.

Eventually the simple mechanical screens and meshes of the "strainer" trap and remove most of the larger solid impurities. But microscopic solid particles, suspended in the hot sugar liquor, still remain and must be extracted by a carbonatation process. For this, a fine-quality limestone is crushed and mixed with water to produce calcium hydroxide or "milk of lime." Carbon dioxide gas is then injected into the solution and a chemical reaction occurs. The result is a precipitate of calcium carbonate or ordinary chalk.

These chalk particles float suspended in the water, and when the sugar liquor is pumped in, while the dissolved sugar element does not react, the microscopic dirt particles attract the chalk and become enlarged.

Once the solid microscopic particles have been enlarged to a sufficient size, they must be removed. This function is performed by the Sweetland Presses, that consist of a series of ultra-fine cloth filters on circular metal frames, mounted in a line. When the carbonated liquor passes through the filter cloths, the enlarged solid particles are trapped and accumulate on the cloth, while the dissolved sugar passes through and now contains no solid matter.

The "pressed" liquor as it comes from the "Sweetlands," although not containing any solids, still retains a golden yellow colour that must be removed by charring, a process by which large cisterns, filled with granular bone char, act as filters to remove the yellow colour from the liquid sugar stream. The resulting clear, colourless syrup coming out of the cistern is called "fine liquor."

After purification, most of the fine liquor is reconverted to solid crystals. This is accomplished by the "vacuum pan" into which the fine liquor is fed. The air in the "pan" is extracted, leaving the sugar to "boil" under a partial vacuum.

This vacuum boiling is essential since sugar boiled at a normal temperature and air pressure would caramelise and be ruined for use as white sugar. Lowering the pressure lowers the temperature at which the water content boils off, thus allowing the sugar to crystallize without being overheated and discoloured.

At precisely the right moment of boiling, the operator injects a small quantity of fine sugar crystals into the boiling mass. These act as a "seed" around which the supersaturated sugar liquor starts to cling, enlarging the crystal size. This "growing" of the crystals continues until, through constant checking and sampling the operator judges that the sugar crystals are at the correct point of growth. The vacuum is "broken," allowing air back into the pan, boiling stops, and the "strike" of recrystallized sugar known as massecuite is "dropped" into a receiver tank. Although the refining process is now technically complete, the massecuite still contains uncrystallized sugar syrup and water, which must be separated from the regrown crystals in the white sugar centrifugals.

The white sugar centrifugals (identical mechanically to the affination centrifugals) are filled with the recrystallized sugar massecuite from the vacuum pans. They then accelerate to over 1,100 R.P.M., and a double wash of clean hot water rinses off much of the uncrystallized sugar syrup from the pure white sugar crystals. The damp white sugar still within the basket is automatically removed through the detachable base of the machine for drying in a granulator while the spun-off syrup is recycled back for reboiling in the remelt vacuum pans to obtain additional sugar. The reclaimed sugar from the remelt stage is reintroduced to the main refining system back at the melter, while the spun-off syrup is collected from the remelt centrifugals and sold off as molasses.

Resembling a giant tumble drier, the granulator tumbles the white sugar crystals while hot, de-humidified air (blown through the machine) dries the crystals. This dry sugar is then stored in refined sugar silos where it is held until it is removed and transferred to the refinery packaging building for final processing. At this stage although the processed sugar is dry and ready for packaging, it must be sorted to obtain the specific granular sizes that correspond to the medium, fine, special fine, and other varieties required by customers. This sorting is performed by sugar screens, which consist of a set of fine wire meshes set in a vibrating cylindrical frame, through which the mixed granular sugar passes. The various sizes of holes in the individual mesh screens separate the required sizes of crystals from the overall volume leaving the sugar ready for packaging.

While approximately 30% of the refinery's sugar production is sold in a bulk granular form to large-scale industrial users, some 40% is packaged for domestic, commercial and smaller industrial uses (the remaining 30% of the refinery production being bulk liquid varieties of sugar).

Redpath Sugars produces a wide selection of sizes and styles of packaged sugars, ranging from the I.S.E. (Individual Serving Envelope) commonly found in restaurants, through the domestic 1, 2, and 4 kilogram granulated sugar bags, to the large 40 kilogram units for commercial uses. In addition, specialized sugars such as pure icing, icing, fruit powdered, golden yellow, and dark brown sugar are each provided in a variety of sizes and types of container.

The many types and sizes of packaged sugar are loaded onto pallets for easy handling. These pallets are then stacked, according to type and size, within the refined sugar warehouse. When a customer's order is to be filled, the appropriate units are moved into the loading bay and on to the trucks by forklift trucks.

As well as manufacturing and packaging sugar, Redpath Sugars has the capability of delivering to customers through its fleet of trucks and tankers. Bagged and boxed sugars on pallets are despatched in the "van" units, while larger orders of granular sugar are loaded directly into bulk granular tankers. Liquid blends of sugar are also available in liquid tanker units.

Finally, to ensure the quality of the sugar produced by Redpath Sugars, the Toronto refinery operates two laboratories. The main laboratory examines the quality of the shipments of the raw sugar received and also extensively tests the finished product to ensure that it meets and surpasses the legal requirements for refined sugar.

The second laboratory is located next to the Control Room in the heart of the refinery and tests samples taken at periodic intervals from each stage of the production. This ensures that the specific stage of production being tested maintains the optimum quality to guarantee the purest possible end product.

Appendix 2

FOUNDING DIRECTORS OF THE WALLACEBURG SUGAR CO. LTD. - JUNE 26, 1901

D.A. Gordon	B. Boutell
S. Eddy	C. Moore
W. Forbes	H.B. Smith
G.W. McCormick	F.W. Gilchrist
J.S. Fraser	J.W. Steinhoff

DIRECTORS OF THE CANADA & DOMINION SUGAR CO. LTD. AND REDPATH INDUSTRIES LTD.

C.H. Houson	December 30, 1930 - February 24, 1942
H.R. Drummond	December 30, 1930 - December 9, 1957
R. Gilchrist	December 30, 1930 - October 8, 1936
A.E. Dyment	December 30, 1930 - Date not recorded
W.J. McGregor	December 30, 1930 - September 21, 1960
H.F. Smith	December 30, 1930 - December 18, 1958
W.W. Mills	December 30, 1930 - April 29, 1937
W.C. Laidlaw	December 30, 1930 - March 14, 1962
G.H. Moulthrop	December 30, 1930 - January 14, 1949
Senator G.G. Foster	December 30, 1930 - May 1, 1931
A.H. Thomson	December 30, 1930 - October 24, 1946
G.B. Foster	January 26, 1932 - August 30, 1973
C.J. Coyle	March 5, 1942 - October 31, 1957
J.F. Lash	May 12, 1943 - October 30, 1950
W.C.J. Meredith	May 15, 1947 - August 28, 1960
G.M. Humphrey	May 12, 1949 - February 5, 1953
G. Fairrie	May 26, 1950 - April 20, 1953
H. Havemeyer Jr.	December 19, 1950 - October 18, 1955
Lord Lyle of Westbourne	April 20, 1953 - March 6, 1954
P.J.B. Lash	July 29, 1953 - April 14, 1959
I.D. Lyle	August 11, 1954 - January 30, 1969
J. Pembroke	July 6, 1956 - January 3, 1970
G.M. Humphrey	October 31, 1957 - February 3, 1960 *
C.J. Coyle	July 23, 1958 - March 17, 1965 *
G.E. Ellsworth	January 30, 1959 - February 29, 1972
P.F. Runge	June 29, 1959 - August 19, 1970
J.O. Whitmee	February 3, 1960 - February 29, 1972
Hon. W. Gagnon	December 14, 1960 - June 10, 1963
H.F. Smith Jr.	December 14, 1960 - September 20, 1965
D.K. MacTavish Q.C.	October 17, 1962 - November 15, 1963
M.D. Oliphant	December 18, 1963 - April 23, 1974
W.H. Punchard	December 18, 1963 - April 23, 1974
Senator L.P. Beaubien	December 18, 1963 - December 18, 1978
Hon. R.H. Winters	December 18, 1963 - January 17, 1966
W.W. Sprague Jr.	March 17, 1965 - September 28, 1971
H.S. Tate	September 20, 1965 - May 1, 1979

J.M. Ferguson	October 25, 1966 - August 29, 1980	J. Forbes	May 6, 1980 - April 30, 1984
J.H. Magee	January 30, 1969 - January 22, 1980	J.M.G. Scott	August 5, 1980 - July 21, 1989
C.F. Harrington	January 29, 1970 - February 17, 1983	C.R. Sharpe	January 8, 1981 - July 21, 1989
C. Lyle	October 27, 1970 - September 22, 1981	L.R. Wilson	May 12, 1981 - September 30, 1989
N.M. Shaw	September 28, 1971 - September 30, 1989	J.R. Kerr Muir	September 22, 1981 - November 24, 1987
R.L. Henry	November 28, 1972 - July 21, 1989	Dr. J. MacNamara	October 20, 1982 - July 21, 1989
D.A. Tate	November 28, 1972 - May 6, 1980	P.E. Martin	October 20, 1982 - November 18, 1988
C.S. MacNaughton	August 30, 1973 - March 31, 1980	M.D. McEwen	May 2, 1984 - September 30, 1989
W.H. Punchard	November 26, 1974 - November 23, 1976*	J.A. Swan	May 2, 1984 - September 30, 1989
R.G. Brownridge	November 26, 1974 - May 12, 1981	R.M. Barford	September 21, 1988 - July 21, 1989
P.S. Newell	November 23, 1976 - June 16, 1982	P.S. Lewis	September 21, 1988 - September 30, 1989
W.D. McKeough	December 18, 1978 - September 30, 1989	W.H. Clement	November 18, 1988 - September 30, 1989
M.J.L. Attfield	May 1, 1979 - October 20, 1982		
J.C.W. Mitchell	January 22, 1980 - November 29, 1985		

* Re-appointed to the Board of Directors

Selected Bibliography

Canada's Illustrated Heritage Series:
>Craig, John: 1977 *The Years of Agony 1910 - 1920* McClelland and Stewart Ltd.

>Franklin, Stephen: 1977 *A Time of Heroes 1940 - 1950* McClelland and Stewart Ltd.

>*Into the 20th Century 1900 - 1910*: 1977 McClelland and Stewart Ltd.

>Ross, Alexander: 1977 *The Booming Fifties 1950 - 1960* McClelland and Stewart Ltd.

>*The Crazy Twenties 1920 - 1930*: 1978 McClelland and Stewart Ltd.

Century of Canada Series:
>Bennett, Paul W.: 1985 *Years of Promise 1896 - 1911* Grolier Ltd.

>Bliss, Michael: 1986 *Years of Change 1967 - 1985* Grolier Ltd.

>Bothwell, Robert: 1987 *Years of Victory 1939 - 1948* Grolier Ltd.

>Horn, Michael: 1986 *Years of Dispair 1929 - 1939* Grolier Ltd.

>Morton, Desmond: 1983 *Years of Conflict 1911 - 1921* Grolier Ltd.

Bothwell, Robert: 1981 *Canada since 1945* University of Toronto Press.

Chalmin, Philippe: 1990 *The Making of a Sugar Giant, Tate and Lyle 1859 - 1989* Harwood Academic Publishers.

Deerr, Noel: 1949 *The History of Sugar*, (2 volumes) Chapman and Hall Ltd.

Francis, R. Douglas and Smith, Donald B.: 1986 (2 volumes) *Readings in Canadian History* Holt, Rinehart and Winston.

Granatstein, J.L.: 1982 *The Ottawa Men, The Civil Service Mandarins 1935 - 1957* Oxford University Press

Harbron, J.D.: 1980 *C.D. Howe* Fitzhenry and Whiteside Ltd.

Mintz, Sidney W.: 1985 *Sweetness and Power, The Place of Sugar in Modern History* Elisabeth Sifton Books - Viking.

Roberts, Leslie: 1957 *C.D. The Life and Times of Clarence Decatur Howe* Clarke, Irwin & Co. Ltd.

Stikeman, H.H.(Editor): 1984 Canada Tax Letter Richard De Boo Publishers.

Strony, L.A.G.: 1954 *The Story of Sugar* George Weidenfeld & Nicolson.

CORPORATE PERIODICALS:

Annual Agriculture Reports: 1931 - 1967 Canada and Dominion Sugar Co. Ltd. Annual Reports: 1930 - 1989 Canada and Dominion sugar Co. Ltd.

Redpath Industries Ltd.

Tate and Lyle P.L.C.

Sugar Facts: Canada and Dominion Sugar Co. Ltd.
Up and Down The Rows: Canada and Dominion Sugar Co. Ltd.

MANUSCRIPTS:
>M.W. Davidson
>Research notes and accounts from unpublished drafts by M.W. Davidson.

Index

A.E. Staley Company 191, 193, 222, 225
Agricultural Consulting Services Division 173, 179
Agricultural Prices Support Board 122, 123
Agro-Industrial Division 192, 199
Alberta Beet Sugar Company Ltd. 58
Albion Co. Ltd. 172, 179, 182, 184, 192 - 194
American Construction and Supply Co. 15
Amstar Sugar Corporation 219, 221, 222, 228
Anti-Inflation Board 191
Anvil Plastics Ltd. 175, 179
Arbour Plastic Products Inc. 218
Archard, Franz Carl 11, 12
Aspartame 219, 227
Atlantic Provinces Economic Commission 124
Atlantic Sugar Refineries Ltd. 48, 50, 125, 141, 154, 158, 175, 178, 198, 204, 206, 208, 214, 217
Austin, Robin 148, 152, 172, 175, 176, 183 - 185
Austin Sugar Refineries Ltd. 177
Automotive, Industrial and Construction Products Division 215, 217
Automotive Industries Division 223
Automotive Industries Inc. 214, 217

B.C. Security Commission 78
B.C.E. Inc. 223
Badger pipe-laying system 174, 175, 184
Bank of England 132
Bank of Montreal 71, 88, 182
Bank of Nova Scotia 223
Beamish Sugar Company 55 - 57
Bennett, R.B. 53
Bonaparte, Napoleon 14
British Columbia Sugar Co. Ltd. 119, 125, 214, 227
C.B. Packaging Ltd. 192, 201, 207, 214
Canada and Dominion Sugar Co. Ltd. 40, 47, 48, 50, 52 - 57, 63 - 65, 67, 70, 73, 76, 82, 85, 87, 89, 96, 99, 102, 105, 106, 108, 111, 115, 117, 119 -121, 124 - 126, 128, 131, 132, 135, 137, 139 - 141, 143, 145, 148, 152, 154, 156 - 158, 163, 164, 175, 177, 178
Canada Car Company 148
Canada Starch Co. Inc. (CaSCo) 140
Canada Steamship Lines 48
Canada Sugar Refinery 13, 111, 154, 193
Canada Sugar Refining Co. Ltd. 43, 44, 47
Canada West Indies Molasses 223
Canadian Beet Growers Association 174
Canadian General Electric 152
Canadian Imperial Bank of Commerce 182

Canadian Mouldings Ltd. 199
Canadian Shipping Board 75
Canadian Shipping Co. 18
Canadian Sugar Factories Ltd. 55
Canadian Sugar Institute 158, 213
Carnation Company 166
Cartier Sugar 152, 154, 156, 158, 172, 175, 181, 184, 194, 197, 198, 206
Castro, Fidel 128
Cello Bags Ltd. 174, 175, 179
Certain-Teed/Daymond Co. 175, 179, 192, 207, 214
Chantecler Wines Ltd. 192
Chatham Board of Trade 19, 110
Chatham & Wallaceburg Land Development Division 177
Chevrier, Lionel 146
Clarkson Gordon & Co. 182
Coca-Cola Company 64, 207
Consumers Association of Canada 174
Colonial Sugars Inc. 215 - 218
Combines Board 197
Combines Department 141, 147, 148, 154, 158, 160, 173, 178, 181, 183
Combines Investigations Act 154
Commonwealth Air Training Scheme 68
Commonwealth Sugar Producers Group 147

Index

Comtrad Ltd. 186, 189, 191, 192, 199, 223
Construction Materials Division 199, 207, 208, 215
Crawford, J.R. 111
Crosse and Blackwell 53, 54
Crystal Estates 179
Cuban Missile Crisis 143
Cyclamates 219
Czarnikow Canada Ltd. 175, 182

Davidson, J.S. 23
Daymond, F.R. 172
Daymond Ltd. 166, 172, 175, 179, 183, 192, 201, 207, 223
De Boo, Richard 213
Delessert, Benjamin 12
Department of Finance 174, 183
Department of Forestry and Rural Development 170
Department of Labour 91, 120
Department of National Revenue 182
Department of Revenue 211
Department of Trade and Commerce 147, 148, 160, 162
Desmond, C. 70
Devonport Trading Ltd. 192
Dewan, P.M. 75, 76
Diefenbaker, John G. 88, 89, 122
Dominion Sugar Beet Co. Ltd. 24, 26, 27, 29, 30, 32, 34 - 39, 41 - 44, 47
Domino Sugar 228
Donlee Manufacturing Industries Ltd. 214, 215, 217
Donlee Plastics 214
Donlee Precision 215, 223
Dresden Sugar Co. Ltd. 15
Drummond, George Alexander 13
Drummond, Guy 131, 132

Drummond, Huntly Redpath 44, 48, 53 - 57, 63, 70, 71, 73, 88, 112, 123
Drummond, Sir George Alexander 123, 124
Drummond Street (Montreal) 123
Duplessis 85
Dyer Co. 15
Dyer, E.H. 13

Eisenhower 129
Employees:
  Balogh, Theresa 205
  Bazinet, G. 198
  Burgess, E.V. 198, 205
  Chandler, Tom 221
  Davidson, M.W. 71, 108, 121, 131, 132, 163, 170, 213
  Easton, B. 78, 120, 121, 158
  Faust, E.J. 158
  Hrudka, G.E. 172
  Irving, Evelyn 182
  Kuzmicz, Jan 193, 205
  Morrison, John 158
  Pinsonneault, Sylvio 120
  Porteous, R. 139, 181
  Punchard, W.H. 172
  Sharpe, P. 221
  Thomson, Andrew 24
  Tulloch, Ralph 205
  Wiese, Herman 24, 30
  Wood, Jack 132
  Wood, John 103

Essex County Associated Growers 121
Expo 67 151, 158, 161, 164, 213

F.I.R.A. 214
Fairrie, Geoffrey 99, 102, 111
Farmers:

Anderson, James 40
Brockman, Wilfred 110
Craven, Wilfred 49
Deweyn, John 40
Fox, W.T. 40
Rabideau, W.H. 49
Racher, W.H. 49
Skinner, Isaac 40
Federal Stabilization Board 160, 163, 164
Federation of Agriculture 121
Fleming, Donald 131
Food Prices Review Board 184
Foreign Investment Review Agency 186, 192, 194, 197, 198, 203
Foster, George B. Q.C. 112, 135, 137, 154
Frost, Leslie 122, 131

General Agreement on Tariffs and Trade (G.A.T.T.) 160, 228
Gardiner, James G. 103, 105
General Agreement on Tariffs and Trade 119
General Gear Co. 215, 223
George Weston Co. Ltd. 176 - 178
Gienow Ltd. 179, 192, 207 - 209
Gienow Sash & Door Co. Ltd. 175
Gilchrist, R. 36, 37, 39
Golden Crystals 227
Gordon, David Alexander 17, 18, 23, 24, 27
Gordon Manufacturing Co. 18
Graham, Dr. 122
Great Western Sugar Co. 215
Greene, J.J. 163

H. & W. Building Products Inc. 218
H.J. Heinz Co. of Canada Ltd. 121
Hanna, W.J. 32

237

Harcourt, Professor Robert 20
Harkness, Hon. D.S. 123
Harvey, D. 147, 148
Heartland Building Products Inc. 218, 223
Henry, Mr. 148, 154, 181
Hodgson Sugar Ltd. 175
Holway Packaging 207, 209
Holway Paper Box Manufacturing Co. Ltd. 187, 192
Houson, Charles Henry 38, 39, 41, 47, 55, 65, 70, 71
Howe, C.D. 107 - 111, 122, 141
Hunt, Herbert 215
Hunt, Nelson 215
Hurricane Hazel 112

International Convention of Sugar Industry Technologists 189
International Development Association 183
International Sugar Agreement 137, 173, 181, 183, 194, 195
International Sugar Conference 57, 65, 105, 111
International Sugar Council 182
International Trade Commission 209
Jannock Inc. 227
Japanese Canadian internees 74, 80
John Labatt Ltd. 193, 195, 197, 208, 209
John Redpath & Son 17
Johnson & Johnson 219
Jones Falls 221

Kennedy, Colonel T.L. 79, 86
Kent Peach Growers Association 121
Kilby Manufacturing Co. 15, 18
King Frederick William III 11
King George V 54

Kitchin, Michael 145
Knight Sugar Co. 23, 29
Krayloy Products Inc. 214

L'Union Franco Canadienne 14
La Compagnie de Sucre de Quebec 14
La Compagnie de Sucre de Betterave de Quebec 14
Lachine Canal 59, 61, 135, 145, 166, 200
Laing Engineering 183
Lake St. Clair 23
Lantic America Inc. 222
Lantic Sugar Ltd. 217, 218, 222, 227
Lash, Johnston, Sheard and Pringle 182
London Plastics Machinery Ltd. 192, 199
Lord Lyle of Westbourne 11
Lyle, Sir Ian 111, 115, 132, 135, 172

Mackay, Justice Kenneth 187
Magee, J.H. 106, 173, 176 - 178, 181, 184
Makin, Ed 222, 223, 228
Manitoba Sugar Co. Ltd. 119
Mansugar Ltd. 175
Marggraf, Andreas Sigismond 11
Martin, Paul 163
McDiarmid, J.S. 53
McEwen, Murray 189, 194, 200, 219, 221 - 223
McGill University 154
McGregor, W.J. 71 - 74, 87, 90, 99, 103, 107 - 111, 114, 115, 121 - 125, 127 - 129, 131, 132, 135, 141
McKeough, W. Darcy 221 - 223
McNeill & Libby of Canada Ltd. 121
McPherson, Robert 78
Merry Packaging Ltd. 187, 192, 207, 214
Michener, Norah 131

Michener, Roland 131
Michigan Sugar Beet Co. 48
Ministry of Agriculture 137
Ministry of Food (U.K.) 99, 106
Montreal Olympics 213
Montreal Products Co. Ltd. 76, 119, 120
Montreal Refinery Closure 200, 201
Mount Royal Hotel 47
MSV/Daymond Ltd. 208
Multi Fittings (U.S.A.) Ltd. 192, 207
Multi-Fittings Ltd. 179, 207, 223
Munich Treaty 59
Munitions and Supply Department 76
Murphy, J.W. 110

N.A.F.T.A. 228
National Sugar Co. Ltd. (see Quebec Sugar Refinery)
Newspapers:
    Canada and Dominion Crystals 139
    Canadian Grocer 53
    Sarnia Observer 17
    Sugar Beet Gazette 24
    Sugar Facts 83, 86, 108
    Toronto Daily Star 131
    Up and Down the Rows 79, 85
    Wallaceburg Advocate 17
    Wallaceburg News 17
Noble, S.R. 64 - 66, 69 -74, 83

Olympic Games 188, 189
Ontario Agricultural College 14, 20, 55, 59, 171
Ontario Beet Growers Association 88, 157, 163
Ontario Historical Society 221
Ontario Hydro 96

Index

Ontario Provincial Police 203
Ontario Sugar Beet Growers Association
    56, 57, 61, 65, 70, 71, 74, 78
Ontario Sugar Beet Growers Marketing
    Board 114, 121, 138, 158, 160, 170
Ontario Sugar Beet Marketing Scheme 72
Ontario Sugar Beet Co. Ltd. 15, 24
Ontario Vegetable Growers Marketing
    Board 121
Order of Prohibition 145, 146, 148, 160,
    162, 172, 197
Oullet, Andre 188

Package Research Corporation 175
Packaging Division 199, 207, 208
Paramount Industries 214
Pearson, Lester B.
Pepsi-Cola Company 64, 207
Perkin, Mr. 72
Perth County Federation of Agriculture 110
Phillips, Nathan 131
Pigeon, Justice 204
Pioneer Sugar Co. 14
Polydextrose 225, 227
Pope John Paul II 213
Pressure Cooker Co. of Canada 18
Prices and Incomes Controls 187
Prince Philip 129, 131
Pringle, Don Q.C. 132

Q.S.R. (see Quebec Sugar Refiners)
Quebec Department of Agriculture 13
Quebec Sugar Refinery 78, 82, 142, 146,
    148, 173, 178, 208, 212, 217, 218
Queen Elizabeth College 218
Queen Elizabeth II 129, 131
Queens Quay East (Toronto) 129

Reagan, Ronald 209
Redpath Consultants International Ltd.
    192, 193
Redpath Holdings Ltd. 200
Redpath Home Improvements Ltd. 183, 184
Redpath Industries Ltd. 179, 181 - 183, 186
    - 189, 191 - 194, 197, 198, 201, 203, 204,
    206 - 209, 211, 214, 215, 217 - 223, 225
Redpath, John 99, 111, 123, 221
Redpath, Peter 123, 154
Redpath Specialty Products 223, 225
Redpath Sugar Museum 193, 199
Redpath Sugars Ltd. 173, 175 - 178, 181,
    183, 184, 186 - 189, 191 - 195, 197 - 201,
    203 - 209, 212 - 214, 216 - 222, 225, 227,
    228
Redpath, the History of a Sugar House 32, 36
Refined Sugars Inc. 207, 208, 216, 219, 222
Refined Syrups and Sugars Inc. 192, 193,
    197 - 199, 203, 207
Restrictive Trade Practices Commission
    127, 174
Rhodes, E.N. 53
Rideau Canal 221
Ross, Premier G.W. 19
Royal Bank of Canada 64
Royal Bank Plaza (Toronto) 194
Rychman, E.B. 50

Saccharin 219
Satola, Robert F. 228
Schultz Die Casting Co. 17
Seaway Insurance Ltd. 192, 207
Sewell, John 199
Shaw, A.M. 122
Shaw, Neil 120, 121, 145, 158, 179, 181,
    186, 198, 199, 203, 204, 223

Shuttleworth, Professor A.E. 14
Smith, H.F. 157
Smith, Henry B. 27
Smith, Sir Donald A. (Baron Strathcoma
    and Mount Royal) 88
South East Toronto Industrial Awareness
    Organization 221
Southwestern Ontario Field Crops
    Employers Association (S.W.O.F.C.A.)
    121, 122, 124, 125
Splenda 227
Spraycool Systems Ltd. 192, 199
St. Lawrence River 31, 59, 195
St. Lawrence Seaway 96, 115, 126, 129,
    136, 195
St. Lawrence Starch Co. 140, 145
St. Lawrence Sugar Refining Co. Ltd. 43,
    48, 64, 77, 85, 87, 111, 137, 141, 154,
    158, 173, 175, 178, 181, 189, 198, 204,
    208, 214
Stachenko, P.S. 181, 184, 189
Staley Canada 223
Standard Sugar Refining Co. 13
Steinberg's Ltd. 158, 194
Steinhoff, J. 17
Stewart, W. 171
Sucralose 218, 225, 227
Sugar Control Board 66
Sugar de-rationed 89
Sugar rationing, implementation 70
Sugar Types:
    Fruit Powdered 161
    Golden Yellow 61, 90, 123, 135
    Granulated 61, 90, 123
    High Fructose Corn Syrup (H.F.C.S.)
        187, 189, 191 - 195, 197, 199, 205 -
        207, 220, 225

Icing Sugar 135, 145
Individual Serving Envelopes (I.S.E.) 136, 145, 161, 166, 188, 189
Liquid Sugar 43, 90, 136, 145, 191, 192
Molasses 42, 172
Quickset 225
Raw Sugar from Natural Cane 225
Special Icing 90
Sugar Cubes 90, 112, 135, 136
Tubelets 175
Supreme Court of Canada 197, 198, 201, 204, 212
Sweeteners Division 207
Sydenham Glass Works 17
Sydenham River 23, 24
Sydenham Trading Co. 17

Tariff Board, 174, 176
Tarte, J.I. 19
Tate & Lyle Ltd. 96, 105, 111, 115, 117, 119 - 121, 128, 131, 132, 135, 137, 145, 154, 157, 170, 171, 175, 179, 184 - 186, 189, 192 - 194, 198, 199, 203, 204, 207, 213, 215, 218, 221 - 223, 225
Tate & Lyle Research and Development 218
Tate & Lyle Technical Services 99
Tate, D.A. 185
Tate, Saxon 157, 158, 163, 172, 176, 178, 179, 185, 223
Taxation Department 183, 187
Taylor, K.W. 99
Tecumseh Park (Chatham) 55
Texas Plastic Industries Inc. 217

Thames River 103
Thompson, L. 209
Titanic 35, 38, 95
Topaz 225
Toronto Harbour Commission 96

U. S. Sugar Act 186
U.S. Farm Bill 219
U.S. Farmers and Manufacturers Beet Sugar Association 139
U.S. Sugar Act 142, 143
United Mine Workers Union 124
University of Toronto 55
Urrutia, Dr. Manuel 128

Vessels:
  Acadia 30
  Atomic 103
  Bolina 195
  Britannia 129
  Brothers 30
  Canadian 50
  Canadian Highlander 115
  Clan Mackay 54
  D.A. Gordon 32
  Easton 99, 101
  Edmonton 39
  Ethel 194, 213
  Federal Schelde 195
  Jack 39
  Libbie and Sadie 32
  Mamie Petrie 32
  Maplebranch 37
  May 189, 191, 194
  Mesler and Pease 32
  Presidente Allende 203
  Ralph Gilchrist 37
  Rook 30
  Senator Hagelson 142
  Sugar Crystal 170

W.H.M.I.S. 220
W.P.T.B. (see Wartime Prices and Trade Board)
Walburn-Swenson Co. 15
Wallaceburg Cooperage Co. 17
Wallaceburg Refinery Closure 142
Wallaceburg Sugar Co. Ltd. 15, 18, 20, 21, 23, 24, 39
Wartime Prices and Trade Board 63 - 66, 72, 78, 99
Westcane 181, 183, 209
Western Sugar Co. (see also Great Western Sugar Co.) 217, 219
Whelan, E. 170, 171, 177
Whitmee, J.O. 132, 135, 154, 164, 176
Wiarton Beet Sugar Manufacturing Co. Ltd. 14, 15
Williams, Mr. 163, 164
Wilson, L.R. (Red) 206, 217, 218, 221, 223
Windmill Point (Montreal) 59, 61, 98, 115, 116
Winters, Robert 164
Workman Bay Co. Ltd. 115

Zymaize Inc. 195, 203, 205 - 209, 211